SPEECHES FOR ILLUSTRATION AND EXAMPLE

GOODWIN F. BERQUIST, JR.

UNIVERSITY OF WISCONSIN-MILWAUKEE

SCOTT, FORESMAN AND COMPANY

CHICAGO, ATLANTA, DALLAS, PALO ALTO, FAIR LAWN, N.J.

PREFACE

Speeches—of statesmen, demagogs, or ordinary citizens—often make fascinating and profitable reading. Much more than most printed documents, a speech text can convey the freshness of the moment. The words and phrases in an anthologized speech have had immediate meaning for a listening audience and, consequently, seldom prove too difficult for a reading audience. A good speech abounds in imagery, vivid word pictures that readers and listeners recall long after other details of the occasion are forgotten. And because clarity usually characterizes the thinking of the effective speaker, principal ideas are emphasized through summary, illustration, and restatement. Even when—as in the case of demagogs—rhetoric is employed to delude the listener, a speech may be a profitable object for study and analysis.

Many collections of speeches are already in print or may easily be purchased in second-hand bookstores—why one more? One reason is that some editors avoid printing complete speech texts, a practice which usually results in ornate bits of oratory being taken out of context. Other editors focus their attention upon breadth. One anthology currently in print, for example, offers the reader well over two hundred excerpts from speeches. Still other collections are limited to recent American speeches, arranged according to subject matter. We think *Speeches for Illustration and Example* serves a purpose that none of these existing anthologies has served; it focuses upon communication problems and the ways in which individuals have met them; and it does this in a way to suggest practical applications to the users of this book.

The five major parts of this book are devoted to five types of communication problems—some common, some less common. The fifteen speeches which appear here were selected from the whole range and history of man's utterances. Each part begins with a brief discussion of the nature of a specific problem in communication, and introductions to individual speeches are designed to help the reader place himself in the speech setting. Each speech text is followed by a description of audience response, review questions, and study projects. Because this book will be extensively used in a first course in speech, an essay on speech as a field of study appears in the appendix. All these materials will lend themselves as well to English composition courses and to other courses in communication skills. In addition, the book has been made sufficiently self-instructional to be used independently by interested readers.

While many persons have contributed to the author's thinking about this book, special thanks are due the following: Professors Frank E. X. Dance, Ted J. McLaughlin, Melvin H. Miller, Raymond H. Myers, and Ralph Leutenegger of the University of Wisconsin-Milwaukee; Professor Franklin H. Knower of Ohio State University; and Dr. Elton Carter, communications consultant for the Singer Sewing Machine Company, State College, Pennsylvania. Miss Margaret Martin of Scott, Foresman and Company deserves particular commendation for her many helpful suggestions in the latter stages of this work. Finally, the author wishes to acknowledge the patience and encouragement of his wife, Nancy. Without her, the writing efforts of this past summer on Washington Island would certainly have been less pleasant and less productive.

GOODWIN F. BERQUIST, JR.

Library of Congress Catalog Card No. 65–17730.

CONTENTS

PART THREE: THE PROBLEM OF PRESENTING SPECIALIZED MATERIAL

PART FOUR: THE PROBLEM OF ADDRESSING VARIED AUDIENCES SIMULTANEOUSLY

PART FIVE: THE PROBLEM OF ESTABLISHING CREDIBILITY

PART ONE

THE PROBLEM OF BEING UNDERSTOOD BY OTHERS

The desire to be understood by others is universal, because understanding is essential to any other response that may be sought. For example, a baby cries for his milk. A child points to her favorite cereal. Parents warn their youngsters to stay away from a hot stove. An artist paints what he "sees" of a lovely sunset. Scientists report the results of their research to other scientists and to the rest of the world. Novelists write about the life they perceive around them. And everybody talks . . . to his neighbors, his relatives, his friends, and sometimes to perfect strangers.

Most of us speak a great deal more than we write. And we listen a great deal more than we speak. So this matter of being understood by others and understanding them when communicating orally is of major importance.

When a person engages in a job interview, much of his success is likely to depend upon his ability to communicate. Who the applicant is (the speaker), what he says (the message), the time of day and the place where the interview is held (the occasion), and the employer (the audience) are key factors in the communication process. But simply listing these factors tells us little. We need to know how this process of oral communication can be made most effective.

EFFECTIVE ORAL COMMUNICATION IN THEORY

Books on communication are much in vogue these days. Some deal with information theory and cybernetics. Others detail the findings of linguists, semanticists, and philologists. Research in mass communication, especially mass persuasion, is published in ever-increasing amounts. Such works, while providing helpful data, are often too specialized to be useful to the average speaker and listener.

Andrew T. Weaver provides a simple, practical explanation of how to communicate more effectively in the following address, which was designed to clarify the role of the speech teacher in improving interpersonal communication. Weaver's speech was delivered at a convention luncheon of the Speech Association of America at St. Louis, Missouri, December 29, 1960. Emeritus Professor of Speech at the University of Wisconsin-Madison, Weaver for over forty years has been actively engaged in speech teaching and speech research. His textbooks in voice science, the fundamentals and forms of speech, and the psychology of speech have exerted wide influence throughout his profession.

Weaver's audience, like many audiences, was a mixed assembly. Seated before him were undergraduate students, grade- and high-school teachers, interested adults, and university colleagues in the field of speech. The common thread uniting all was the desire to hear the words of a distinguished man who devoted his life to the teaching of speech.

TOWARD UNDERSTANDING THROUGH SPEECH

ANDREW T. WEAVER

Today I shall not discuss the "sales-talk" uses of speech. I shall not concern myself with the clever arguments of candidates competing for the prize of public office. I shall not be thinking of such mighty rhetoric as that which Cicero hurled against Catiline. What we have thought and taught about the power speech gives us over others is not now the object of my consideration. For the few moments you lend me, I am asking that we focus our attention upon a nobler and more basic role of speech in the lives of men. I suggest that we raise our sights above the lowlands where speech serves self-interest to the higher plateau where it brings the satisfactions of companionship and mutual understanding. All too often, I

From **Vital Speeches of the Day** (February 1, 1961), 244–247. Text emended by the speaker and used with permission. The first two paragraphs have been omitted. An analysis of Weaver's many contributions to the field of speech may be found in **The Speech Teacher** (March 1963), 85–91.

think, we have emphasized the objective of manipulating and controlling our fellow man to satisfy our egoistic drives, and have neglected the loftier goals of cooperation and understanding. /1

There is no deeper craving of the human heart than the hunger for understanding. Individuals, communities, and peoples yearn to be understood. The other day I read a touching statement by Pearl Buck, in which she relates the experiences that have come to her as the result of having a mentally retarded daughter. She testifies that her contacts with other parents of similarly afflicted children have brought her the rare happiness of knowing that her problems have been completely understood. Misery does indeed love company, and, most of all, the chance to *talk with* such company. Professor Carl Rogers[1] has demonstrated the therapeutic power of providing unhappy, maladjusted people with sympathetic listeners into whose understanding ears they can pour their thoughts and feelings without restraint. . . .[2] /2

The other day I read the strange story of a worker in the steel mills down in the Chicago area who, in his spare time, had earned a graduate degree in psychology. He had given his thesis the title "Why the Foreman Hates the Boss." His graduate committee changed it to read, "Emotional Coefficient Correlative in Interpersonal Relationships Between Management and Supervising Echelons." A well-known columnist, who relates the incident, adds this stinging comment: "To my mind this sums up many of the unattractive traits of the academic personality. . . . For failing to communicate with the community at large, it is mostly to blame." /3

Contributing to fuller understanding among men is no minor mission in education; it is the vital core of our obligation as teachers of speech. I am not one of those who maintain that, if we just understood each other perfectly, the millennium would dawn and "man to man the world o'er would brithers be," but I do hold that, by building increased understanding, we relax some of the stresses and strains that plague our lives and help to bring in a better day for all men everywhere. /4

Confused and defective speech always limits understanding. Both Lenin and Lincoln realized this fact; both said that the way to destroy a nation is to confuse its speech. Indeed, this is very ancient wisdom. Twenty-five hundred years ago, Confucius was asked how he would begin to govern his nation if he were placed in power. He answered: "I would begin by establishing correct use of speech." He went on to explain how destructive incorrect speech is to the social and political structure. He concluded by saying, "A gentleman never uses his speech indiscriminately." Or, for another illustration, read the story of the Tower of Babel in Genesis 11:6–18: "And the Lord said, behold the people is *one*, and they have all

[1]Staff member of Western Behavioral Sciences Institute, La Jolla, California, and author of **Client-Centered Therapy** (Boston: Houghton Mifflin Company, 1951) and several other works.

[2]A paragraph dealing with the late Marilyn Monroe was deleted at the request of the speaker. (Editor's note)

one language . . . and now nothing will be restrained from them which they have imagined to do . . . let us go down and confound their language, that they may not understand one another's speech." The antithesis of this tale is to be found in the second chapter of the Book of Acts where we are told that every man heard the apostles speak in his own tongue. George Orwell, in his depressing novel *Nineteen Eighty-Four*, paints a picture of the utter and final ruin of a free society by a totalitarian tyranny whose secret weapon in degrading men to the level of robots is a distorted, controlled, and ever-shrinking vocabulary. /5

But now we come to the practical question: just how we, as teachers of speech, can promote understanding. /6

First, we must realize that meaning always originates in the nervous system of a speaker and seeks its complement in the nervous system of a listener. We must think of speech as a stimulating or stirring-up process, rather than as a transmitting or transferring process. All any speaker can do is issue sight-and-sound drafts on the listener's bank account of experience. We talk about "giving and getting meaning" without bothering to ask ourselves what meaning actually *is*. Meaning is always in the *responses of persons* to things or symbols. Meaning is a fusion of present responses with the residues of past responses. Meaning is not something *done to us:* it is something *we ourselves do*. /7

From these fundamental propositions, important practical implications emerge. When we look for meanings in words, we are barking up the wrong tree. When we suppose that, by some strange hocus-pocus, we can stir up meanings out of a vacuum, we are doomed to disappointment. Meaning always has to be manufactured on the spot by the one who "gets" it. If the listener does not have in his experience the stuff out of which the desired meaning can be made, there is no way in which the speaker can "give" it to him. /8

I am sure that should the ghost of Albert Einstein come to me in the hope of stirring up in me the concept of relativity, his mission would be hopeless; I simply do not have in my experience the ingredients out of which I could construct Einstein's theory. Or, take a simpler example: A motorist stopped at a farmhouse and inquired the way to the Miller place. The farmer said, "Go down the road till you come to the Johnson farm—." "But," broke in the traveler, "I don't know which the Johnson farm is." "Well," said the farmer, "Go down the road till you come to a small grove of beech trees—." "But," interrupted the traveler, "I wouldn't know a beech tree if I saw one." The farmer scratched his head and then tried once more: "Go down till you come to a fence with some hop vines trailing along the top—." "I never have seen a hop vine in my life," said the traveler. The exasperated farmer looked at him for a moment and then remarked: "Well, stranger, I guess you just don't know enough for me to tell you how to get to the Miller place!" /9

A good many years ago, Professor I. A. Richards made his startling statement: "When people talk with each other, misunderstanding is the rule and understanding, a happy accident." This hyperbole points up a truth we often overlook: Satisfactory communication is more rare than we realize. We naively assume that, since what we say is clear to *us*, it therefore will be equally clear to *others*. We fail to comprehend the fact that the speech signs we make have to be filtered through the nervous systems of other persons, on their way to minds made up of experiences different from our own. Those of us who read students' examination papers should easily grasp this point! */10*

When we consider the structure of the human nervous systems which, through speech, try to come to terms of understanding with each other, we must marvel that any real correspondence ever occurs. The late Judson Herrick of the University of Chicago is authority for the statement that if there were 1,000,000 cells in the human body, connected in pairs, the number of possible combinations would be 10 to the 2,783,000th power—a number so unimaginably large that 250 book-sized pages would be required to print it. But, instead of 1,000,000 nerve cells, there are from 10,000,000,000 to 12,000,000,000 which can be interconnected in infinitely complex patterns. In their film "Communication Primer," Charles and Ray Eames tell us that, if each potential combination were represented by a single dot, there would be enough dots to blacken the surfaces of several earths. When we contemplate such incredible complexities of the human nervous structure, we are amazed that any correlation between the thinking and feeling of one person and the thinking and feeling of another is possible at all; understanding becomes the miracle of miracles. */11*

How then shall we account for the fact that some measure of understanding actually can be achieved? */12*

To begin with, there is the fact of *common structure.* Within the rather vague range of what we call "normal," we human beings are structurally more alike than different. We all have sense organs, nervous sytems, muscles, and glands. Then there is the fact of *common environment.* We all experience rain and sunshine, summer and winter, grass and trees, automobiles and telephones, houses and streets, food and drink, radio and television, fellow human beings, etc., etc. The more similar our environments, the more easily we understand each other. The specialist limits his environment and, *ipso facto,* finds it difficult to communicate with lay people. He and his fellow specialists understand each other very well. The sharing of common experience always generates understanding; that is the reason why professional conferences are so satisfying. */13*

When we seek to promote understanding, there are certain additional facts we should keep in mind. */14*

First, we should realize that individuals differ in their ability to react to words. There is a world of sense objects and there is a world of words. Some people live mainly in one of these worlds and some in the other. In *Hamlet,* Shakespeare sets before us a vivid contrast between these two worlds. The melancholy, meditative Dane is the perfect type of the man of words, one in whom "the native hue of resolution is sicklied o'er, by the pale cast of thought." How different is young Fortinbras who has Hamlet's "dying voice" to succeed him on the throne. He strides into the final scene, orders his servants to carry out the bodies, "bid the cannon shoot," clear up the confusion, and get things moving. To men of his direct-action type, much of Hamlet's wordy wisdom seems so detached from their world of things as to be sheer nonsense. The lesson for us is that, if we want to understand others and be understood by them, we must live in the same world with them sufficiently to acquire the necessary common references. */15*

Second, as we work to promote understanding, we should train ourselves to avoid the semantic error of identification. Three centuries ago Thomas Hobbes observed, "Words are wise men's counters; they do but reckon with them, but they are the money of fools." We must constantly remind ourselves that names are not people, flags are not nations, paper currency is not wealth—*words are not things.* All of us who have managed multi-sectioned courses know how easy it is to equalize the numbers of enrollment cards for the several classes, but how very different is the problem of shifting the students! */16*

In this connection, I often contemplate the amazing performance of Woodrow Wilson with his Fourteen Points. You will remember how, in the quiet of his study, he pounded out, on his old Hammond typewriter, his plan for reorganizing the world, and then handed it to the waiting news reporters. But, alas, when he met the other war leaders at Versailles, he found that reality stubbornly refused to fall into the neat word molds he had formulated. Irreverent old Clemenceau wryly observed: "God Almighty had only ten points, Wilson has fourteen." Please understand that I intend no disparagement of Woodrow Wilson, whom I greatly admire; I am merely pointing out that his great dream failed because men who lived, not in his world of *words*, but in their world of *things*, either could not or would not understand it. */17*

Some years ago, when my wife and I were taken aboard the submarine *USS Starfish* in Pearl Harbor, this error of identification was brought home to me. It was shortly after the *Squalus* disaster off Portsmouth, New Hampshire, in which a crew of twenty-six men had gone to their death on the bottom of the Atlantic. I asked our host, Commander Wills, what had become of the *Squalus* after the Navy had refloated it. "This is it," he said. "What caused it to sink?" I inquired. "The induction valve stuck," he said. "What made it stick?" I asked. "We never found out. That is it," he answered, pointing to it. Who would have served on the ship if the old name had been retained? */18*

Third, in trying to build understanding, we must be extremely careful in our use of abstract terms; they are loaded with potential misunderstanding. When we talk about an apple, we can all see it, touch it, smell it, taste it, etc. We can compare our sense experiences with those of others. When we talk about it, we *talk sense.* But, when we discuss democracy, Americanism, Communism, patriotism, justice, etc., we are not dealing with objects which we can perceive through our senses. Such words signify personal, individual experiences which have lost their direct connections with the world of sense. As Gray and Wise[3] say: "Abstractions are unavoidable in the use of language. . . . What is important is that in our use of words we should be conscious of the fact that they are abstractions. . . . Unless we are especially conscious of how far we have gone in our abstracting . . . our language will be meaningless, even to ourselves." As abstractions take us further and further from sense experience, we finally find ourselves talking *nonsense.* /19

Field trips, clinics, demonstrations, and laboratories are helpful teaching devices because they provide constant opportunity for common checking of sense experiences. Therefore, they do not easily degenerate into blowing word bubbles. But, political speeches abound in cloudy abstractions; only rarely are they couched in concrete, object-oriented words. The more closely we can stick to the specific and the concrete, the more understanding we shall generate. This fact has been recognized by all great speakers from Demosthenes to Churchill. /20

On February 12, 1861, Abraham Lincoln, on his way to Washington for his inauguration, addressed the Indiana legislature. In his speech, he remarked: "Solomon says, 'There is a time to keep silence,' and when men wrangle by the mouth with no certainty that they mean the same thing while using the same word, it were perhaps as well if they would keep silence. The words *coercion* and *invasion* are much used in these days, and often with some temper and hot blood. Let us make sure if we can, that we do not misunderstand the meaning of those who use them. Let us get exact definitions of these words, *not from dictionaries but from the men themselves.*" How well Lincoln understood that the meanings were in the men, not in their words! /21

We should not conclude our discussion of understanding without at least a word about the role of listening. In my judgment, one of the most vital recent developments in our field is our increased emphasis on the receiving end of speech. For this significant improvement we have to thank President-Elect Nichols,[4] who has done more than any other person to produce this salutary change. /22

It is a distressing paradox that in a world like ours, so unbelievably rich in listening opportunities, we seem to become poorer and poorer listeners. My good friend, the late Halford Luccock, warned us that we are in danger of having our tongues wear out before our ears do! Half a century ago, John Dewey wrote: "The one thing that people tend to take for granted when talking to others is that they understand each other. In the give and take of talk, things go so fast and one is so busy organizing his reply that

[3]Giles Wilkeson Gray and Claude Merton Wise, authors of **The Bases of Speech**, 3rd ed. (New York: Harper & Brothers, 1959), p. 507.

[4]Ralph G. Nichols, who was President-Elect of the Speech Association of America in 1960, has spent much of his professional career investigating listening. See, for example, **Are You Listening?** by Nichols and Leonard A. Stevens (New York: McGraw-Hill Book Co., Inc., 1957).

he doesn't take time to make sure what he is replying to." This sort of behavior does not promote understanding! */23*

One reason why we are poor listeners is that we are intolerant of ideas not congenial to us. As George F. Kennan says, "There is no uglier tendency in American nature than the quickness to moral indignation which many of us display when others do not think as we do." It takes us from one national election to the next to get into the proper frame of mind for understanding the arguments of the opposing side. The attitude of the intolerant, ego-centered listener inevitably awakens in others feelings of hostility which make it difficult for *them* to understand *him.* We all should ponder thoughtfully the great words of Herbert Spencer: "In proportion as we love truth more and victory less, we shall become anxious to know what it is that leads our opponents to think as they do. We shall begin to suspect that the pertinacity of belief exhibited by them comes from a perception of something we have not perceived and we shall learn to supplement that portion of truth which we have found with the portion found by them." This tolerant approach is the royal road to understanding. */24*

But tolerance is not enough. If we would develop *understanding* we must also cultivate *sensitiveness* and *imagination.* Insensitiveness renders us incapable of interpreting the audible and visible signs of others' thoughts and feelings. The unimaginative individual lacks the ability to put himself into the shoes of others; he simply cannot conceive of their sincerely thinking and feeling differently from the way he does. On the other hand, the imaginative individual avoids the tragic blunders against which Edward Roland Sill warns us in his lines:

> ". . . These hard, well-meaning hands we thrust
> Among the heart strings of a friend.
>
> "The ill-timed truth we might have kept—
> Who knows how sharp it pierced and stung?
> The word we had not sense to say—
> Who knows how grandly it had rung?" */25*

How many stupidly unnecessary wounds we inflict by playing with words, not knowing that they are loaded! Our own homely poet, Will Carleton, once said:

> "Careful with fire," is good advice we know:
> "Careful with words," is ten times doubly so

or, as Joseph Conrad puts the matter, in *Lord Jim:* "There is a weird power in a spoken word—a word carries far and deals destruction through time as bullets go flying through space." */26*

Now as I come in sight of my conclusion, let me try to lift this whole discussion, for a moment, to the level of national and world problems. */27*

It was our late-lamented friend and leader, William Norwood Brigance, who first made us fully aware of the significance of what Arnold Toynbee had been saying about the imperative necessity for skill on the part of democratic leaders in winning the confidence of the masses. Somehow, working understandings between the gifted and creative leaders, on the one hand, and the great body of ordinary citizens on the other, must be established and maintained. This is the central, perennial problem in a democracy. At long last, we are coming to appreciate the fact that it is not enough for technical experts and specialists to reach cooperative understandings with each other. Such rapport is essential, of course, but it is relatively easy to achieve. The real problem is how to get the masses to understand enough of what men of genius, the small creative minority, are about so that they will permit and encourage them to function in freedom and will be able to evaluate the solutions which these leaders make available to them. Such understanding is absolutely prerequisite to the safety and progress of our democratic society, and *we are still far short of having achieved it!* /28

How well I recall a national convention, many years ago, when Dean Dennis[5] of Northwestern proposed his revolutionary criteria of artistic values. He contended that the noblest art is that which appeals to the many and to the judicious few; that the next lower level of art is that which appeals to the many without offending the judicious few; and finally, below that, he rated the art which appeals to the many even though it offends the judicious few. His sharp rejection of the test laid down by Hamlet in his advice to the players provoked a storm of discussion. Particularly disturbed were those who insisted that the greatest art is that which can be understood and appreciated only by the judicious few and, *ipso facto*, must remain meaningless to the unsophisticated many. Those who aligned themselves with Dean Dennis contended that this view was tantamount to saying that the greatest art is that which nobody can understand. Sometimes, as I look at modern art, I fear that we have adopted that false doctrine! However, the philosophy expressed by Dennis highlights the central idea which I want to leave with you. I think we desperately need more of the type of communication which brings the many and the judicious few together in common appreciation and understanding. Here lies fertile ground which, thus far, we have failed to appropriate and cultivate. It is my conviction that the best defense against the ever-present danger of misunderstanding is to speak in words which will stir the clearest and deepest common experiences of humanity. Abstract language which passes over the heads of ordinary people is as empty as a broken promise. /29

In November 1863, standing on the Gettysburg battlefield, still terrible with the scars of wrath and destruction, an eloquent former United States

[5]Ralph Brownell Dennis (1876–1942), Director and Dean of The School of Speech, Northwestern University, from 1913 to 1942.

Senator, Massachusetts Governor, Harvard President, and Phi Beta Kappa poet, delivered a long oration described in *Harper's Weekly* as "smooth, cold, and spoken with grace, but wanting one stirring thought, one vivid picture, one thrilling appeal." Then, the gaunt, homely son of the Western prairie stepped forward and, in 135 seconds, gave voice to such universal longings and hopes of humanity that his words still strike home to the hearts of common men the world around. The same reporter who had so casually dismissed Everett's ponderous rhetoric wrote: "The few words of the President were from the heart to the heart. They cannot even be read without kindling emotion." Lincoln's speech will be remembered at least as long as his native tongue is spoken. To understand and appreciate what he said does not require a graduate degree! */30*

What then is the sum and substance of the matter? Many of the calamities that afflict mankind are, for the present at least, beyond our control. Hurricanes, blizzards, earthquakes, and floods wreak their havoc upon us despite our utmost efforts to guard against their assaults. But even more devastating than these natural disasters are the catastrophies which we ourselves precipitate—the daily and hourly tragedies of misunderstanding which we might prevent by improving our skill in speech. */31*

Hear the sage words of F. L. Lucas: "We are all serving life sentences of solitary confinement in our own bodies; like prisoners, we tap in awkward code to our fellow men in their neighboring cells." Or, if you will permit me to change the figure of speech, each of us lives on a tiny island in a vast archipelago. On each of the islands around us, one of our fellow beings awaits the satisfactions which can reach him and return to us only if there is a free flow of thought and feeling between us. John Donne's great metaphor "every man is a piece of the continent, a part of the main," comes true only when the islands are bound together by adequate communication. If we would escape isolation and loneliness, we must keep our antennae high and our sending and receiving equipment in efficient working order. As teachers of speech, our supreme task is to open satisfactory communication channels among men. It is our special mission to see to it that our fellow human beings, with all their getting, get understanding. May we ever keep our eyes lifted to that great goal. */32*

> Weaver's speech was warmly received at the convention at which it was given, and it reached a larger audience when printed in *Vital Speeches of the Day*.

QUESTIONS

1. Is Weaver opposed to using speech as a tool to influence human behavior? If not, why does he avoid this common theme?

2. Why does Weaver believe that it is impossible to transfer an idea from one mind to another? How does he account for the measure of understanding which does exist among us?

3. Have you ever attempted to explain any special technique to a person unfamiliar with it? What happened? Would Weaver approve, or conclude that you were attempting the impossible?

4. Weaver relates the story (par. 3) of a graduate committee altering the title of a student thesis to make it sound more "academic." From your own experience, can you present evidence to demonstrate the existence of an "academic language"? If so, what role does such a language play in furthering the notion of a college as an "ivory tower"?

5. The tendency of some young girls to squirm uneasily when hearing the word *snake* exemplifies what phenomenon? Cite three similar incidents from your own experience which illustrate this barrier to effective communication.

6. Can a speaker avoid the use of abstract words completely? If not, what can he do to enhance the understanding of his listeners when using abstractions?

7. Compose a single sentence summarizing Weaver's theory of effective communication. Using this theory as a standard, evaluate the effectiveness of his speech—how successfully does he communicate with you?

PROJECTS

1. Describe the forms of communication behavior which occur when a class is exposed to student-centered teaching. (See Carl Rogers, *Client-Centered Therapy* [Boston: Houghton Mifflin Company, 1951], Ch. 9.) How does this teaching approach differ from the traditional one, from the standpoint of student and of instructor? What reactions do students have to this approach?

2. Prepare a 500-word essay on "Newspeak," George Orwell's fictional language in *Nineteen Eighty-Four* (New York: Harcourt, Brace & Company, 1949). Defend or refute Orwell's thesis that strict language control can destroy a civilization.

3. Abraham Lincoln maintained that meanings are in men, not in their words. Support this contention by describing the language of three acquaintances. Pay particular attention to the connotations, or strictly personal meanings, of the words your subjects use.

4. Prepare a list of the barriers to effective listening you encounter over a two-day period. Record each incident in detail as it occurs. What do you find to be the most common obstacle to understanding through speech? Why do you suppose this is so?

5. Read Franklin D. Roosevelt's public speeches given in 1933 during the first hundred days of his administration. What elements in these addresses were apparently designed to inspire popular confidence in the federal government?

6. Read Carl Sandburg's account of Lincoln's Gettysburg Address in *Abraham Lincoln: The War Years, 1861–1864,* Vol. II [New York: Dell Publishing Co., Inc., 1959], 400–415). Explain the varied reaction of the press to Lincoln's speech. Would this address be as well known today if the South had won the Civil War? If the speech were three times as long? If Lincoln had died a natural death in 1870?

THEORY PUT INTO PRACTICE

If one were to summarize Andrew T. Weaver's theory of effective communication (as in answering Question 7, p. 11), he would probably state the matter something like this: *Effective oral communication is the ability of a speaker to transmit meanings by stirring up within his listeners an awareness of background experiences similar to his own.* Weaver's point is clear enough, but how does a speaker know for sure which of his experiences are most likely to correspond with those of his listeners? Furthermore, doesn't this problem of experience-matching increase with the size and anonymity of an audience?

One way to implement Weaver's philosophy is to supply so many illustrations of the central theme that one or more are bound to prove meaningful to every listener. Russell Conwell, a prominent Baptist preacher, followed this approach early in the century.[1] Conwell prepared a public lecture, "Acres of Diamonds," in which he related sixteen illustrations of a single idea. Despite the fact that this lecture was over two hours long, people flocked to hear it—many people paid to hear it several times. Before he died, the speaker had told the famous story of the man in search of riches over five thousand times!

Customs in speaking have changed since the days of our grandparents. These days almost no one listens to a single speaker for two hours. In fact, now we are more likely to time speeches in minutes, or even seconds when the message is broadcast. How then can the modern speaker be reasonably assured of reaching his listeners in a brief time?

Weaver's emphasis upon *common structure* and *common environment* ("Toward Understanding Through Speech," par. 13) appears to suggest an answer. The speaker whose examples relate to the personal or vicarious experiences of his listeners is the speaker who best communicates his message, whether that message is purely informative, or whether it is persuasive in nature.

The following speech took five and one-half minutes to deliver. It was given May 14, 1964, to fulfill an assignment in a course in beginning public speaking. As you will observe, it is based on four simple illustrations.

The speaker, Clarence Yurk, was a junior majoring in economics. His theme is one that dozens of students choose to speak about. Few develop their material as effectively as he, however.

[1]For an account of Conwell's career and the speech which made him famous, see **Acres of Diamonds** (New York: Harper & Brothers, 1915). The money Conwell received for delivering this lecture helped to found Temple University in Philadelphia.

The audience was composed of the speech instructor and a dozen students.

Notice as you read this speech how common the illustrations are. It would be difficult to find an American anywhere who has not shared in one or more experiences of the kind Yurk describes.

LOST: FOUR FRIENDS

CLARENCE YURK

In the last four years I have lost four friends. /1

During January of this year a friend of mine was driving on a highway late at night. Out of the darkness a car sped toward her. Her car was involved in a head-on collision and Gladys was killed. I lost a friend. /2

Four years ago a friend of mine scored thirty-eight points against Green Bay West in a high-school basketball game. That was on a Friday night. Two nights later the car in which he was riding slammed into a tree at ninety miles an hour. John was cut in half, and I lost another friend. /3

Two years ago Susie Hinz was killed. As usual, her mother picked her up after school and, as usual, they took the same side road home. They lived in the country. On that road they came upon a railroad crossing they had crossed a thousand times. However, on that particular day, because they had crossed the railroad crossing a thousand times and there wasn't a train scheduled for that time anyway, they started across the tracks without looking. A train smashed into their car at seventy miles an hour, dragging their car over a hundred feet. Susie was killed. I lost another friend. /4

All three of these accidents were a result of some form of carelessness. Let's go back over them again. As I said, Gladys was killed in a head-on collision. That means that either one or both of the cars involved crossed the centerline of the highway. One or both drivers were guilty of negligence. /5

John was killed in a car traveling at ninety miles per hour. Need I say more? That was foolishness. /6

Susie was killed because of inattentiveness. Had either she or her mother bothered to look before crossing those tracks they'd probably be alive today. /7

By this time you've probably guessed what I'm getting at. I'm talking to you about the age-old theme of "Drive Carefully." Oh, I know, you're probably saying, "Now look, Clarence, I heard this sermon a thousand times. What do you expect me to do?" There's *no reason* why you and me as college students should *ever* be guilty of negligence, foolishness, or inattentiveness. *Think* when you get behind the wheel of your car. If I can

Text supplied by the speaker and used with permission. For a memorable example of a speech built effectively upon a single illustration, see Bruce Barton's "Which Knew Not Joseph" in **Classified Speech Models**, ed. W. N. Brigance (New York: S. F. Crofts, 1928).

leave you with just one thought today, it's that. I want you to think when you drive. I don't know why it is, but a man can spend his whole day on the job thinking, or a college student can spend hours in a library, thinking, but when he gets into his car at night he completely forgets to think and relies entirely on natural instinct. A car is a two thousand-pound battering ram. That "tin lizzy" out there, or whatever affectionate name you've given it, kills more people in one year than we lost during the whole Korean conflict. *Think* when you drive. Always expect the unexpected. The shortstop for the Milwaukee Braves always expects the next play to come to him. That way he stays on his toes. You, too, should be on your toes when you drive. Always expect the unexpected. Always think. /8

Perhaps you've noticed by now that I said I lost four friends in four years and I've only told you about three. This afternoon I'm going to Sheboygan to attend a funeral. One of my best friends was killed in an auto accident on Tuesday. Gene was twenty-five, married, and had a seven-months-old son. What am I going to say to his wife? /9

Four friends in four years. At that rate, if I live to the age of seventy, I'm going to lose forty-five more friends. My definition of a friend is someone I know and like. *You* are all my friends. /10

As the speaker sat down, an observer could sense the intense concentration of the audience. Not a chair moved, not a sound was heard. As one listener later remarked, "I remember that speech every time I drive back and forth to school."

QUESTIONS

1. What is Yurk's purpose in this speech? How many times does he refer to his purpose, either directly or by implication? Would the speech have been stronger if he had simply mentioned the idea of safe driving once and then moved on to one or two other ideas?

2. If you were asked to speak on traffic safety, what sorts of supporting material would you use besides the example or illustration? Would Yurk's speech have been stronger if he had used a greater variety of speech supports? Would it have been more interesting?

3. How many facts does the speaker reveal about each incident? Should he tell us more than he does? Should he stress material other than that included here? Would one *detailed example be* preferable to the four short ones?

4. Beginning speakers often say that if they had thirty minutes in which to speak, oral communication would be relatively simple. Do you think Yurk's speech would have been improved if he had talked six times as long? Is a good short speech harder to prepare than a good long one?

5. Did you notice grammatical errors as you read this speech? Assuming that such errors exist, is this weakness as serious in a speaker as in a writer? Why or why not?

6. Did you find it hard to believe that a student could lose four friends in automobile accidents in four years? Did the speaker's succinct wording strike you as an artificial striving for effect, or would you have developed these examples in much the same way? Should a speaker "perform" before an audience as an actor does?

7. How did you react to the speaker's concealment of the fourth incident until the end of the speech? Did the fact that this example was the most recent of the four make it more effective than the others? Would this speech have been better organized if the speaker began by presenting his last example first?

8. All of Yurk's examples are from his own experience. Would he have been more effective if he had supplemented personal experience with relevant material from books, magazines, and newspapers? Why is personal experience sometimes an inadequate source of speech material? Are there sources of material other than those we have mentioned?

PROJECTS

1. Select three speeches concerned with safety from *Vital Speeches of the Day*. Summarize the central theme of each in a single sentence. Were these three speeches as meaningful to you as the Yurk speech? Why or why not?

2. Examine the results of psychological studies on the organization of persuasive arguments as reported in Carl I. Hovland, Irving L. Janis, and Harold H. Kelley, *Communication and Persuasion* (New Haven: Yale University Press, 1953). When should the strongest argument in a persuasive speech be presented? Defend your answer.

3. Compare the treatment of speech standards in Irving J. Lee's "Four Ways of Looking at a Speech," *The Quarterly Journal of Speech*, XXVIII (April 1942), 148–155 (reprinted in *The Speaker's Resource Book*, ed. Carroll C. Arnold, Douglas Ehninger, and John C. Gerber [Chicago: Scott, Foresman and Company, 1961], pp. 18–23) with that in James H. McBurney and Ernest J. Wrage, *The Art of Good Speech* (New York: Prentice-Hall, Inc., 1953), pp. 21–32. What significant differences do you find in these two treatments?

4. Some readers may respond to the Yurk speech by dismissing it as mere emotionalism. Most of us like to think that in important matters we are basically logical. But read the account of nonlogical persuasion in Lew Sarrett and William T. Foster, *Basic Principles of Speech*, rev. ed. (Boston: Houghton Mifflin Company, 1946), pp. 478–504. If you had been a member of the audience in the situation described on pp. 481–485, could you have resisted the pressure to sign up for the draft?

5. Much of the impact that a speaker has upon his audience results from stimuli other than the speaker's words. We are all aware of the irritation a harsh voice may produce. But we are less conscious of the cultural variables Edward Hall describes in *The Silent Language* (New York: Premier Books, 1961). Write a 500-word essay describing Hall's "Vocabulary of Culture." Illustrate each of his message systems with an appropriate example from American society.

PART TWO

THE PROBLEM OF SPEAKING ON BEHALF OF A GROUP

Carefully developed qualities and skills are necessary if a group spokesman is to do his job well. First, before a speaker can put the views of his associates into words, he must know what those views are. His *grasp of group attitudes* must be as complete as that of a sociologist studying an isolated segment of society.

A group spokesman is also expected to be *well informed about those issues which affect group welfare*. Because of his ready access to sources of information, his presentation of the group's position is usually thorough, and his recommendations for action, practical and far-sighted.

A group spokesman, especially a national leader, is also expected to demonstrate *acute awareness of time and place*. Other international aid programs had been started before 1960 but it was the Kennedy injunction to "ask not what your country can do for you, ask what you can do for your country" that gave impetus to the Peace Corps. This nation was ready to support an ambitious program of service abroad.

As important as these three qualities is *the speaker's command of language*. The ability to word an idea clearly, directly, and in a memorable fashion is one that any speaker covets.

SPEAKING ON BEHALF OF THE COMMON PEOPLE

An instructive example of a speech on behalf of constituents is one by John Pym which was given many years ago in London. The date was April 17, 1640. The speaker was a fifty-six-year-old country squire from western England. Pym's immediate audience was the House of Commons, though his remarks were soon to be read with keen interest throughout the British Isles.

Pym's speech was delivered at the opening of the Fourth Parliament of Charles I. Charles had succeeded to the throne of England upon the death of his father, James I, in 1625. Charles' relations with his first three Parliaments had been so stormy that for eleven years he ruled the country alone, resorting to taxation by executive decree. The role of the House of Commons as keeper of the nation's purse strings was therefore by-passed. Though Stuart supporters may have agreed that "the King can do no wrong," others did not. One faction, which included large numbers of Puritans and merchants, was strongly resentful of Charles' policies. The issues of the times were complex, and views were divided. But with no Parliaments in session, people had little hope of having their grievances heard.

Charles' reign continued autocratic until the religious controversy of the period came to a crisis. William Laud, Archbishop of Canterbury and *de facto* head of the state church, introduced greater ritual in religious services; Charles then enjoined these changes upon the church in Scotland as well, while endeavoring to further the episcopal system of church government over the presbyterian form favored there.

In England, opinion differed regarding the changes in ritual, with many people opposing them, especially the Puritans. But in Scotland, the changes were more openly resented. So incensed were the Scots by Charles' acting on his authority as King of Scotland and without the approval of the Scottish Parliament or the General Assembly of the Scottish Church in enjoining these changes that they issued a call to arms. Now north of the River Tweed was an army which might invade England to make war against Charles' forces.

The King's immediate needs were an army and more than his customary revenue. Thomas Wentworth, perhaps the ablest of his ministers, recommended a new Parliament as the means of securing them. Wentworth assumed that in this hour of national crisis, the members would rally to Charles' support.

The new Parliament gave Charles' opponents a chance to demand concessions from him. But the concessions Commons had won from the Crown in the past had come as the result of united efforts, and no consensus was apparent in mid-April 1640. Members were divided in their counsel: some supported the King; a Puritan faction led by John Pym desired sweeping concessions; and the majority cautiously awaited the developments of the session before making up their minds.

At the opening of Parliament, the King's ministers explained that Charles needed subsidies with which to fight the Scots; once these were granted, the King would listen to grievances. Older members of the House recalled that this King did not always keep his promises; granted supply, he might dissolve Parliament at once, as he had in the 1620's. To correct grievances or to grant subsidies—this was the issue before the House.

Pym's speech came on the second day of general debate. As Edward Hyde, who was seated in the chamber, wrote, "Whilst men gazed upon each other, looking who should begin (much the greater part having never before sat in Parliament), Mr. Pym, a man of good reputation, but much better known afterward, who had been as long in these assemblies as any man then living, broke the ice, and in a set discourse of about two hours . . ." addressed the House.

Pym's speech is long; the reader is at once aware of its broad scope. Above all, his speech is a remarkable documentation of group attitudes. Note as you read the speech Pym's references to precedent, the language and arguments he uses, and the solution he recommends.

ON THE NATION'S GRIEVANCES

JOHN PYM

Never Parliament had greater business to dispatch, nor more difficulties to encounter; therefore we have reason to take all advantages of order and address, and hereby we shall not only do our own work, but dispose and enable ourselves for the better satisfaction of his Majesty's desire of supply. The grievances being removed, our affections will carry us with speed and cheerfulness, to give his Majesty that which may be sufficient both for his honor and support. Those that in the very first place shall endeavor to redress the grievances, will be found not to hinder, but to be the best furtherers of his Majesty's service. He that takes away weights, doth as much advantage motion, as he that addeth wings. Divers pieces of this main work have been already propounded; his endeavor should be to

Text, somewhat modernized for this book, from Charles Kendall Adams, **Representative British Orations**, Vol. I (New York: G. P. Putnam and Sons, 1884), 38–84. Adams' text, except for changes in spelling and punctuation, corresponds exactly with one corrected by Pym. For a detailed account of the speech and its implications see Goodwin F. Berquist, "Revolution Through Persuasion: John Pym's Appeal to the Moderates in 1640," **The Quarterly Journal of Speech** (February 1963), 23–30.

present to the House a model of the whole.[1] In the creation, God made the world according to that idea or form which was eternally preëxistent in the Divine mind. Moses was commanded to frame the tabernacle after the pattern showed him in the mount. Those actions are seldom well perfected in the execution, which are not first well molded in the design and proposition. /1

He said he would labor to contract those manifold affairs both of the church and state, which did so earnestly require the wisdom and faithfulness of this House, into a double method of grievances and cures. And because there wanted not some who pretended that these things, wherewith the commonwealth is now grieved, are much for the advantage of the King, and that the redress of them will be to his Majesty's great disadvantage and loss, he doubted not but to make it appear, that in discovering the present great distempers and disorders, and procuring remedy for them, we should be no less serviceable to his Majesty, who hath summoned us to this great council, than useful to those whom we do here represent. For the better effecting whereof, he propounded three main branches of his discourse. In the first, he would offer them the several heads of some principal grievances, under which the kingdom groaned. In the second, he undertook to prove that the disorders from whence those grievances issued, were as hurtful to the King as to the people. In the third, he would advise such a way of healing, and removing those grievances, as might be equally effectual to maintain the honor and greatness of the King, and to procure the prosperity and contentment of the people. /2

In the handling whereof he promised to use such expressions as might mitigate the sharpness and bitterness of those things whereof he was to speak, so far as his duty and faithfulness would allow. It is a great prerogative to the King, and a great honor attributed to him, in a maxim of our law, that he can do no wrong; he is the fountain of justice; and, if there be any injustice in the execution of his commands, the law casts it upon the ministers, and frees the King.[2] /3

Activity, life, and vigor are conveyed into the sublunary creatures by the influence of heaven; but the malignity and distemper, the cause of so many epidemical diseases, do proceed from the noisome vapors of the earth, or some ill-affected qualities of the air, without any infection or alteration of those pure, celestial, and incorruptible bodies. In the like manner, he said, the authority, the power, and countenance of princes may concur in the actions of evil men, without partaking in the injustice and obliquity of them. These matters whereof we complain have been presented to his Majesty, either under the pretense of royal prerogatives,

[1]As a parliamentary diarist in the 1620's, Pym developed the habit of referring to himself in the third person, a practice he continues in this report of his speech where, occasionally, he will refer to his own remarks with "He said."

[2]The divine right of a king to govern as he saw fit was a favorite doctrine of Charles I. Members of Parliament might affect royal policy by attacking royal ministers and seeking their removal, but to attack the King personally was to guarantee a trip to the Tower and imprisonment there for days, months, or even years, at the King's pleasure.

which he is bound to maintain, or of public good, which is the most honorable object of regal wisdom. But the covetous and ambitious designs of others have interposed betwixt his royal intentions and the happiness of his people, making those things pernicious and hurtful, which his Majesty apprehended as just and profitable. /4

He said, the things which he was to propound were of a various nature, many of them such as required a very tender and exquisite consideration. In handling of which, as he would be bold to use the liberty of the place and relation wherein he stood, so he would be very careful to express that modesty and humility which might be expected by those of whose actions he was to speak. And if his judgment or his tongue should slip into any particular mistake, he would not think it so great a shame to fail by his own weakness as he should esteem it an honor and advantage to be corrected by the wisdom of that House to which he submitted himself, with this protestation, that he desired no reformation as much as to reform himself. /5

The greatest liberty of the kingdom is religion; thereby we are freed from spiritual evils, and no impositions are so grievous as those that are laid upon the soul. /6

The next great liberty is justice, whereby we are preserved from injuries in our persons and estates; from this is derived into the commonwealth, peace, and order, and safety; and when this is interrupted, confusion and danger are ready to overwhelm all. /7

The third great liberty consists in the power and privilege of parliaments; for this is the fountain of law, the great council of the kingdom, the highest court; this is enabled by the legislative and conciliary power, to prevent evils to come; by the judiciary power, to suppress and remove evils present. If you consider these three great liberties in the order of dignity, this last is inferior to the other two, as means are inferior to the end; but, if you consider them in the order of necessity and use, this may justly claim the first place in our care, because the end cannot be obtained without the means: and if we do not preserve this, we cannot long hope to enjoy either of the others. Therefore being to speak of those grievances which lie upon the kingdom, he would observe this order. /8

1. To mention those which were against the privilege of parliaments. 2. Those which were prejudicial to the religion established in the kingdom. 3. Those which did interrupt the justice of the realm in the liberty of our persons and propriety of our estates. /9

The privileges of Parliament were not given for the ornament or advantage of those who are the members of Parliament. They have a real use and efficacy toward that which is the end of parliaments. We are free from suits that we may the more entirely addict ourselves to the public services; we have, therefore, liberty of speech, that our counsels may not be corrupted with fear, or our judgments perverted with self respects. Those three great faculties and functions of Parliament, the legislative, judiciary, and conciliary power, cannot be well exercised without such privileges as these.

The wisdom of our laws, the faithfulness of our counsels, the righteousness of our judgments, can hardly be kept pure and untainted if they proceed from distracted and restrained minds. /10

It is a good rule of the moral philosopher: *Et non laedas mentem gubernatricem omnium actionum.* These powers of Parliament are to the body politic as the rational faculties of the soul to a man; that which keeps all the parts of the commonwealth in frame and temper, ought to be most carefully preserved in that freedom, vigor, and activity, which belongs to itself. Our predecessors in this House have ever been most careful in the first place to settle and secure their privileges; and he hoped, that we, having had greater breaches made upon us than heretofore, would be no less tender of them, and forward in seeking reparation for that which is past, and prevention of the like for the time to come. /11

Then he propounded divers particular points wherein the privileges of Parliament had been broken. First, in restraining the members of the House from speaking. Secondly, in forbidding the Speaker to put any question. /12

These two were practiced the last day of the last Parliament (and, as was alleged, by his Majesty's command); and both of them trench upon the very life and being of parliaments; for if such a restraining power as this should take root, and be admitted, it will be impossible for us to bring any resolution to perfection in such matters as shall displease those about the King. /13

Thirdly, by imprisoning divers members of the House, for matters done in Parliament. Fourthly, by indictments, informations, and judgments in ordinary and inferior courts, for speeches and proceedings in Parliaments. Fifthly, by the disgraceful order of the King's bench, whereby some members of this House were enjoined to put in security of their good behavior; and for refusal thereof, were continued in prison divers years, without any particular allegation against them. One of them was freed by death. Others were not dismissed till his Majesty had declared his intention to summon the present Parliament. And this he noted not only as a breach of privilege, but as a violation of the common justice of the kingdom. Sixthly, by the sudden and abrupt dissolution of Parliaments, contrary to the law and custom. /14

Often hath it been declared in Parliaments, that the Parliament should not be dissolved, till the petitions be answered. This (he said) was a great grievance because it doth prevent the redress of other grievances. It were a hard case that a private man should be put to death without being heard. As this representative body of the Commons receives a being by the summons, so it receives a civil death by the dissolution. Is it not a much more heavy doom by which we lose our being, to have this civil death inflicted on us in displeasure, and not to be allowed time and liberty to answer for ourselves? That we should not only die, but have this mark of infamy laid upon us? to be made intestabiles, disabled to make our wills, to dispose of our business, as this House hath always used to do before adjournments or dissolutions? Yet this hath often been our case! We have not been permitted to pour out our last sighs and groans into the bosom of our dear sovereign. The words of dying men are full of piercing affections; if we might be heard to speak, no doubt we should so fully express our love and faithfulness to our prince, as might take off the false suggestions and aspersions of others; at least we should in our humble supplications recommend some such things to him in the name of his people, as would make for his own honor, and the public good of his kingdom. */15*

Thus he concluded the first sort of grievances, being such as were against the privilege of Parliament, and passed on to the next, concerning religion; all which he conveyed under these four heads. The first, was the great encouragement given to popery, of which he produced these particular evidences.[3] 1. A suspension of all laws against papists, whereby they enjoy a free and almost public exercise of that religion. Those good statutes which were made for restraint of idolatry and superstition, are now a ground of security to them in the practice of both; being used to no other end but to get money into the King's purse; which as it is clearly against the intentions of the law, so it is full of mischief to the kingdom. By this means a dangerous party is cherished and increased, who are ready to close with any opportunity of disturbing the peace and safety of the state. Yet he did not desire any new laws against popery, or any rigorous courses in the execution of those already in force; he was far from seeking the ruin of their persons or estates; only he wished they might be kept in such a condition as should restrain them from doing hurt. */16*

It may be objected, there are moderate and discreet men amongst them, men of estates, such as have an interest in the peace and prosperity of the kingdom as well as we. These (he said) were not to be considered according to their own disposition, but according to the nature of the body whereof they are parties. The planets have several and particular motions of their own, yet they are all rapt and transported into a contrary course by the superior orb which comprehends them all. The principles of popery are such as are incompatible with any other religion. There may be a suspension of violence for some by certain respects; but the ultimate end even of that moderation is, that they may with more advantage extirpate that which is opposite to them. Laws will not restrain them. Oaths will not. The Pope can dispense with both these, and where there is occasion, his command will move them to the disturbance of the realm—against their own private disposition—yea, against their own reason and judgment—to obey him; to whom they have (especially the Jesuitical party) absolutely and entirely obliged themselves, not only in spiritual matters, but in temporal, as they are in order *ad spiritualia*. Henry III and Henry IV of France were

[3]*Popery* refers to the practice of Roman Catholicism. Pym was born in the days of the Spanish Armada—a period in English history during which allegiance to the Pope in Rome was frequently identified with alliance with Catholic Spain. Since the time of the Armada, English Catholics were required by law to pay recusant fees for nonattendance at services of the Anglican Church.

no Protestants themselves, yet were murdered because they tolerated Protestants. The King and the kingdom can have no security but in their weakness and disability to do hurt. /17

2. A second encouragement is, their admission into places of power and trust in the commonwealth, whereby they get many dependents and adherents, not only of their own, but even of such as make profession to be Protestants. /18

3. A third, their freedom of resorting to London and the court, whereby they have opportunity, not only of communicating their counsels and designs, one to another, but of diving into his Majesty's counsels, by the frequent access of those who are active men amongst them, to the tables and company of great men; and under subtle pretenses and disguises they want not means of cherishing their own projects, and of endeavoring to mold and bias the public affairs to the great advantage of that party. /19

4. A fourth, that as they have a congregation of cardinals at Rome, to consider of the aptest ways and means of establishing the Pope's authority and religion in England, so they have a nuncio here, to act and dispose that party to the execution of those counsels, and, by the assistance of such cunning and Jesuitical spirits as swarm in this town, to order and manage all actions and events, to the furtherance of that main end.[4] /20

The second grievance of religion, was from those manifold innovations lately introduced into several parts of the kingdom, all inclining to popery, and disposing and fitting men to entertain it. The particulars were these: 1. Divers of the chiefest points of religion in difference betwixt us and the papists have been publicly defended, in licensed books, in sermons, in university acts and disputations. 2. Divers popish ceremonies have been not only practiced but countenanced, yea, little less than enjoined, as altars, images, crucifixes, bowings, and other gestures and observances, which put upon our churches a shape and face of popery. He compared this to the dry bones in Ezekiel. First, they came together; then the sinews and the flesh came upon them; after this the skin covered them; and then breath and life was put into them! So (he said) after these men had molded us into an outward form and visage of popery, they would more boldly endeavor to breathe into us the spirit of life and popery. /21

The third grievance was the countenancing and preferring those men who were most forward in setting up such innovations; the particulars were so well known that they needed not to be named.[5] /22

The fourth was, the discouragement of those who were known to be most conscionable and faithful professors of the truth. Some of the ways of effecting this he observed to be these: 1. The courses taken to enforce and enlarge those unhappy differences, for matters of small moment,

[4]The Queen was a devout Catholic whose presence at court ensured a haven for priests and for foreign visitors of Roman persuasion.

[5]Pym and his Puritan friends opposed the ritualistic innovations of Archbishop Laud as much as the rebelling Scots.

which have been amongst ourselves, and to raise up new occasions of further division, whereby many have been induced to forsake the land, not seeing the end of those voluntary and human injunctions in things appertaining to God's worship. Those who are indeed lovers of religion, and of the churches of God, would seek to make up those breaches, and to unite us more entirely against the common enemy. 2. The overrigid prosecution of those who are scrupulous in using some things enjoined, which are held by those who enjoin them, to be in themselves indifferent. It hath been ever the desire of this House, expressed in many Parliaments in Queen Elizabeth's time and since, that such might be tenderly used. It was one of our petitions delivered at Oxford to his Majesty that now is; but what little moderation it hath produced is not unknown to us all! Any other vice almost may be better endured in a minister than inconformity. 3. The unjust punishments and vexations of sundry persons for matters required without any warrant of law: as, for not reading the book concerning recreation on the Lord's day; for not removing the communion table to be set altarwise at the east end of the chancel; for not coming up to the rails to receive the sacrament; for preaching the Lord's day in the afternoon; for catechising in any other words and manner than in the precise words of the short catechism in the common prayer book. */23*

The fifth and last grievance concerning religion, was the encroachment and abuse of ecclesiastical jurisdiction. The particulars mentioned were these: 1. Fining and imprisoning in cases not allowed by law. 2. The challenging their jurisdiction to be appropriate to their order, which they allege to be *jure divino*. 3. The contriving and publishing of new articles, upon which they force the churchwardens to take oaths, and to make inquiries and presentments, as if such articles had the force of canons; and this was an effect of great presumption and boldness, not only in the bishops, but in the archdeacons, officials, and chancellors, taking upon themselves a kind of synodal authority. The injunctions of this kind might, indeed, well partake in name with that part of the common law which is called the extravagants! */24*

Having dispatched these several points, he proceeded to the third kind of grievances, being such as are against the common justice of the realm, in the liberty of our persons, and propriety of our estates, of which he had many to propound: in doing whereof, he would rather observe the order of time, wherein they were acted, than of consequence; but when he should come to the cure, he should then persuade the House to begin with those which were of most importance, as being now in execution, and very much pressing and exhausting the commonwealth. */25*

He began with the tonnage and poundage and other impositions not warranted by law; and because these burdens had long lain upon us, and the principles which produced them are the same from whence divers others are derived, he thought it necessary to premise a short narrative and relation of the grounds and proceedings of the power of imposing herein practiced. It was a fundamental truth, essential to the Constitution and government of this kingdom — an hereditary liberty and privilege of all the freeborn subjects of the land — that no tax, tallage, or other charge might be laid upon us, without common consent in Parliament. This was acknowledged by the Conqueror; ratified in that contract which he made with this nation, upon his admittance to the kingdom; declared and confirmed in the laws which he published. This hath never been denied by any of our kings — though broken and interrupted by some of them, especially by King John and Henry III. Then, again, it was confirmed by Magna Charta, and other succeeding laws; yet not so well settled but that it was sometime attempted by the two succeeding Edwards, in whose times the subjects were very sensible of all the breaches made upon the common liberty, and, by the opportunity of frequent Parliaments, pursued them with fresh complaints, and for the most part found redress, and procured the right of the subject to be fortified by new statutes. */26*

He observed that those kings, even in the acts whereby they did break the law, did really affirm the subject's liberty, and disclaim that right of imposing which is now challenged: for they did usually procure the merchants' consent to such taxes as were laid, thereby to put a color of justice upon their proceeding; and ordinarily they were limited to a short time, and then propounded to the ratification of the Parliament, where they were canceled or confirmed, as the necessity and state of the kingdom did require. But for the most part such charges upon merchandise were taken by authority of Parliament, and granted for some short time, in a greater or lesser proportion, as was requisite for supply of the public occasions — six or twelve in the pound, for one, two, or three years, as they saw cause to be employed for the defense of the sea: and it was acknowledged so clearly to be in the power of Parliament, that they have sometimes been granted to noblemen, and sometimes to merchants, to be disposed for that use. Afterward they were granted to the King for life, and so continued for divers descents, yet still as a gift and grant of the Commons. */27*

Betwixt the time of Edward III and Queen Mary, never prince (that he could remember) offered to demand any imposition but by grant in Parliament. Queen Mary laid a charge upon cloth, by the equity of the statute of tonnage and poundage, because the rate set upon wool was much more than upon cloth; and, there being little wool carried out of the kingdom unwrought, the Queen thought she had reason to lay on somewhat more; yet not full so much as brought them to an equality, but that still there continued a less charge upon wool wrought into cloth, than upon wool carried out unwrought; until King James' time when upon Nicholson's project, there was a further addition of charge, but still upon pretense of the statute, which is that we call the pretermitted custom. */28*

In Queen Elizabeth's time, it is true, one or two little impositions crept in, the general prosperity of her reign overshadowing small errors and innovations. One of these was upon currants, by occasion of the merchants' complaints that the Venetians had laid a charge upon the English cloth, that so we might be even with them, and force them the sooner to take it off. But this being demanded by King James, was denied by one Bates, a merchant, and upon a suit in the exchecquer, was adjudged for the King. Now the manner of that judgment was thus: There were then but three judges in that court, all differing from one another in the grounds of their sentences. The first was of opinion, the King might impose upon such commodities as were foreign and superfluous, as currants were, but not upon such as were native and to be transported, or necessary, and to be imported for the use of the kingdom. The second judge was of opinion, he might impose upon all foreign merchandise, whether superfluous or no, but not upon native. The third, that forasmuch as the King had the custody of the ports, and the guard of the seas, and that he might open and shut up the ports as he pleased, he had a prerogative to impose upon all merchandise, both exported and imported. Yet this single, distracted, and divided judgment, is the foundation of all the impositions now in practice; for, after this, King James laid new charges upon all commodities outward and inward, not limited to a certain time and occasion, but reserved to himself, his heirs and successors, forever—the first impositions in fee simple that were ever heard of in this kindgom. This judgment, and the right of imposing thereupon assumed, was questioned *in septimo* and *duodecimo* of that King, and was the cause of the breach of both those Parliaments. In 18 and 21 Jacobi, indeed, it was not agitated by this House, but only that they might preserve the favor of the King, for the dispatch of some other great businesses, upon which they were more especially attentive. But in the first of his present Majesty, it necessarily came to be remembered, upon the proposition on the King's part, for renewing the bill of tonnage and poundage; yet so moderate was that Parliament, that they thought rather to confirm the impositions already set by a law to be made, than to abolish them by a judgment in Parliament; but that and divers ensuing Parliaments have been unhappily broken, before that endeavor could be accomplished: only at the last meeting a remonstrance was made concerning the liberty of the subject in this point;[6] and it hath always been expressed to be the meaning of the House, and so it was (as he said) his own meaning in the proposition now made, to settle and restore the right according to law, and not to diminish the King's profit, but to establish it by a free grant in Parliament. */29*

However, since the breach of the last Parliament, his Majesty hath, by a new book of rates, very much increased the burden upon merchandise, and now tonnage and poundage, old and new impositions, are all taken by prerogative, without any grant in Parliament, or authority of law, as we conceive; from whence divers inconveniences and mischiefs are produced. 1. The danger of the precedent, that a judgment in one court, and in one case, is made binding to all the kingdom. 2. Men's goods are seized, their legal suits are stopped, and justice denied to those that desire to take the

[6]Pym's reference is to the Petition of Right of 1628, which prohibited arbitrary taxation. In exchange for subsidies King Charles had signed the Petition.

benefit of the law. 3. The great sums of money received upon these impositions, intended for the guard of the seas, claimed and defended upon no ground but of public trust, for protection of merchants and defense of the ports, are dispersed to other uses, and a new tax raised for the same purposes. 4. These burdens are so excessive, that trade is thereby very much hindered, the commodities of our own growth extremely abased, and those imported much enhanced; all which lies not upon the merchant alone, but upon the generality of the subject; and by this means the stock of the kingdom is much diminished, our exportation being less profitable, and our importation more changeable. And if the wars and troubles in the neighbor parts had not brought almost the whole stream of trade into this kingdom, we should have found many more prejudicial effects of these impositions, long before this time, than yet we have done. Especially they have been insupportable to the poor plantations, whither many of his Majesty's subjects have been transported, in divers parts of the continent and islands of America, in furtherance of a design tending to the honor of the kingdom, and the enlargement of his Majesty's dominions.[7] The adventurers in this noble work have for the most part no other support but tobacco, upon which such a heavy rate is set, that the King receives twice as much as the true value of the commodity to the owner. 5. Whereas these great burdens have caused divers merchants to apply themselves to a way of traffic abroad by transporting goods from one country to another, without bringing them home into England. But now it hath been lately endeavored to set an imposition upon this trade, so that the King will have a duty even out of those commodities which never come within his dominions, to the great discouragement of such active and industrious men. */30*

The next general head of civil grievances, was enforcing men to compound for knighthood; which though it may seem past, because it is divers years since it was used, yet upon the same grounds the King may renew it, as often as he pleaseth, for the composition looks backward, and the offense continuing, is subject to a new fine. The state of that business he laid down thus: Heretofore, when the services due by tenure were taken in kind, it were fit there were some way of trial and approbation of those that were bound to such services. Therefore, it was ordained, that such as were to do knight's services, after they came of age, and had possession of their lands, should be made knights; that is, publicly declared to be fit for that service. Divers ceremonies and solemnities were in use for this purpose; and if by the party's neglect this was not done, he was punishable by fine; there being in those times an ordinary and open way to get knighthood, for those who were born to it. Now it is quite true, that although the use of this hath for divers ages been discontinued, yet there have passed very few kings under whom there hath not been a general summons, re-

[7]The speaker was especially knowledgeable about colonial settlements in the New World, having served for the previous eleven years as treasurer of the Providence Island Company (a joint stock venture in the Caribbean) and as a patentee of the Saybrook Colony in Connecticut.

quiring those who had lands of such value as the law prescribes, to appear at the coronation, or some other great solemnity, and to be knighted, and yet nothing intended but the getting of some small fines. So this grievance is not altogether new in the kind; but it is new in the manner, and in the excess of it, and that in divers respects. 1. First, it hath been extended beyond all intention and color of law. Not only inn-holders, but likewise leaseholders, copyholders, merchants, and others; scarce any man free from it. 2. The fines have been immoderate, far beyond the proportion of former times. 3. The proportion has been without any example, precedent, or rule of justice. For though those that were summoned did appear, yet distresses infinite were made out against them, and issues increased and multiplied, and no way open to discharge those issues, by plea or otherwise, but only by compounding with the commissioners at their own pleasure. */31*

The third general head of civil grievances was, the great inundation of monopolies; whereby heavy burdens are laid, not only upon foreign, but also native commodities. These began in the soap patent. The principal undertakers in this were divers popish recusants, men of estate and quality, such as in likelihood did not only aim at their private gain, but that by this open breach of law, the King and his people might be more fully divided, and the ways of Parliament men more thoroughly obstructed. Amongst the infinite inconveniences and mischiefs which this did produce, these few may be observed: 1. The impairing the goodness, and enhancing the price of most of the commodities and manufactures of the realm, yea, of those which are of most necessary and common use, as salt, soap, beer, coals, and infinite others. 2. That, under color of licenses, trades and manufactures are restrained to a few hands, and many of the subjects deprived of their ordinary way of livelihood. 3. That, upon such illegal grants, a great number of persons had been unjustly vexed by pursuivants, imprisonments, attendance upon the council table, forfeiture of goods, and many other ways. */32*

The fourth head of civil grievances was that great and unparalleled grievance of the ship money, which, though it may seem to have more warrant of law than the rest, because there hath a judgment passed for it, yet in truth it is thereby aggravated, if it be considered that the judgment is founded upon the naked opinion of some judges without any written law, without any custom, or authority of law books, yea, without any one precedent for it.[8] Many express laws, many declarations in Parliaments, and the constant practice and judgment at all times being against it! Yea, in the very nature of it, it will be found to be disproportionable to the case of "necessity" which is pretended to be the ground of it! Necessity excludes all formalities and solemnities. It is no time then to make levies and taxes to build and prepare ships. Every man's person, every man's ships are to

[8]The famous Ship-Money Trial of John Hampden, Pym's friend, in 1637 aroused a great deal of resentment against this form of taxation.

be employed for the resisting of an invading enemy. The right on the subject's part was so clear, and the pretenses against it so weak, that he thought no man would venture his reputation or conscience in the defense of that judgment, being so contrary to the grounds of the law, to the practice of former times, and so inconsistent in itself. */33*

Amongst many inconveniences and obliquities of this grievance, he noted these: 1. That it extendeth to all persons, and to all times; it subjecteth our goods to distress, and our persons to imprisonment; and, the causes of it being secret and invisible, referred to his Majesty's breast alone, the subject was left without possibility of exception and relief. 2. That there were no rules or limits for the proportion; so that no man knew what estate he had, or how to order his course or expenses. 3. That it was taken out of the subject's purse by a writ, and brought into the King's coffers by instructions from the lords of his most honorable privy council. Now, in the legal defense of it, the writ only did appear; of the instructions there was no notice taken, which yet in the real execution of it were most predominant. It carries the face of service in the writ, and of revenue in the instructions. Why, if this way had not been found to turn the ship into money, it would easily have appeared how incompatible this service is with the office of a sheriff, in the inland counties; and how incongruous and inconvenient for the inhabitants! The law in a body politic is like nature, which always prepareth and disposeth proper and fit instruments and organs for every natural operation. If the law had intended any such charge as this, there should have been certain rules, suitable means, and courses, for the levying and managing of it. */34*

The fifth head was the enlargement of the forests beyond the bounds and perambulations appointed and established by act of Parliament, 27 and 28 Edward I; and this is done upon the very reasons and exceptions which had been on the King's part propounded, and by the Commons answered, in Parliament, not long after that establishment. It is not unknown to many in this House that those perambulations were the fruit and effect of that famous charter which is called "Charta de Forrestâ," whereby many tumults, troubles, and discontents had been taken away, and composed between the King and his subjects; and it is full of danger, that by reviving those old questions, we may fall into the like distempers. Hereby, however, no blame could fall upon that great lord, who is now justice in Eyre,[9] and in whose name these things were acted; it could not be expected that he should take notice of the laws and customs of the realm; therefore he was careful to procure the assistance and direction of the judges; and if anything were done against law, it was for them to answer, and not for him. */35*

[9]Sir Thomas Wentworth, first Earl of Strafford (1593–1641), was lord deputy in Ireland and perhaps the ablest and most resented adviser of Charles I. Many of the King's policies were attributed to him, and the second Parliament of 1640 was to enact a bill of attainder to bring about his execution.

The particular irregularities and obliquities of this business were these: 1. The surreptitious procuring a verdict for the King, without giving notice to the country whereby they might be prepared to give in evidence for their own interest and indemnity, as was done in Essex. 2. Whereas the judges in the justice seat in Essex were consulted with about the entry of the former verdict, and delivered their opinion touching that alone, without meddling with the point of right; this opinion was after enforced in other counties as if it had been a judgment upon the matter, and the council for the county discountenanced in speaking, because it was said to be already adjudged. 3. The inheritance of divers of the subjects have been hereupon disturbed, after the quiet possession of three or four hundred years, and a way opened for the disturbance of many others. 4. Great sums of money have been drawn from such as have lands within these pretended bounds, and those who have forborne to make composition have been threatened with the execution of these forest laws. 5. The fifth was the selling of nuisances, or at least some such things as are supposed to be nuisances. The King, as father of the commonwealth, is to take care of the public commodities and advantages of his subjects, as rivers, highways, common sewers, and suchlike, and is to remove whatsoever is prejudicial to them; and for the trial of those there are legal and ordinary writs of *ad quod damnum;* but of late a new and extrajudicial way hath been taken, of declaring matters to be nuisances; and divers have thereupon been questioned, and if they would not compound, they have been fined; if they do compound, that which was first prosecuted as a common nuisance is taken into the King's protection and allowed to stand; and having yielded the King money, no further care is taken whether it be good or bad for the commonwealth. By this a very great and public trust is either broken or abused. If the matter compounded for be truly a nuisance, then it is broken to the hurt of the people; if it be not a nuisance, then it is abused to the hurt of the party. The particulars mentioned were: First, the commission for buildings in and about this town, which heretofore hath been presented by this House as a grievance in King James' time, but now of late the execution hath been much more frequent and prejudicial than it was before. Secondly, commission for depopulation, which began some few years since, and is still in hot prosecution. By both these the subject is restrained from disposing of his own. Some have been commanded to demolish their houses; others have been forbidden to build; others, after great trouble and vexation, have been forced to redeem their peace with large sums, and they still remain, by law, as liable to a new question as before; for it is agreed by all that the King cannot license a common nuisance; and although indeed these are not such, yet it is a matter of very ill consequence that, under that name, they should be compounded for, and may in ill times hereafter be made a precedent for the kings of this realm to claim a power of licensing such things as are nuisances indeed. */36*

The seventh great civil grievance hath been, the military charges laid upon the several counties of the kingdom; sometimes by warrant under his Majesty's signature, sometimes by letters from the council table, and sometimes (such had been the boldness and presumption of some men), by the order of the Lord Lieutenants, or deputy-lieutenant alone. This is a growing evil; still multiplying and increasing from a few particulars to many, from small sums to great. It began first to be practiced as a loan, for supply of coat and conduct money; and for this it hath some countenance from the use in Queen Elizabeth's time, when the lords of the council did often desire the deputy-lieutenants to procure so much money to be laid out in the country as the service did require, with a promise to pay it again in London; for which purpose there was a constant warrant in the exchequer. This was the practice in her time, and in a great part of King James'. But the payments were then so certain, as it was little otherwise than taking up money upon bills of exchange. At this day they follow these precedents in the manner of the demand (for it is with a promise of a repayment), but not in the certainty and readiness of satisfaction. */37*

The first particular brought into a tax (as he thought) was the muster master's wages, at which many repined; but being for small sums, it began to be generally digested; yet, in the last Parliament, this House was sensible of it, and to avoid the danger of the precedent that the subjects should be forced to make any payments without consent in Parliament, they thought upon a bill that might be a rule to the lieutenants what to demand, and to the people what to pay. But the hopes of this bill were dashed in the dissolution of that Parliament. Now of late divers other particulars are growing into practice, which make the grievance much more heavy. Those mentioned were these: 1. Pressing men against their will, and forcing them which are rich or unwilling to serve, to find others in their place. 2. The provision of public magazines for powder, and other munition, spades and pickaxes. 3. The salary of divers officers besides the muster master. 4. The buying of cart-horses and carts, and hiring of carts for carriages. */38*

The eighth head of civil grievances was the extrajudicial declarations of judges, whereby the subjects have been bound in matters of great importance without hearing of counsel or argument on their part, and are left without legal remedy, by writ of error or otherwise. He remembered the expression used by a former member of the House, of a "teeming Parliament." This, he said, was a teeming grievance; from hence have issued most of the great grievances now in being. The ship-money—the pretended nuisances already mentioned—and some others which have not yet been touched upon—especially that concerning the proceedings of ecclesiastical courts. */39*

The ninth general head was—that the authority and wisdom of the council table have been applied to the contriving and managing of several monopolies, and other great grievances. The institution of the council table was much for the advantage and security of the subject, to avoid surreptitious and precipitate courts in the great affairs of the kingdom. But by law an oath should be taken by all those of the King's council, in which, amongst other things it is expressed that they should for no cause forbear to do right to all the King's people. If such an oath be not now taken, he wished it might be brought into use again. */40*

It was the honor of that table, to be, as it were, incorporated with the King; his royal power and greatness did shine most conspicuously in their actions and in their counsels. We have heard of projectors and referees heretofore; and what opinion and relish they have found in this House is not unknown. But that any such thing should be acted by the council table which might give strength and countenance to monopolies, as it hath not been used till now of late, so it cannot be apprehended without the just grief of the honest subject, and encouragement of those who are ill affected. He remembered that *in tertio* of this King, a noble gentleman, then a very worthy member of the Commons' House, now a great lord and eminent counsellor of state, did in this place declare an opinion concerning that clause used to be inserted in patents of monopoly, whereby justices of peace are commanded to assist the patentees; and that he urged it to be a great dishonor to those gentlemen which are in commission to be so meanly employed—with how much more reason may we, in jealousy of the honor of the council table, humbly desire that their precious time, their great abilities, designed to the public care and service of the kingdom, may not receive such a stain, such a diminution as to be employed in matters of so ill report, in the estimation of the law; of so ill effect in the apprehension of the people! */41*

The tenth head of civil grievances was comprised in the high court of Star Chamber, which some think succeeded that which in the Parliament rolls is called *magnum concilium*, and to which Parliaments were wont so often to refer those important matters which they had no time to determine. But now this court, which in the late restoration or erection of it in Henry VII's time, was especially designed to restrain the oppression of great men, and to remove the obstructions and impediments of the law—this, which is both a court of counsel and a court of justice—hath been made an instrument of erecting and defending monopolies and other grievances; to set a face of right upon those things which are unlawful in their own nature; a face of public good upon such as are pernicious in their use and execution. The soap patent and divers other evidences thereof may be given, so well known as not to require a particular relation. And as if this were not enough, this court hath lately intermeddled with the ship money! Divers sheriffs have been questioned for not levying and collecting such sums as their counties have been charged with; and if this beginning be not prevented, the Star Chamber will become a court of revenue, and it shall be made crime not to collect or pay such taxes as the state shall require! */42*

The eleventh head of civil grievance was now come to. He said, he was gone very high, yet he must go a little higher. That great and most eminent power of the King, of making edicts and proclamations, which are said to be *leges temporis*, and by means of which our princes have used to encounter with such sudden and unexpected danger, as would not endure so much delay, as assembling the great council of the kingdom—this, which is one of the most glorious beams of majesty, most rigorous in commanding reverence and subjection, hath, to our unspeakable grief, been often exercised of late for the enjoining and maintaining sundry monopolies and other grants; exceeding burdensome and prejudicial to the people. */43*

The twelfth next. Now, although he was come as high as he could upon earth, yet the presumption of evil men did lead him one step higher—even as high as heaven—as high as the throne of God! It was now (he said) grown common for ambitious and corrupt men of the clergy to abuse the truth of God and the bond of conscience; preaching down the laws and liberties of the kingdom; and pretending divine authority for an absolute power in the King, to do what he would with our persons and goods. This hath been so often published in sermons and printed books, that it is now the highway to preferment! */44*

In the last Parliament we had a sentence of an offense of this kind against one Manwaring, then a doctor, now a bishop; concerning whom (he said) he would say no more but this, that when he saw him at that bar, in the most humble and dejected posture that ever he observed, he thought he would not so soon have leaped into a bishop's chair! But his success hath emboldened others; therefore (he said) this may well be noted as a double grievance, that such doctrine should be allowed, and that such men should be preferred; yea, as a root of grievances, whereby they endeavor to corrupt the King's conscience, and, as much as in them lies, to deprive the people of that royal protection to which his Majesty is bound by the fundamental laws of the kingdom, and by his own personal oath. */45*

The thirteenth head of civil grievances he would thus express: The long intermission of Parliaments, contrary to the two statutes yet in force, whereby it is appointed there should be Parliaments once a year, at the least; and most contrary to the public good of the kingdom; since, this being well remedied, it would generate remedies for all the rest. */46*

Having gone through the several heads of grievances, he came to the second main branch, propounded in the beginning; that the disorders from whence these grievances issued were as hurtful to the King as to the people, of which he gave divers reasons. */47*

1. The interruption of the sweet communion which ought to be betwixt the King and his people, in matters of grace and supply. They have need of him by his general pardon; to be secured from projectors and informers; to be freed from obsolete laws; from the subtle devices of such as seek to restrain the prerogative to their own private advantage, and the public hurt; and he hath need of them for counsel and support in great and extraordinary occasions. This mutual intercourse, if indeed sustained, would so weave the affections and interests of his subjects into his actions and designs that their wealth and their persons would be his; his own estate would be managed to most advantage; and public undertakings would be prosecuted at the charge and adventure of the subject. The victorious attempts

in Queen Elizabeth's time upon Portugal, Spain, and the Indies, were for the greatest part made upon the subjects' purses, and not upon the Queen's; though the honor and profit of the success did most accrue to her. */48*

2. Those often breaches and discontentments betwixt the King and the people are very apt to diminish his reputation abroad, and disadvantage his treaties and alliances. */49*

3. The apprehension of the favor and encouragement given to popery hath much weakened his Majesty's party beyond the sea, and impaired that advantage which Queen Elizabeth and his royal father have heretofore made, of being heads of the Protestant union. */50*

4. The innovations in religion and rigor of ecclesiastical courts have forced a great many of his Majesty's subjects to forsake the land; whereby not only their persons and their posterity, but their wealth and their industry are lost to this kingdom, much to the reduction, also, of his Majesty's customs and subsidies. And, amongst other inconveniences of such a sort, this was especially to be observed, that divers clothiers, driven out of the country, had set up the manufacture of cloth beyond the seas; whereby this state is like to suffer much by abatement of the price of wools, and by want of employment for the poor; both which likewise tend to his Majesty's particular loss. */51*

5. It puts the King upon improper ways of supply, which, being not warranted by law, are much more burdensome to the subject than advantageous to his Majesty. In France, not long since, upon a survey of the King's revenue, it was found that two parts in three never came to the King's purse, but were diverted to the profit of the officers or ministers of the Crown, and it was thought a very good service and reformation to reduce two parts to the King, leaving still a third part to the instruments that were employed about getting it in. It may well be doubted that the King may have the like or worse success in England, which appears already in some particulars. The King, for instance, hath reserved upon the monopoly of wines thirty thousand pounds rent a year; the vintner pays forty shillings a ton, which comes to ninety thousand pounds; the price upon the subject by retail is increased twopence a quart, which comes to eight pounds a ton, and for forty-five thousand tons brought in yearly, amounts to three hundred and sixty thousand pounds; which is three hundred and thirty thousand pounds loss to the kingdom, above the King's rent! Other monopolies also, as that of soap, have been very chargeable to the kingdom and brought very little treasure into his Majesty's coffers. Thus it is that the law provides for that revenue of the Crown which is natural and proper, that it may be safely collected and brought to account; but this illegal revenue, being without any such provision, is left to hazard and much uncertainty, either not to be retained, or not duly accounted of. */52*

6. It is apt to weaken the industry and courage of the subject; if they be left uncertain, whether they shall reap the benefit of their own pains

and hazard. Those who are brought into the condition of slaves will easily grow to a slavish disposition, who, having nothing to lose, do commonly show more boldness in disturbing than defending a kingdom. */53*

7. These irregular courses do give opportunity to ill instruments, to insinuate themselves into the King's service, for we cannot but observe, that if a man be officious in furthering their inordinate burdens of ship money, monopolies, and the like, it varnisheth over all other faults, and makes him fit both for employment and preferment; so that out of their offices, they are furnished for vast expenses, purchases, buildings; and the King loseth often more in desperate debts at their death, than he got by them all their lives. Whether this were not lately verified in a western man, much employed while he lived, he leaves to the knowledge of those who were acquainted with his course; and he doubted not but others might be found in the like case. The same course, again, has been pursued with those that are affected to popery, to profaneness, and to superstitious innovations in matters of religion. All kinds of spies and intelligencers, have means to be countenanced and trusted if they will be but zealous in these kind of services, which, how much it detracts from his Majesty, in honor, in profit, and prosperity of public affairs, lies open to every man's apprehension. And from these reasons or some of them, he thought it proceeded, that through the whole course of the English story it might be observed, that those kings who had been most respectful of the laws, had been most eminent in greatness, in glory, and success, both at home and abroad; and that others, who thought to subsist by the violation of them, did often fall into a state of weakness, poverty, and infortunity. */54*

8. The differences and discontents betwixt his Majesty and the people at home, have in all likelihood diverted his royal thoughts and counsels from those great opportunities which he might have, not only to weaken the House of Austria, and to restore the Palatinate, but to gain himself a higher pitch of power and greatness than any of his ancestors.[10] For it is not unknown how weak, how distracted, how discontented the Spanish colonies are in the West Indies. There are now in those parts in New England, Virginia, and the Caribbean Islands, and in the Bermudas, at least sixty thousand able persons of this nation, many of them well armed, and their bodies seasoned to that climate, which with a very small charge, might be set down in some advantageous parts of these pleasant, rich, and fruitful countries, and easily make his Majesty master of all that treasure, which not only foments the war, but is the great support of popery in all parts of Christendom. */55*

9. And lastly, those courses are likely to produce such distempers in the state as may not be settled without great charge and loss; by which

[10]Charles' sister had married the Protestant Elector of the Palatine, a German state west of the Rhine. The Elector's lands were overrun by the Austrians, precipitating bitter war between Catholics and Protestants on the Continent.

means more may be consumed in a few months than shall be gotten by such ways in many years. */56*

Having thus passed through the two first general branches, he was now come to the third, wherein he was to set down the ways of healing and removing those grievances which consisted of two main branches: first, in declaring the law where it was doubtful; the second, in better provision for the execution of law, where it is clear. But (he said) because he had already spent much time, and begun to find some confusion in his memory,[11] he would refer the particulars to another opportunity, and for the present only move that which was general to all, and which would give weight and advantage to all the particular ways of redress. That is, that we should speedily desire a conference with the Lords, and acquaint them with the miserable condition wherein we find the church and state; and as we have already resolved to join in a religious seeking of God, in a day of fast and humiliation, so to entreat them to concur with us in a parliamentary course of petitioning the King, as there should be occasion; and in searching out the causes and remedies of these many insupportable grievances under which we lie. That so, by the united wisdom and authority of both Houses, such courses may be taken as (through God's blessing) may advance the honor and greatness of his Majesty, and restore and establish the peace and prosperity of the kingdom. */57*

This, he said, we might undertake with comfort and hope of success; for though there be a darkness upon the land, a thick and palpable darkness, like that of Egypt, yet, as in that, the sun had not lost his light, nor the Egyptians their sight (the interruption was only in the medium), so with us, there is still (God be thanked) light in the sun—wisdom and justice in his Majesty—to dispel this darkness; and in us there remains a visual faculty, whereby we are enabled to apprehend, and moved to desire, light. And when we shall be blessed in the enjoying of it, we shall thereby be incited to return his Majesty such thanks as may make it shine more clearly in the world, to his own glory, and in the hearts of his people, to their joy and contentment. */58*

According to the clerk of the House of Commons, cries of "a good oration!" greeted Pym as he sat down. As he requested, the assembly appointed a committee to consult with the Lords about national grievances. The King's hopes of quick revenue were destroyed forever.

Pym's leadership of the House of Commons was now established. The subjects he introduced in April would become the first order of business when the Long Parliament convened in November.

[11]To this day members of the House of Commons are expected to deliver their remarks without notes; in view of the length of Pym's address, it is not surprising that his memory began to fail him.

QUESTIONS

1. Would Pym's speech have been equally influential with the Englishmen of 1640 if it had been half as long? Why or why not?

2. How many specific grievances does Pym enumerate? Is the quantity of a speaker's supporting evidence more, or less, persuasive than its quality? Explain.

3. The House of Commons was a natural forum for a speaker, like Pym, who desired a nation-wide audience. Why wouldn't the House of Lords, the upper house which roughly corresponds to our Senate, have suited Pym's purpose as well?

4. In the fifth paragraph of his speech Pym conveys his sense of humility. What effect do you think such a statement had, coming as it did from one of the oldest and most experienced members of Commons?

5. What were the "privileges of Parliament" Pym refers to (par. 10)? What sort of image does the phrase *parliamentary privilege* convey to an American today?

6. Pym argues (par. 15) that parliaments, like men, should be allowed certain rights before they die. Do you find this comparison valid, or would you agree with Charles that a parliament should sit only as long as it pleased the Crown?

7. Pym refers to the Magna Charta as justification for what parliamentary right? Why is this right generally considered the most important privilege in the history and development of the House of Commons?

8. What is Pym's principal objection to "enforcing men to compound for knighthood?"

9. Thomas Carlyle described Pym's style of speaking as "barren as brick clay." Why do you agree or disagree with this estimate?

10. What were the provisions of the Petition of Right of 1628? Compare the King's interpretation of this document with that of John Pym.

11. What relationship existed between the English clergy and the Crown in Pym's time? Why do you think Charles enforced acceptance of Laud's religious innovations?

PROJECTS

1. Prepare a topical outline of Pym's speech. If you were classifying his primary purpose, would you say it is informative or persuasive? That is, is Pym most concerned with providing his listeners with factual information or swaying them to his way of thinking? Defend your answer.

2. Pym makes a number of references throughout his speech to the Bible. If you had lived in 1640, would this have been the most appropriate means of proof and rhetorical embellishment? Or would references to such writers as Shakespeare, Ben Jonson, and Francis Bacon have been more apropos? Compose a 500-word essay supporting your answer.

3. What did the term *Puritan* stand for in the seventeenth century? Discuss specific passages in Pym's speech that would appeal to the Puritans of his day.

4. Read the biographical account of William Laud in the *Dictionary of National Biography*. What position did Laud take toward Puritans and Roman Catholics? Why was he so frequently misunderstood?

5. Some readers will object to Pym's treatment of Roman Catholicism on the grounds of religious intolerance. Read the account of Pym and the Short Parliament of 1640 by Esme Wingfield-Stratford in *King Charles and King Pym, 1637–1643* (London: Hollis and Carter, Ltd., 1949).

6. When were Catholics first allowed to vote in national elections in Britain? When were they formally admitted to Parliament? What are the provisions of the Coronation Oath Act of 1689, still in effect? See Carl Stephenson and Frederick G. Marcham, *Sources of English Constitutional History* (New York: Harper & Brothers, 1937). What obstacles, if any, did Benjamin Disraeli, a Jew, encounter in becoming Queen Victoria's Prime Minister?

7. Describe how the three functions of the English Parliament originated. What specific needs did early parliamentary assemblies satisfy?

8. Enumerate the principal provisions of the British Constitution. Do you think that the British political system is more, or less, flexible than our own? Why?

9. Read C. V. Wedgwood's account of the Ship Money Trial of 1637 in *The King's Peace, 1637–1641*, Vol. I of *The Great Rebellion* (New York: The Macmillan Company, 1955). Is Pym's objection to the verdict in this trial valid?

10. Pym argued that annual parliaments were necessary to remedy the nation's grievances. Support or refute this position.

11. Read the account of Pym's life in the *Dictionary of National Biography*. What action did Charles intend to take against Pym in 1641? This action, though thwarted, has been described as the spark which started the English Civil War. Why?

SPEAKING ON BEHALF OF THE AMERICAN COLONISTS

Though it may seem strange today, some of the greatest speeches ever delivered were apparent failures when measured by a common standard of effectiveness—audience approval or agreement. Such a speech was that of Edmund Burke before the House of Commons, March 22, 1775.

Burke was born in Ireland in 1729 or 1730. He was tutored by a Quaker schoolmaster, spent six years at Trinity College, Dublin, and then embarked on a lifetime of scholarly activity, writing, and public service. Burke's interests included politics, philosophy, and literature, both classical and modern. Samuel Johnson said, "No man of sense could meet Burke by accident under a gateway to avoid a shower, without being convinced that he was the first man in England."

Burke's investigations centered upon America, India, and France—three major trouble spots in the reign of George III. It is the first of these three areas which concerns us here.

In 1758, Burke became the editor and principal contributor to a new British journal, the *Annual Register.* Among the varied functions of the new magazine, two in particular explain Burke's grasp of American affairs: the *Register* regularly included summaries of debates in Parliament and it printed news from abroad, including reports on activities of English colonies in the New World. So great did Burke's comprehension of American affairs become that he gained a reputation as a knowledgeable friend of the colonists. (In fact, Chauncey A. Goodrich reports in *Select British Eloquence* that in 1771 Burke accepted a commission of a thousand pounds per year as parliamentary agent for the colony of New York.)

Burke was not a wealthy man. His early attempts to eke out an existence as a man of letters achieved limited success financially, though his writings did gain him recognition among the intelligentsia of England. Later he became private secretary to Lord Rockingham, the Whig leader who then was Prime Minister, and who helped him secure a seat in the House of Commons. In this arena Burke was to remain active from 1765 until just before his death in 1797.

Relations between England and America had been both good and bad since 1761. On the one hand, British troops, supplemented by colonial militiamen, decisively defeated the French in North America, thereby making future settlement west of the Ohio legal and relatively safe. William Pitt, the Prime Minister who engineered these victories, became a colonial hero; an era of good feeling between colonies and mother country seemed inevitable. But on the other hand, the expenses of the war had to be met. Pitt's successors at Whitehall decided that the colonies should foot the bill for the recently concluded French and Indian War. Toward this end, Parliament enacted a series of revenue bills, the most famous of which was the Stamp Act of 1765. This act was so widely attacked in the New World that its repeal was made the first order of business in the new Rockingham Administration a year later.

In repealing the Stamp Act, however, Parliament reiterated its right to tax the American colonies. Here lay the seed of future trouble, as later ministries were to discover. New taxes gave rise to new protests and partial repeals; collection of royal revenue in America became more and more hazardous. On April 19, 1774, Burke discussed American taxation in the House. Supporting a proposal by another member to repeal the tax on tea, he said, "Leave America, if she has taxable matter in her, to tax herself. . . . Be content to bind America by the bonds of trade; you have always done it." In addition to speaking out against the principle of taxing the colonies for revenue, he delivered a stinging attack on ministerial vacillation. Tension mounted as the colonists awaited the Crown's next move in 1775.

Lord North, the King's Prime Minister from 1769 to 1781, brought a new proposal before the House on February 20, 1775. It was an act, North said, for "conciliating the differences with America." North's bill was a scheme for dividing and thereby subduing the rebellious colonies. He proposed to exempt individual colonies from parliamentary taxation if they voluntarily paid their share for the common defense.

The reintroduction of the American question gave Burke another opportunity to speak on a topic he knew better than any other member. "On Conciliation with America" was his eleventh-hour attempt to keep the American colonies British. *No taxation without representation* was his central theme. Since three thousand miles of ocean separated England from America, he considered regular colonial representation at Westminster unfeasible. Consequently, he proposed that American colonial assemblies be allowed to tax themselves, for only in their own bodies could they be truly represented. The benefits of the British Constitution were to be extended beyond the seas—a startling proposal in 1775 but accepted practice today in the British Commonwealth of Nations.

As you read his speech, notice Burke's many appeals to history, his phrasing of political maxims, and his extended analysis of Lord North's bill in contrast to his own resolutions. Put yourself in the place of a New York merchant in 1775. How would this last-minute effort at conciliation by your colonial agent in England have struck you?

ON CONCILIATION WITH AMERICA

EDMUND BURKE

I hope, sir, that notwithstanding the austerity of the Chair, your good nature will incline you to some degree of indulgence towards human frailty. You will not think it unnatural that those who have an object depending, which strongly engages their hopes and fears, should be somewhat inclined to superstition. As I came into the House, full of anxiety about the event of my motion, I found, to my infinite surprise, that the grand penal bill, by which we had passed sentence on the trade and sustenance of America, is to be returned to us from the other House.[1] I do confess, I could not help looking on this event as a fortunate omen. I look upon it as a sort of providential favor, by which we are put once more in possession of our deliberative capacity upon a business so very questionable in its nature, so very uncertain in its issue. By the return of this bill, which seemed to have taken its flight forever, we are at this very instant nearly as free to choose a plan for our American government as we were on the first day of the session. If, sir, we incline to the side of conciliation, we are not at all embarrassed (unless we please to make ourselves so) by any incongruous mixture of coercion and restraint. We are therefore called upon, as it were by a superior warning voice, again to attend to America, to attend to the whole of it together, and to review the subject with an unusual degree of care and calmness. *|1*

Surely it is an awful subject, or there is none so on this side of the grave. When I first had the honor of a seat in this House, the affairs of that continent pressed themselves upon us as the most important and most delicate object of parliamentary attention. My little share in this great deliberation oppressed me. I found myself a partaker in a very high trust; and having no sort of reason to rely on the strength of my natural abilities for the proper execution of that trust, I was obliged to take more than common pains to instruct myself in everything which relates to our colonies. I was not less under the necessity of forming some fixed ideas concerning the general policy of the British Empire. Something of this sort seemed to be indispensable, in order, amidst so vast a fluctuation of passions and opinions, to concenter my thoughts, to ballast my conduct, to

Text, somewhat modernized for this book, from **The Writings and Speeches of Edmund Burke**, Vol. II (Boston: Little, Brown & Co., 1901), 101 – 182. Burke as a speaker and man of letters is the subject of articles by Donald C. Bryant in **The Quarterly Journal of Speech** and elsewhere.

[1]Burke refers to an act to restrain the trade and commerce of the provinces of Massachusetts Bay and New Hampshire and the colonies of Connecticut and Rhode Island and Providence Plantation to Great Britain, Ireland, and the British islands in the West Indies, and to prohibit the provinces and colonies from carrying on any fishing on the banks of Newfoundland and other places, under certain conditions and limitations.

preserve me from being blown about by every wind of fashionable doctrine. I really did not think it safe or manly to have fresh principles to seek upon every fresh mail which should arrive from America. /2

At that period I had the fortune to find myself in perfect concurrence with a large majority in this House. Bowing under that high authority, and penetrated with the sharpness and strength of that early impression, I have continued ever since, without the least deviation, in my original sentiments. Whether this be owing to an obstinate perseverance in error, or to a religious adherence to what appears to me truth and reason, it is in your equity to judge. /3

Sir, Parliament, having an enlarged view of objects, made, during this interval, more frequent changes in their sentiments and their conduct than could be justified in a particular person upon the contracted scale of private information. But though I do not hazard anything approaching to a censure on the motives of former Parliaments to all those alterations, one fact is undoubted—that under them the state of America has been kept in continual agitation. Everything administered as remedy to the public complaint, if it did not produce, was at least followed by, an heightening of the distemper, until, by a variety of experiments, that important country has been brought into her present situation—a situation which I will not miscall, which I dare not name, which I scarcely know how to comprehend in the terms of any description. /4

In this posture, sir, things stood at the beginning of the session. About that time, a worthy member of great parliamentary experience, who in the year 1766 filled the chair of the American Committee with much ability, took me aside, and, lamenting the present aspect of our politics, told me things were come to such a pass that our former methods of proceeding in the House would be no longer tolerated—that the public tribunal (never too indulgent to a long and unsuccessful opposition) would now scrutinize our conduct with unusual severity—that the very vicissitudes and shiftings of ministerial measures, instead of convicting their authors of inconstancy and want of system, would be taken as an occasion of charging us with a predetermined discontent which nothing could satisfy, whilst we accused every measure of vigor as cruel and every proposal of lenity as weak and irresolute. The public, he said, would not have patience to see us play the game out with our adversaries; we must produce our hand. It would be expected that those who for many years had been active in such affairs should show that they had formed some clear and decided idea of the principles of colony government, and were capable of drawing out something like a platform of the ground which might be laid for future and permanent tranquillity. /5

I felt the truth of what my honorable friend represented; but I felt my situation, too. His application might have been made with far greater propriety to many other gentlemen. No man was, indeed, ever better disposed, or worse qualified, for such an undertaking, than myself. Though I gave so far into his opinion that I immediately threw my thoughts into a sort of parliamentary form, I was by no means equally ready to produce them. It generally argues some degree of natural impotence of mind, or some want of knowledge of the world, to hazard plans of government, except from a seat of authority. Propositions are made, not only ineffectually, but somewhat disreputably, when the minds of men are not properly disposed for their reception; and for my part, I am not ambitious of ridicule, not absolutely a candidate for disgrace. /6

Besides, sir, to speak the plain truth, I have in general no very exalted opinion of the virtue of paper government, nor of any politics in which the plan is to be wholly separated from the execution. But when I saw that anger and violence prevailed every day more and more, and that things were hastening towards an incurable alienation of our colonies, I confess my caution gave way. I felt this as one of those few moments in which decorum yields to a higher duty. Public calamity is a mighty leveler; and there are occasions when any, even the slightest, chance of doing good must be laid hold on, even by the most inconsiderable person. /7

To restore order and repose to an empire so great and so distracted as ours is, merely in the attempt, an undertaking that would ennoble the flights of the highest genius, and obtain pardon for the efforts of the meanest understanding. Struggling a good while with these thoughts, by degrees I felt myself more firm. I derived, at length, some confidence from what in other circumstances usually produces timidity. I grew less anxious, even from the idea of my own insignificance. For, judging of what you are by what you ought to be, I persuaded myself that you would not reject a reasonable proposition because it had nothing but its reason to recommend it. On the other hand, being totally destitute of all shadow of influence, natural or adventitious, I was very sure that if my proposition were futile or dangerous, if it were weakly conceived or improperly timed, there was nothing exterior to it of power to awe, dazzle, or delude you. You will see it just as it is, and you will treat it just as it deserves. /8

The proposition is peace. Not peace through the medium of war; not peace to be hunted through the labyrinth of intricate and endless negotiations; not peace to arise out of universal discord, fomented from principle, in all parts of the empire; not peace to depend on the juridical determination of perplexing questions, or the precise marking the shadowy boundaries of a complex government. It is simple peace, sought in its natural course and in its ordinary haunts. It is peace sought in the spirit of peace, and laid in principles purely pacific. I propose, by removing the ground of the difference, and by restoring the *former unsuspecting confidence of the colonies in the mother country*, to give permanent satisfaction to your people, and (far from a scheme of ruling by discord) to reconcile them to each other in the same act and by the bond of the very same interest which reconciles them to British government. /9

My idea is nothing more. Refined policy ever has been the parent of confusion, and ever will be so, as long as the world endures. Plain good intention, which is as easily discovered at the first view as fraud is surely detected at last, is, let me say, of no mean force in the government of mankind. Genuine simplicity of heart is an healing and cementing principle. My plan, therefore, being formed upon the most simple grounds imaginable, may disappoint some people when they hear it. It has nothing to recommend it to the pruriency of curious ears. There is nothing at all new and captivating in it. It has nothing of the splendor of the project which has been lately laid upon your table by the noble lord in the blue riband.[2] It does not propose to fill your lobby with squabbling colony agents, who will require the interposition of your mace at every instant to keep the peace amongst them. It does not institute a magnificent auction of finance, where captivated provinces come to general ransom by bidding against each other, until you knock down the hammer, and determine a proportion of payments beyond all the powers of algebra to equalize and settle. */10*

The plan which I shall presume to suggest derives, however, one great advantage from the proposition and registry of that noble lord's project. The idea of conciliation is admissible. First, the House, in accepting the resolution moved by the noble lord, has admitted, notwithstanding the menacing front of our address, notwithstanding our heavy bill of pains and penalties, that we do not think ourselves precluded from all ideas of free grace and bounty. */11*

The House has gone farther: it has declared conciliation admissible *previous* to any submission on the part of America. It has even shot a good deal beyond that mark, and has admitted that the complaints of our former mode of exerting the right of taxation were not wholly unfounded. That right thus exerted is allowed to have had something reprehensible in it—something unwise, or something grievous—since, in the midst of our heat and resentment, we, of ourselves, have proposed a capital alteration, and, in order to get rid of what seemed so very exceptionable, have instituted a mode that is altogether new—one that is, indeed, wholly alien from all the ancient methods and forms of Parliament. */12*

The *principle* of this proceeding is large enough for my purpose. The means proposed by the noble lord for carrying his ideas into execution, I think, indeed, are very indifferently suited to the end; and this I shall

[2]"That when the governor, council, and assembly, or general court, of any of his Majesty's provinces or colonies in America shall *propose* to make provision, *according to the condition, circumstances,* and *situation* of such province or colony, for contributing their *proportion* to the *common defense* (such *proportion* to be raised under the authority of the general court or general assembly of such province or colony, and disposable by Parliament), and shall *engage* to make provision also for the support of the civil government and the administration of justice in such province or colony, it will be proper, *if such proposal shall be approved by his Majesty and the two Houses of Parliament,* and for so long as such provision shall be made accordingly, to forbear, *in respect of such province or colony,* to levy any duty, tax, or assessment, or to impose any further duty, tax, or assessment, except only such duties as it may be expedient to continue to levy or to impose for the regulation of commerce: the net produce of the duties last mentioned to be carried to the account of such province or colony respectively."—Resolution moved by Lord North in the Committee, and agreed to by the House February 27, 1775. [Here and elsewhere Burke refers to Lord North as "the lord in the blue riband"—the badge of the Order of the Garter.]

endeavor to show you before I sit down. But, for the present, I take my ground on the admitted principle. I mean to give peace. Peace implies reconciliation; and where there has been a material dispute, reconciliation does in a manner always imply concession on the one part or on the other. In this state of things I make no difficulty in affirming that the proposal ought to originate from us. Great and acknowledged force is not impaired, either in effect or in opinion, by an unwillingness to exert itself. The superior power may offer peace with honor and with safety. Such an offer from such a power will be attributed to magnanimity. But the concessions of the weak are the concessions of fear. When such a one is disarmed, he is wholly at the mercy of his superior; and he loses forever that time and those chances which, as they happen to all men, are the strength and resources of all inferior power. */13*

The capital leading questions on which you must this day decide are these two: First, whether you ought to concede; and secondly, what your concession ought to be. On the first of these questions we have gained (as I have just taken the liberty of observing to you) some ground. But I am sensible that a good deal more is still to be done. Indeed, sir, to enable us to determine both on the one and the other of these great questions with a firm and precise judgment, I think it may be necessary to consider distinctly the true nature and the peculiar circumstances of the object which we have before us; because, after all our struggle, whether we will or not, we must govern America according to that nature and to those circumstances, and not according to our own imaginations, not according to abstract ideas of right, by no means according to mere general theories of government, the resort to which appears to me, in our present situation, no better than arrant trifling. I shall therefore endeavor, with your leave, to lay before you some of the most material of these circumstances in as full and as clear a manner as I am able to state them. */14*

The first thing that we have to consider with regard to the nature of the object is the number of people in the colonies. I have taken for some years a good deal of pains on that point. I can by no calculation justify myself in placing the number below two millions of inhabitants of our own European blood and color, besides at least 500,000 others, who form no inconsiderable part of the strength and opulence of the whole. This, sir, is, I believe, about the true number. There is no occasion to exaggerate, where plain truth is of so much weight and importance. But whether I put the present numbers too high or too low is a matter of little moment. Such is the strength with which population shoots in that part of the world that, state the numbers as high as we will, whilst the dispute continues, the exaggeration ends. Whilst we are discussing any given magnitude, they are grown to it. Whilst we spend our time in deliberating on the mode of governing two millions, we shall find we have millions more to manage. Your children do not grow faster from infancy to manhood than they spread from families to communities, and from villages to nations. */15*

I put this consideration of the present and the growing numbers in the front of our deliberation because, sir, this consideration will make it evident to a blunter discernment than yours that no partial, narrow, contracted, pinched, occasional system will be at all suitable to such an object. It will show you that it is not to be considered as one of those *minima* which are out of the eye and consideration of the law, not a paltry excrescence of the state, not a mean dependent, who may be neglected with little damage and provoked with little danger. It will prove that some degree of care and caution is required in the handling such an object; it will show that you ought not, in reason, to trifle with so large a mass of the interests and feelings of the human race. You could at no time do so without guilt; and be assured you will not be able to do it long with impunity. */16*

But the population of this country, the great and growing population, though a very important consideration, will lose much of its weight if not combined with other circumstances. The commerce of your colonies is out of all proportion beyond the numbers of the people. This ground of their commerce, indeed, has been trod some days ago, and with great ability, by a distinguished person[3] at your bar. This gentleman, after thirty-five years—it is so long since he first appeared at the same place to plead for the commerce of Great Britain—has come again before you to plead the same cause, without any other effect of time than that, to the fire of imagination and extent of erudition which even then marked him as one of the first literary characters of his age, he has added a consummate knowledge in the commercial interest of his country, formed by a long course of enlightened and discriminating experience. */17*

Sir, I should be inexcusable in coming after such a person with any detail if a great part of the members who now fill the House had not the misfortune to be absent when he appeared at your bar. Besides, sir, I propose to take the matter at periods of time somewhat different from his. There is, if I mistake not, a point of view from whence, if you will look at this subject, it is impossible that it should not make an impression upon you. */18*

I have in my hand two accounts: one a comparative state of the export trade of England to its colonies, as it stood in the year 1704, and as it stood in the year 1772; the other a state of the export trade of this country to its colonies alone, as it stood in 1772, compared with the whole trade of England to all parts of the world (the colonies included) in the year 1704. They are from good vouchers: the latter period from the accounts on your table; the earlier from an original manuscript of Davenant, who first established the Inspector-General's office, which has been ever since his time so abundant a source of parliamentary information. */19*

The export trade to the colonies consists of three great branches: the African, which, terminating almost wholly in the colonies, must be put to the account of their commerce; the West Indian; and the North Ameri-

[3]Burke refers to Richard Glover (1712–1785), a poet, who had been a Member of Parliament for Weymouth, 1761–1768.

can. All these are so interwoven that the attempt to separate them would tear to pieces the contexture of the whole, and, if not entirely destroy, would very much depreciate the value of all the parts. I therefore consider these three denominations to be, what in effect they are, one trade. /20

The trade to the colonies, taken on the export side, at the beginning of this century, that is, in the year 1704, stood thus:

Exports to North America and the West Indies . .	£483,265	
To Africa	86,665	
	£569,930	/21

In the year 1772, which I take as a middle year between the highest and lowest of those lately laid on your table, the account was as follows:

To North America and the West Indies	£4,791,734	
To Africa	866,398	
To which if you add the export trade from Scotland, which had in 1704 no existence . .	364,000	
	£6,022,132	/22

From five hundred and odd thousand, it has grown to six millions. It has increased no less than twelvefold. This is the state of the colony trade, as compared with itself at these two periods, within this century; and this is matter for meditation. But this is not all. Examine my second account. See how the export trade to the colonies alone in 1772 stood in the other point of view, that is, as compared to the whole trade of England in 1704.

The whole export trade of England, including that to the colonies, in 1704	£6,509,000	
Export to the colonies alone, in 1772	6,022,000	
Difference	£ 487,000	/23

The trade with America alone is now within less than £500,000 of being equal to what this great commercial nation, England, carried on at the beginning of this century with the whole world! If I had taken the largest year of those on your table, it would rather have exceeded. But, it will be said, is not this American trade an unnatural protuberance, that has drawn the juices from the rest of the body? The reverse. It is the very food that has nourished every other part into its present magnitude. Our general trade has been greatly augmented, and augmented more or less in almost every part to which it ever extended, but with this material difference: that of the six millions which in the beginning of the century constituted the whole mass of our export commerce, the colony trade was but one twelfth part; it is now (as a part of sixteen millions) considerably more than a third of the whole. This is the relative proportion of the importance of the colonies at these two periods; and all reasoning concerning our mode of treating them must have this proportion as its basis, or it is a reasoning weak, rotten, and sophistical. /24

Mr. Speaker, I cannot prevail on myself to hurry over this great consideration. It is good for us to be here. We stand where we have an immense view of what is, and what is past. Clouds indeed, and darkness, rest upon the future. Let us, however, before we descend from this noble eminence, reflect that this growth of our national prosperity has happened within the short period of the life of man. It has happened within sixty-eight years. There are those alive whose memory might touch the two extremities. For instance, my Lord Bathurst might remember all the stages of the progress. He was in 1704 of an age at least to be made to comprehend such things. He was then old enough *acta parentum jam legere, et quae sit poterit cognoscere virtus*. Suppose, sir, that the angel of this auspicious youth, foreseeing the many virtues which made him one of the most amiable, as he is one of the most fortunate men of his age, had opened to him in vision that when, in the fourth generation, the third prince of the House of Brunswick had sat twelve years on the throne of that nation which (by the happy issue of moderate and healing councils) was to be made Great Britain, he should see his son, Lord Chancellor of England, turn back the current of hereditary dignity to its fountain, and raise him to a higher rank of peerage, whilst he enriched the family with a new one—if, amidst these bright and happy scenes of domestic honor and prosperity, that angel should have drawn up the curtain, and unfolded the rising glories of his country, and whilst he was gazing with admiration on the then commercial grandeur of England, the genius should point out to him a little speck, scarce visible in the mass of the national interest, a small seminal principle rather than a formed body, and should tell him, "Young man, there is America, which at this day serves for little more than to amuse you with stories of savage men and uncouth manners, yet shall, before you taste of death, show itself equal to the whole of that commerce which now attracts the envy of the world. Whatever England has been growing to by a progressive increase of improvement, brought in by varieties of people, by succession of civilizing conquests and civilizing settlements in a series of seventeen hundred years, you shall see as much added to her by America in the course of a single life!" If this state of his country had been foretold to him, would it not require all the sanguine credulity of youth, and all the fervid glow of enthusiasm, to make him believe it? Fortunate man, he has lived to see it! Fortunate indeed, if he lives to see nothing that shall vary the prospect, and cloud the setting of his day! */25*

Excuse me, sir, if, turning from such thoughts, I resume this comparative view once more. You have seen it on a large scale; look at it on a small one. I will point out to your attention a particular instance of it in the single province of Pennsylvania. In the year 1704, that province called for £11,459 in value of your commodities, native and foreign. This was the whole. What did it demand in 1772? Why, nearly fifty times as much; for in that year the export to Pennsylvania was £507,909, nearly equal to the export to all the colonies together in the first period. */26*

I choose, sir, to enter into these minute and particular details because generalities, which in all other cases are apt to heighten and raise the subject, have here a tendency to sink it. When we speak of the commerce with our colonies, fiction lags after truth, invention is unfruitful, and imagination cold and barren. */27*

So far, sir, as to the importance of the object in the view of its commerce, as concerned in the exports from England. If I were to detail the imports, I could show how many enjoyments they procure which deceive the burden of life, how many materials which invigorate the springs of national industry and extend and animate every part of our foreign and domestic commerce. This would be a curious subject indeed, but I must prescribe bounds to myself in a matter so vast and various. */28*

I pass, therefore, to the colonies in another point of view—their agriculture. This they have prosecuted with such a spirit that, besides feeding plentifully their own growing multitude, their annual export of grain, comprehending rice, has some years ago exceeded a million in value. Of their last harvest, I am persuaded, they will export much more. At the beginning of the century some of these colonies imported corn from the mother country. For some time past the Old World has been fed from the New. The scarcity which you have felt would have been a desolating famine, if this child of your old age, with a true filial piety, with a Roman charity, had not put the full breast of its youthful exuberance to the mouth of its exhausted parent. */29*

As to the wealth which the colonies have drawn from the sea by their fisheries, you had all that matter fully opened at your bar. You surely thought those acquisitions of value, for they seemed even to excite your envy; and yet the spirit by which that enterprising employment has been exercised ought rather, in my opinion, to have raised your esteem and admiration. And pray, sir, what in the world is equal to it? Pass by the other parts, and look at the manner in which the people of New England have of late carried on the whale fishery. Whilst we follow them among the tumbling mountains of ice, and behold them penetrating into the deepest frozen recesses of Hudson's Bay and Davis's Straits, whilst we are looking for them beneath the Arctic Circle, we hear that they have pierced into the opposite region of polar cold, that they are at the antipodes, and engaged under the frozen Serpent of the South. Falkland Island, which seemed too remote and romantic an object for the grasp of national ambition, is but a stage and resting-place in the progress of their victorious industry. Nor is the equinoctial heat more discouraging to them than the accumulated winter of both the poles. We know that, whilst some of them draw the line and strike the harpoon on the coast of Africa, others run the longitude, and pursue their gigantic game along the coast of Brazil. No sea but what is vexed by their fisheries. No climate that is not witness to their toils. Neither the perseverance of Holland, nor the activity of France, nor the dexterous and firm sagacity of English enterprise, ever carried this most perilous mode of hardy industry to the extent to which it has been pushed by this recent people—a people who are still, as it were, but in the gristle, and not yet hardened into the bone of manhood. When I contemplate these things—when I know that the colonies in general owe little or nothing to any care of ours, and that they are not squeezed into this happy form by the constraints of watchful and suspicious government, but that, through a wise and salutary neglect, a generous nature has been suffered to take her own way to perfection—when I reflect upon these effects—when I see how profitable they have been to us—I feel all the pride of power sink, and all presumption in the wisdom of human contrivances melt and die away within me; my rigor relents; I pardon something to the spirit of liberty. */30*

I am sensible, sir, that all which I have asserted in my detail is admitted in the gross, but that quite a different conclusion is drawn from it. America, gentlemen say, is a noble object—it is an object well worth fighting for. Certainly it is, if fighting a people be the best way of gaining them. Gentlemen in this respect will be led to their choice of means by their complexions and their habits. Those who understand the military art will of course have some predilection for it. Those who wield the thunder of the state may have more confidence in the efficacy of arms. But I confess, possibly for want of this knowledge, my opinion is much more in favor of prudent management than of force, considering force not as an odious but a feeble instrument for preserving a people so numerous, so active, so growing, so spirited as this, in a profitable and subordinate connection with us. */31*

First, sir, permit me to observe that the use of force alone is but *temporary*. It may subdue for a moment, but it does not remove the necessity of subduing again; and a nation is not governed which is perpetually to be conquered. */32*

My next objection is its *uncertainty*. Terror is not always the effect of force, and an armament is not a victory. If you do not succeed, you are without resource: for, conciliation failing, force remains; but, force failing, no further hope of reconciliation is left. Power and authority are sometimes bought by kindness; but they can never be begged as alms by an impoverished and defeated violence. */33*

A further objection to force is that you *impair the object* by your very endeavors to preserve it. The thing you fought for is not the thing which you recover, but depreciated, sunk, wasted, and consumed in the contest. Nothing less will content me than *whole America*. I do not choose to consume its strength along with our own, because in all parts it is the British strength that I consume. I do not choose to be caught by a foreign enemy at the end of this exhausting conflict, and still less in the midst of it. I may escape, but I can make no insurance against such an event. Let me add that I do not choose wholly to break the American spirit, because it is the spirit that has made the country. */34*

Lastly, we have no sort of *experience* in favor of force as an instrument in the rule of our colonies. Their growth and their utility has been owing to methods altogether different. Our ancient indulgence has been said to be pursued to a fault. It may be so; but we know, if feeling is evidence, that our fault was more tolerable than our attempt to mend it, and our sin far more salutary than our penitence. */35*

These, sir, are my reasons for not entertaining that high opinion of untried force by which many gentlemen, for whose sentiments in other particulars I have great respect, seem to be so greatly captivated. But there is still behind a third consideration concerning this object, which serves to determine my opinion on the sort of policy which ought to be pursued in the management of America, even more than its population and its commerce: I mean its *temper and character.* */36*

In this character of the Americans a love of freedom is the predominating feature which marks and distinguishes the whole; and as an ardent is always a jealous affection, your colonies become suspicious, restive, and untractable whenever they see the least attempt to wrest from them by force, or shuffle from them by chicane, what they think the only advantage worth living for. This fierce spirit of liberty is stronger in the English colonies, probably, than in any other people of the earth, and this from a great variety of powerful causes, which, to understand the true temper of their minds, and the direction which this spirit takes, it will not be amiss to lay open somewhat more largely. */37*

First, the people of the colonies are descendants of Englishmen. England, sir, is a nation which still, I hope, respects, and formerly adored, her freedom. The colonists emigrated from you when this part of your character was most predominant; and they took this bias and direction the moment they parted from your hands. They are therefore not only devoted to liberty, but to liberty according to English ideas and on English principles. Abstract liberty, like other mere abstractions, is not to be found. Liberty inheres in some sensible object; and every nation has formed to itself some favorite point, which by way of eminence becomes the criterion of their happiness. It happened, you know, sir, that the great contests for freedom in this country were from the earliest times chiefly upon the question of taxing. Most of the contests in the ancient commonwealths turned primarily on the right of election of magistrates, or on the balance among the several orders of the state. The question of money was not with them so immediate. But in England it was otherwise. On this point of taxes the ablest pens and most eloquent tongues have been exercised, the greatest spirits have acted and suffered. In order to give the fullest satisfaction concerning the importance of this point, it was not only necessary for those who in argument defended the excellence of the English Constitution to insist on this privilege of granting money as a dry point of fact, and to prove that the right had been acknowledged in ancient parchments and blind usages to reside in a certain body called a House of Commons; they went much further—they attempted to prove, and they succeeded, that in theory it ought to be so, from the particular nature of a House of Commons as an immediate representative of the people, whether the old records had delivered this oracle or not. They took infinite pains to inculcate, as a fundamental principle, that in all monarchies the people must in effect themselves, mediately or immediately, possess the power of granting their own money, or no shadow of liberty could subsist. The colonies draw from you, as with their lifeblood, these ideas and principles. Their love of liberty, as with you, fixed and attached on this specific point of taxing. Liberty might be safe or might be endangered in twenty other particulars without their being much pleased or alarmed. Here they felt its pulse; and as they found that beat, they thought themselves sick or sound. I do not say whether they were right or wrong in applying your general arguments to their own case. It is not easy, indeed, to make a monopoly of theorems and corollaries. The fact is that they did thus apply those general arguments; and your mode of governing them, whether through lenity or indolence, through wisdom or mistake, confirmed them in the imagination that they, as well as you, had an interest in these common principles. */38*

They were further confirmed in this pleasing error by the form of their provincial legislative assemblies. Their governments are popular in a high degree: some are merely popular; in all, the popular representative is the most weighty; and this share of the people in their ordinary government never fails to inspire them with lofty sentiments, and with a strong aversion from whatever tends to deprive them of their chief importance. */39*

If anything were wanting to this necessary operation of the form of government, religion would have given it a complete effect. Religion, always a principle of energy, in this new people is no way worn out or impaired; and their mode of professing it is also one main cause of this free spirit. The people are Protestants, and of that kind which is the most adverse to all implicit submission of mind and opinion. This is a persuasion not only favorable to liberty, but built upon it. I do not think, sir, that the reason of this averseness in the dissenting churches from all that looks like absolute government is so much to be sought in their religious tenets as in their history. Everyone knows that the Roman Catholic religion is at least coeval with most of the governments where it prevails, that it has generally gone hand in hand with them, and received great favor and every kind of support from authority. The Church of England, too, was formed from her cradle under the nursing care of regular government. But the dissenting interests have sprung up in direct opposition to all the ordinary powers of the world, and could justify that opposition only on a strong claim to natural liberty. Their very existence depended on the powerful and unremitted assertion of that claim. All Protestantism, even the most cold and passive, is a sort of dissent. But the religion most prevalent in our northern colonies is a refinement on the principle of resistance: it is the dissidence of dissent, and the protestantism of the Protestant religion. This religion, under a variety of denominations agreeing in nothing but in the communion of the spirit of liberty, is predominant in most of the northern provinces, where the Church of England, notwithstanding its legal rights, is in reality no more than a sort of private sect, not composing, most probably, the tenth of the people. The colonists left England when this spirit was high, and in the emigrants was the highest of all; and even that stream of foreigners which has been constantly flowing into these colonies has, for the greatest part, been composed of dissenters from the establishments of their several countries, and have brought with them a temper and character far from alien to that of the people with whom they mixed. */40*

Sir, I can perceive, by their manner, that some gentlemen object to the latitude of this description, because in the southern colonies the Church of England forms a large body, and has a regular establishment. It is certainly true. There is, however, a circumstance attending these colonies, which, in my opinion, fully counterbalances this difference, and makes the spirit of liberty still more high and haughty than in those to the northward. It is that in Virginia and the Carolinas they have a vast multitude of slaves. Where this is the case in any part of the world, those who are free are by far the most proud and jealous of their freedom. Freedom is to them not only an enjoyment, but a kind of rank and privilege. Not seeing there that freedom, as in countries where it is a common blessing and as broad and general as the air, may be united with much abject toil, with great misery, with all the exterior of servitude, liberty looks amongst them like something that is more noble and liberal. I do not mean, sir, to commend the superior morality of this sentiment, which has at least as much pride as virtue in it; but I cannot alter the nature of man. The fact is so; and these people of the southern colonies are much more strongly, and with a higher and more stubborn spirit, attached to liberty, than those to the northward. Such were all the ancient commonwealths; such were our Gothic ancestors; such in our days were the Poles; and such will be all masters of slaves, who are not slaves themselves. In such a people, the haughtiness of domination combines with the spirit of freedom, fortifies it, and renders it invincible. */41*

Permit me, sir, to add another circumstance in our colonies, which contributes no mean part towards the growth and effect of this untractable spirit: I mean their education. In no country, perhaps, in the world is the law so general a study. The profession itself is numerous and powerful, and in most provinces it takes the lead. The greater number of the deputies sent to the Congress were lawyers. But all who read, and most do read, endeavor to obtain some smattering in that science. I have been told by an eminent bookseller that in no branch of his business, after tracts of popular devotion, were so many books as those on the law exported to the plantations. The colonists have now fallen into the way of printing them for their own use. I hear that they have sold nearly as many of Blackstone's *Commentaries* in America as in England. General Gage marks out this disposition very particularly in a letter on your table. He states that all the people in his government are lawyers, or smatterers in law; and that in Boston they have been enabled, by successful chicane, wholly to evade many parts of one of your capital penal constitutions. The smartness of debate will say that this knowledge ought to teach them more clearly the rights of legislature, their obligations to obedience, and the penalties of rebellion. All this is mighty well. But my honorable and learned friend[4] on the floor, who condescends to mark what I say for animadversion, will disdain that ground. He has heard, as well as I, that when great honors and great emoluments do not win over this knowledge to the service of the state, it is a formidable adversary to government. If the spirit be not tamed and broken by these happy methods, it is stubborn and litigious. *Abeunt studia in mores.* This study renders men acute, inquisitive, dexterous, prompt in attack, ready in defense, full of resources. In other countries the people, more simple, and of a less mercurial cast, judge of an ill principle in government only by an actual grievance; here they anticipate the evil, and judge of the pressure of the grievance by the badness of the principle. They augur misgovernment at a distance, and snuff the approach of tyranny in every tainted breeze. */42*

The last cause of this disobedient spirit in the colonies is hardly less powerful than the rest, as it is not merely moral, but laid deep in the natural constitution of things. Three thousand miles of ocean lie between you and them. No contrivance can prevent the effect of this distance in weakening government. Seas roll, and months pass, between the order and the execution; and the want of a speedy explanation of a single point is enough to defeat a whole system. You have, indeed, winged ministers of vengeance, who carry your bolts in their pounces to the remotest verge of the sea; but there a power steps in that limits the arrogance of raging passions and furious elements, and says, "So far shalt thou go, and no farther." Who are you, that should fret and rage, and bite the chains of nature? Nothing worse happens to you than does to all nations who have extensive empire; and it happens in all the forms into which empire can be thrown. In large bodies, the circulation of power must be less vigorous at the extremities. Nature has said it. The Turk cannot govern Egypt, and Arabia, and Kurdistan, as he governs Thrace; nor has he the same dominion in Crimea and Algiers which he has at Brusa and Smyrna. Despotism itself is obliged to truck and huckster. The Sultan gets such obedience as he can. He governs with a loose rein, that he may govern at all; and the whole of the force and vigor of his authority in his center is derived from a prudent relaxation in all his borders. Spain, in her provinces, is perhaps not so well obeyed as you are in yours. She complies, too; she submits; she watches times. This is the immutable condition, the eternal law, of extensive and detached empire. */43*

Then, sir, from these six capital sources, of descent, of form of government, of religion in the northern provinces, of manners in the southern, of education, of the remoteness of situation from the first mover of govern-

[4]Burke refers to Edward Thurlow (1731 – 1806), who was appointed Attorney General in 1771 and was made Chancellor and the first Baron Thurlow in 1778.

ment—from all these causes a fierce spirit of liberty has grown up. It has grown with the growth of the people in your colonies, and increased with the increase of their wealth: a spirit that, unhappily meeting with an exercise of power in England, which, however lawful, is not reconcilable to any ideas of liberty, much less with theirs, has kindled this flame that is ready to consume us. /44

I do not mean to commend either the spirit in this excess, or the moral causes which produce it. Perhaps a more smooth and accommodating spirit of freedom in them would be more acceptable to us. Perhaps ideas of liberty might be desired more reconcilable with an arbitrary and boundless authority. Perhaps we might wish the colonists to be persuaded that their liberty is more secure when held in trust for them by us (as their guardians during a perpetual minority) than with any part of it in their own hands. But the question is not whether their spirit deserves praise or blame—what, in the name of God, shall we do with it? You have before you the object, such as it is, with all its glories, with all its imperfections on its head. You see the magnitude, the importance, the temper, the habits, the disorders. By all these considerations we are strongly urged to determine something concerning it. We are called upon to fix some rule and line for our future conduct, which may give a little stability to our politics, and prevent the return of such unhappy deliberations as the present. Every such return will bring the matter before us in a still more untractable form. For what astonishing and incredible things have we not seen already! What monsters have not been generated from this unnatural contention! Whilst every principle of authority and resistance has been pushed, upon both sides, as far as it would go, there is nothing so solid and certain, either in reasoning or in practice, that has not been shaken. Until very lately, all authority in America seemed to be nothing but an emanation from yours. Even the popular part of the colony constitution derived all its activity, and its first vital movement, from the pleasure of the Crown. We thought, sir, that the utmost which the discontented colonists could do was to disturb authority; we never dreamt they could of themselves supply it, knowing in general what an operose business it is to establish a government absolutely new. But having, for our purposes in this contention, resolved that none but an obedient assembly should sit, the humors of the people there, finding all passage through the legal channel stopped, with great violence broke out another way. Some provinces have tried their experiment, as we have tried ours; and theirs has succeeded. They have formed a government sufficient for its purposes, without the bustle of a revolution, or the troublesome formality of an election. Evident necessity and tacit consent have done the business in an instant. So well they have done it, that Lord Dunmore (the account is among the fragments on your table) tells you that the new institution is infinitely better obeyed than the ancient government ever was in its most fortunate periods. Obedience is what makes government, and not the names by which it is called: not the name of Governor, as formerly, or

Committee, as at present. This new government has originated directly from the people, and was not transmitted through any of the ordinary artificial media of a positive constitution. It was not a manufacture ready formed, and transmitted to them in that condition from England. The evil arising from hence is this: that the colonists having once found the possibility of enjoying the advantages of order in the midst of a struggle for liberty, such struggles will not henceforward seem so terrible to the settled and sober part of mankind as they had appeared before the trial. */45*

Pursuing the same plan of punishing by the denial of the exercise of government to still greater lengths, we wholly abrogated the ancient government of Massachusetts. We were confident that the first feeling, if not the very prospect of anarchy, would instantly enforce a complete submission. The experiment was tried. A new, strange, unexpected face of things appeared. Anarchy is found tolerable. A vast province has now subsisted, and subsisted in a considerable degree of health and vigor, for near a twelvemonth, without governor, without public council, without judges, without executive magistrates. How long it will continue in this state, or what may arise out of this unheard-of situation, how can the wisest of us conjecture? Our late experience has taught us that many of those fundamental principles formerly believed infallible are either not of the importance they were imagined to be, or that we have not at all adverted to some other far more important and far more powerful principles which entirely overrule those we had considered as omnipotent. I am much against any further experiments which tend to put to the proof any more of these allowed opinions which contribute so much to the public tranquillity. In effect, we suffer as much at home by this loosening of all ties, and this concussion of all established opinions, as we do abroad. For, in order to prove that the Americans have no right to their liberties, we are every day endeavoring to subvert the maxims which preserve the whole spirit of our own. To prove that the Americans ought not to be free, we are obliged to depreciate the value of freedom itself; and we never seem to gain a paltry advantage over them in debate, without attacking some of those principles, or deriding some of those feelings, for which our ancestors have shed their blood. */46*

But, sir, in wishing to put an end to pernicious experiments, I do not mean to preclude the fullest inquiry. Far from it. Far from deciding on a sudden or partial view, I would patiently go round and round the subject, and survey it minutely in every possible aspect. Sir, if I were capable of engaging you to an equal attention, I would state that, as far as I am capable of discerning, there are but three ways of proceeding relative to this stubborn spirit which prevails in your colonies and disturbs your government. These are: to change that spirit, as inconvenient, by removing the causes; to prosecute it, as criminal; or to comply with it, as necessary. I would not be guilty of an imperfect enumeration; I can think of but these three. Another has, indeed, been started, that of giving up the colonies; but it met so slight a reception that I do not think myself obliged to dwell a great while upon it. It is nothing but a little sally of anger, like the frowardness of peevish children, who, when they cannot get all they would have, are resolved to take nothing. */47*

The first of these plans—to change the spirit, as inconvenient, by removing the causes—I think is the most like a systematic proceeding. It is radical in its principle; but it is attended with great difficulties, some of them little short, as I conceive, of impossibilities. This will appear by examining into the plans which have been proposed. */48*

As the growing population of the colonies is evidently one cause of their resistance, it was last session mentioned in both Houses, by men of weight, and received not without applause, that, in order to check this evil, it would be proper for the Crown to make no further grants of land. But to this scheme there are two objections. The first, that there is already so much unsettled land in private hands as to afford room for an immense future population, although the Crown not only withheld its grants, but annihilated its soil. If this be the case, then the only effect of this avarice of desolation, this hoarding of a royal wilderness, would be to raise the value of the possessions in the hands of the great private monopolists, without any adequate check to the growing and alarming mischief of population. */49*

But if you stopped your grants, what would be the consequence? The people would occupy without grants. They have already so occupied in many places. You cannot station garrisons in every part of these deserts. If you drive the people from one place, they will carry on their annual tillage, and remove with their flocks and herds to another. Many of the people in the back settlements are already little attached to particular situations. Already they have topped the Appalachian Mountains. From thence they behold before them an immense plain—one vast, rich, level meadow—a square of five hundred miles. Over this they would wander without a possibility of restraint; they would change their manners with the habits of their life; would soon forget a government by which they were disowned; would become hordes of English Tartars, and, pouring down upon your unfortified frontiers a fierce and irresistible cavalry, become masters of your governors and your counsellors, your collectors and comptrollers, and of all the slaves that adhered to them. Such would, and, in no long time, must be, the effect of attempting to forbid as a crime, and to suppress as an evil, the command and blessing of Providence, "Increase and multiply." Such would be the happy result of an endeavor to keep as a lair of wild beasts that earth which God by an express charter has given to the children of men. Far different, and surely much wiser, has been our policy hitherto. Hitherto we have invited our people, by every kind of bounty, to fixed establishments. We have invited the husbandman to look to authority for his title. We have taught him piously to believe in the mysterious virtue of wax and parchment. We have thrown each tract of land, as it was peopled, into districts, that the ruling power should never be wholly out of sight. We have settled all we could; and we have carefully attended every settlement with government. /50

Adhering, sir, as I do, to this policy, as well as for the reasons I have just given, I think this new project of hedging in population to be neither prudent nor practicable. /51

To impoverish the colonies in general, and in particular to arrest the noble course of their marine enterprises, would be a more easy task. I freely confess it. We have shown a disposition to a system of this kind—a disposition even to continue the restraint after the offense—looking on ourselves as rivals to our colonies, and persuaded that of course we must gain all that they shall lose. Much mischief we may certainly do. The power inadequate to all other things is often more than sufficient for this. I do not look on the direct and immediate power of the colonies to resist our violence as very formidable. In this, however, I may be mistaken. But when I consider that we have colonies for no purpose but to be serviceable to us, it seems to my poor understanding a little preposterous to make them unserviceable in order to keep them obedient. It is, in truth, nothing more than the old, and, as I thought, exploded problem of tyranny, which proposes to beggar its subjects into submission. But remember, when you have completed your system of impoverishment, that nature still proceeds in her ordinary course; that discontent will increase with misery; and that there are critical moments in the fortune of all states, when they who are too weak to contribute to your prosperity may be strong enough to complete your ruin. *Spoliatis arma supersunt.* /52

The temper and character which prevail in our colonies are, I am afraid, unalterable by any human art. We cannot, I fear, falsify the pedigree of this fierce people, and persuade them that they are not sprung from a nation in whose veins the blood of freedom circulates. The language in which they would hear you tell them this tale would detect the imposition; your speech would betray you. An Englishman is the unfittest person on earth to argue another Englishman into slavery. /53

I think it is nearly as little in our power to change their republican religion as their free descent, or to substitute the Roman Catholic as a penalty, or the Church of England as an improvement. The mode of inquisition and dragooning is going out of fashion in the Old World, and I should not confide much to their efficacy in the New. The education of the Americans is also on the same unalterable bottom with their religion. You cannot persuade them to burn their books of curious science, to banish their lawyers from their courts of law, or to quench the lights of their assemblies by refusing to choose those persons who are best read in their privileges. It would be no less impracticable to think of wholly annihilating the popular assemblies in which these lawyers sit. The army, by which we must govern in their place, would be far more chargeable to us, not quite so effectual, and perhaps, in the end, full as difficult to be kept in obedience. /54

With regard to the high aristocratic spirit of Virginia and the southern colonies, it has been proposed, I know, to reduce it by declaring a general enfranchisement of their slaves. This project has had its advocates and panegyrists; yet I never could argue myself into any opinion of it. Slaves are often much attached to their masters. A general wild offer of liberty would not always be accepted. History furnishes few instances of it. It is sometimes as hard to persuade slaves to be free as it is to compel freemen to be slaves; and in this auspicious scheme we should have both these pleasing tasks on our hands at once. But when we talk of enfranchisement, do we not perceive that the American master may enfranchise, too, and arm servile hands in defense of freedom?—a measure to which other people have had recourse more than once, and not without success, in a desperate situation of their affairs. */55*

Slaves as these unfortunate black people are, and dull as all men are from slavery, must they not a little suspect the offer of freedom from that very nation which has sold them to their present masters—from that nation, one of whose causes of quarrel with those masters is their refusal to deal any more in that inhuman traffic? An offer of freedom from England would come rather oddly, shipped to them in an African vessel, which is refused an entry into the ports of Virginia or Carolina with a cargo of three hundred Angola Negroes. It would be curious to see the Guinea captain attempting at the same instant to publish his proclamation of liberty and to advertise his sale of slaves. */56*

But let us suppose all these moral difficulties got over. The ocean remains. You cannot pump this dry; and as long as it continues in its present bed, so long all the causes which weaken authority by distance will continue. "Ye Gods! annihilate but space and time,/And make two lovers happy," was a pious and passionate prayer, but just as reasonable as many of the serious wishes of very grave and solemn politicians. */57*

If, then, sir, it seems almost desperate to think of any alterative course for changing the moral causes (and not quite easy to remove the natural) which produce prejudices irreconcilable to the late exercise of our authority, but that the spirit infallibly will continue, and, continuing, will produce such effects as now embarrass us, the second mode under consideration is, to prosecute that spirit in its overt acts, as *criminal*. */58*

At this proposition I must pause a moment. The thing seems a great deal too big for my ideas of jurisprudence. It should seem, to my way of conceiving such matters, that there is a very wide difference, in reason and policy, between the mode of proceeding on the irregular conduct of scattered individuals, or even of bands of men, who disturb order within the state, and the civil dissensions which may, from time to time, on great questions, agitate the several communities which compose a great empire. It looks to me to be narrow and pedantic to apply the ordinary ideas of criminal justice to this great public contest. I do not know the method of drawing up an indictment against an whole people. I cannot insult and ridicule the feelings of millions of my fellow creatures as Sir Edward Coke insulted one excellent individual (Sir Walter Raleigh) at the bar. I am not ripe to pass sentence on the gravest public bodies, entrusted with magistracies of great authority and dignity, and charged with the safety of their fellow citizens, upon the very same title that I am. I really think that for wise men this is not judicious, for sober men not decent, for minds tinctured with humanity not mild and merciful. */59*

Perhaps, sir, I am mistaken in my idea of an empire, as distinguished from a single state or kingdom. But my idea of it is this: that an empire is the aggregate of many states under one common head, whether this head be a monarch or a presiding republic. It does, in such constitutions, frequently happen (and nothing but the dismal, cold, dead uniformity of servitude can prevent its happening) that the subordinate parts have many local privileges and immunities. Between these privileges and the supreme common authority the line may be extremely nice. Of course disputes, often, too, very bitter disputes, and much ill blood, will arise. But though every privilege is an exemption (in the case) from the ordinary exercise of the supreme authority, it is no denial of it. The claim of a privilege seems rather, *ex vi termini*, to imply a superior power; for to talk of the privileges of a state or of a person who has no superior is hardly any better than speaking nonsense. Now in such unfortunate quarrels among the component parts of a great political union of communities, I can scarcely conceive anything more completely imprudent than for the head of the empire to insist that if any privilege is pleaded against his will or his acts, that his whole authority is denied; instantly to proclaim rebellion, to beat to arms, and to put the offending provinces under the ban. Will not this, sir, very soon teach the provinces to make no distinctions on their part? Will it not teach them that the government against which a claim of liberty is tantamount to high treason is a government to which submission is equivalent to slavery? It may not always be quite convenient to impress dependent communities with such an idea. */60*

We are, indeed, in all disputes with the colonies, by the necessity of things, the judge. It is true, sir. But I confess that the character of judge in my own cause is a thing that frightens me. Instead of filling me with pride, I am exceedingly humbled by it. I cannot proceed with a stern, assured judicial confidence, until I find myself in something more like a judicial character. I must have these hesitations as long as I am compelled to recollect that, in my little reading upon such contests as these, the sense of mankind has at least as often decided against the superior as the subordinate power. Sir, let me add, too, that the opinion of my having some abstract right in my favor would not put me much at my ease in passing sentence, unless I could be sure that there were no rights which, in their exercise under certain circumstances, were not the most odious of all wrongs and the most vexatious of all injustice. Sir, these considerations have great weight with me, when I find things so circumstanced that I see the same party at once a civil litigant against me in a point of right and a culprit before me, while I sit as criminal judge on acts of his whose moral quality is to be decided upon the merits of that very litigation. Men are every now and then put, by the complexity of human affairs, into strange situations; but justice is the same, let the judge be in what situation he will. /61

There is, sir, also a circumstance which convinces me that this mode of criminal proceeding is not (at least in the present stage of our contest) altogether expedient, which is nothing less than the conduct of those very persons who have seemed to adopt that mode by lately declaring a rebellion in Massachusetts Bay, as they had formerly addressed to have traitors brought hither, under an act of Henry the Eighth, for trial. For, though rebellion is declared, it is not proceeded against as such; nor have any steps been taken towards the apprehension or conviction of any individual offender, either on our late or our former address; but modes of public coercion have been adopted, and such as have much more resemblance to a sort of qualified hostility towards an independent power than the punishment of rebellious subjects. All this seems rather inconsistent; but it shows how difficult it is to apply these juridical ideas to our present case. /62

In this situation, let us seriously and coolly ponder. What is it we have got by all our menaces, which have been many and ferocious?-What advantage have we derived from the penal laws we have passed, and which, for the time, have been severe and numerous? What advances have we made towards our object by the sending of a force, which, by land and sea, is no contemptible strength? Has the disorder abated? Nothing less. When I see things in this situation, after such confident hopes, bold promises, and active exertions, I cannot, for my life, avoid a suspicion that the plan itself is not correctly right. /63

If, then, the removal of the causes of this spirit of American liberty be, for the greater part, or rather entirely, impracticable—if the ideas of criminal process be inapplicable, or, if applicable, are in the highest degree inexpedient, what way yet remains? No way is open, but the third and last—to comply with the American spirit as necessary, or, if you please, to submit to it as a necessary evil. /64

If we adopt this mode, if we mean to conciliate and concede, let us see of what nature the concession ought to be. To ascertain the nature of our concession, we must look at their complaint. The colonies complain that they have not the characteristic mark and seal of British freedom. They complain that they are taxed in a Parliament in which they are not represented. If you mean to satisfy them at all, you must satisfy them with regard to this complaint. If you mean to please any people, you must give them the boon which they ask—not what you may think better for them, but of a kind totally different. Such an act may be a wise regulation, but it is no concession; whereas our present theme is the mode of giving satisfaction. /65

Sir, I think you must perceive that I am resolved this day to have nothing at all to do with the question of the right of taxation. Some gentlemen startle, but it is true: I put it totally out of the question. It is less than nothing in my consideration. I do not indeed wonder, nor will you, sir, that gentlemen of profound learning are fond of displaying it on this profound subject. But my consideration is narrow, confined, and wholly limited to the policy of the question. I do not examine whether the giving away a man's money be a power excepted and reserved out of the general trust of government, and how far all mankind, in all forms of polity, are entitled to an exercise of that right by the charter of nature—or whether, on the contrary, a right of taxation is necessarily involved in the general principle of legislation, and inseparable from the ordinary supreme power. These are deep questions, where great names militate against each other, where reason is perplexed, and an appeal to authorities only thickens the confusion; for high and reverend authorities lift up their heads on both sides, and there is no sure footing in the middle. This point is the great "Serbonian bog/Betwixt Damiata and Mount Casius old, /Where armies whole have sunk." I do not intend to be overwhelmed in that bog, though in such respectable company. The question with me is not whether you have a right to render your people miserable, but whether it is not your interest to make them happy. It is not what a lawyer tells me I *may* do, but what humanity, reason, and justice tell me I ought to do. Is a politic act the worse for being a generous one? Is no concession proper, but that which is made from your want of right to keep what you grant? Or does it lessen the grace or dignity of relaxing in the exercise of an odious claim because you have your evidence-room full of titles, and your magazines stuffed with arms to enforce them? What signify all those titles and all those arms? Of what avail are they, when the reason of the thing tells me that the assertion of my title is the loss of my suit, and that I could do nothing but wound myself by the use of my own weapons? */66*

Such is steadfastly my opinion of the absolute necessity of keeping up the concord of this empire by a unity of spirit, though in a diversity of operations, that, if I were sure the colonists had, at their leaving this country, sealed a regular compact of servitude, that they had solemnly abjured all the rights of citizens, that they had made a vow to renounce all ideas of liberty for them and their posterity to all generations, yet I should hold myself obliged to conform to the temper I found universally prevalent in my own day, and to govern two million of men, impatient of servitude, on the principles of freedom. I am not determining a point of law; I am restoring tranquillity; and the general character and situation of a people must determine what sort of government is fitted for them. That point nothing else can or ought to determine. */67*

My idea, therefore, without considering whether we yield as matter of right or grant as matter of favor, is *to admit the people of our colonies into an interest in the Constitution*, and, by recording that admission in the journals of Parliament, to give them as strong an assurance as the nature of the thing will admit that we mean forever to adhere to that solemn declaration of systematic indulgence. */68*

Some years ago, the repeal of a revenue act, upon its understood principle, might have served to show that we intended an unconditional abatement of the exercise of a taxing power. Such a measure was then sufficient to remove all suspicion and to give perfect content. But unfortunate events since that time may make something further necessary—and not more necessary for the satisfaction of the colonies than for the dignity and consistency of our own future proceedings. */69*

I have taken a very incorrect measure of the disposition of the House, if this proposal in itself would be received with dislike. I think, sir, we have few American financiers. But our misfortune is, we are too acute, we are too exquisite in our conjectures of the future, for men oppressed with such great and present evils. The more moderate among the opposers of parliamentary concession freely confess that they hope no good from taxation; but they apprehend the colonists have further views, and if this point were conceded, they would instantly attack the trade laws. These gentlemen are convinced that this was the intention from the beginning, and the quarrel of the Americans with taxation was no more than a cloak and cover to this design. Such has been the language even of a gentleman[5] of real moderation, and of a natural temper well adjusted to fair and equal government. I am, however, sir, not a little surprised at this kind of discourse, whenever I hear it; and I am the more surprised on account of the arguments which I constantly find in company with it, and which are often urged from the same mouths and on the same day. */70*

For instance, when we allege that it is against reason to tax a people under so many restraints in trade as the Americans, the noble lord in the blue riband shall tell you that the restraints on trade are futile and useless, of no advantage to us, and of no burden to those on whom they are imposed—that the trade to America is not secured by the Acts of Navigation, but by the natural and irresistible advantage of a commercial preference. */71*

Such is the merit of the trade laws in this posture of the debate. But when strong internal circumstances are urged against the taxes, when the scheme is dissected, when experience and the nature of things are brought to prove, and do prove, the utter impossibility of obtaining an effective revenue from the colonies—when these things are pressed, or rather press themselves, so as to drive the advocates of colony taxes to a clear admission of the futility of the scheme—then, sir, the sleeping trade laws revive from their trance, and this useless taxation is to be kept sacred, not for its own sake, but as a counterguard and security of the laws of trade. */72*

Then, sir, you keep up revenue laws which are mischievous in order to preserve trade laws that are useless. Such is the wisdom of our plan in

[5]Burke refers to George Rice (1724–1779), who represented Carmarthenshire in Parliament, 1754–1779.

both its members. They are separately given up as of no value; and yet one is always to be defended for the sake of the other. But I cannot agree with the noble lord, nor with the pamphlet from whence he seems to have borrowed these ideas concerning the inutility of the trade laws. For, without idolizing them, I am sure they are still, in many ways, of great use to us; and in former times they have been of the greatest. They do confine, and they do greatly narrow, the market for the Americans. But my perfect conviction of this does not help me in the least to discern how the revenue laws form any security whatsoever to the commercial regulations, or that these commercial regulations are the true ground of the quarrel, or that the giving way, in any one instance, of authority is to lose all that may remain unconceded. */73*

One fact is clear and indisputable: The public and avowed origin of this quarrel was on taxation. This quarrel has, indeed, brought on new disputes on new questions, but certainly the least bitter, and the fewest of all, on the trade laws. To judge which of the two be the real, radical cause of quarrel, we have to see whether the commercial dispute did, in order of time, precede the dispute on taxation. There is not a shadow of evidence for it. Next, to enable us to judge whether at this moment a dislike to the trade laws be the real cause of quarrel, it is absolutely necessary to put the taxes out of the question by a repeal. See how the Americans act in this position, and then you will be able to discern correctly what is the true object of the controversy, or whether any controversy at all will remain. Unless you consent to remove this cause of difference, it is impossible, with decency, to assert that the dispute is not upon what it is avowed to be. And I would, sir, recommend to your serious consideration, whether it be prudent to form a rule for punishing people, not on their own acts, but on your conjectures. Surely it is preposterous, at the very best. It is not justifying your anger by their misconduct, but it is converting your ill will into their delinquency. */74*

But the colonies will go further. Alas! alas! when will this speculating against fact and reason end? What will quiet these panic fears which we entertain of the hostile effect of a conciliatory conduct? Is it true that no case can exist in which it is proper for the sovereign to accede to the desires of his discontented subjects? Is there anything peculiar in this case, to make a rule for itself? Is all authority of course lost, when it is not pushed to the extreme? Is it a certain maxim that, the fewer causes of dissatisfaction are left by government, the more the subject will be inclined to resist and rebel? */75*

All these objections being in fact no more than suspicions, conjectures, divinations, formed in defiance of fact and experience, they did not, sir, discourage me from entertaining the idea of a conciliatory concession, founded on the principles which I have just stated. */76*

In forming a plan for this purpose, I endeavored to put myself in that frame of mind which was the most natural and the most reasonable, and which was certainly the most probable means of securing me from all error. I set out with a perfect distrust of my own abilities, a total renunciation of every speculation of my own, and with a profound reverence for the wisdom of our ancestors, who have left us the inheritance of so happy a Constitution and so flourishing an empire, and, what is a thousand times more valuable, the treasury of the maxims and principles which formed the one and obtained the other. /77

During the reigns of the kings of Spain of the Austrian family, whenever they were at a loss in the Spanish councils, it was common for their statesmen to say that they ought to consult the genius of Philip the Second. The genius of Philip the Second might mislead them; and the issue of their affairs showed that they had not chosen the most perfect standard. But, sir, I am sure that I shall not be misled, when, in a case of constitutional difficulty, I consult the genius of the English Constitution. Consulting at that oracle (it was with all due humility and piety), I found four capital examples in a similar case before me: those of Ireland, Wales, Chester, and Durham. /78

Ireland, before the English conquest, though never governed by a despotic power, had no parliament. How far the English Parliament itself was at that time modeled according to the present form is disputed among antiquarians. But we have all the reason in the world to be assured that a form of parliament, such as England then enjoyed, she instantly communicated to Ireland; and we are equally sure that almost every successive improvement in constitutional liberty, as fast as it was made here, was transmitted thither. The feudal baronage, and the feudal knighthood, the roots of our primitive Constitution, were early transplanted into that soil, and grew and flourished there. Magna Charta, if it did not give us originally the House of Commons, gave us at least a House of Commons of weight and consequence. But your ancestors did not churlishly sit down alone to the feast of Magna Charta. Ireland was made immediately a partaker. This benefit of English laws and liberties, I confess, was not at first extended to *all* Ireland. Mark the consequence. English authority and English liberty had exactly the same boundaries. Your standard could never be advanced an inch before your privileges. Sir John Davies shows beyond a doubt that the refusal of a general communication of these rights was the true cause why Ireland was five hundred years in subduing; and after the vain projects of a military government, attempted in the reign of Queen Elizabeth, it was soon discovered that nothing could make that country English, in civility and allegiance, but your laws and your forms of legislature. It was not English arms, but the English Constitution, that conquered Ireland. From that time, Ireland has ever had a general Parliament, as she had before a partial Parliament. You changed the people, you altered the religion, but you never touched the form or the vital substance of free government in that kingdom. You deposed kings; you restored them; you altered the succession to theirs, as well as to your own Crown; but you never altered their Constitution, the principle of which was respected by usurpation, restored with the restoration of monarchy, and established, I trust, forever by the glorious Revolution. This has made Ireland the great and flourishing kingdom that it is, and, from a disgrace and a burden intolerable to this nation, has rendered her a principal part of our strength and ornament. This country cannot be said to have ever formally taxed her. The irregular things done in the confusion of mighty troubles, and on the hinge of great revolutions, even if all were done that is said to have been done, form no example. If they have any effect in argument, they make an exception to prove the rule. None of your own liberties could stand a moment, if the casual deviations from them, at such times, were suffered to be used as proofs of their nullity. By the lucrative amount of such casual breaches in the Constitution, judge what the stated and fixed rule of supply has been in that kingdom. Your Irish pensioners would starve, if they had no other fund to live on than taxes granted by English authority. Turn your eyes to those popular grants from whence all your great supplies are come, and learn to respect that only source of public wealth in the British Empire. */79*

My next example is Wales. This country was said to be reduced by Henry the Third. It was said more truly to be so by Edward the First. But though then conquered, it was not looked upon as any part of the realm of England. Its old Constitution, whatever that might have been, was destroyed; and no good one was substituted in its place. The care of that tract was put into the hands of Lords Marchers—a form of government of a very singular kind, a strange, heterogeneous monster, something between hostility and government—perhaps it has a sort of resemblance, according to the modes of those times, to that of commander-in-chief at present, to whom all civil power is granted as secondary. The manners of the Welsh nation followed the genius of the government: The people were ferocious, restive, savage, and uncultivated; sometimes composed, never pacified. Wales, within itself, was in perpetual disorder; and it kept the frontier of England in perpetual alarm. Benefits from it to the state there were none. Wales was only known to England by incursion and invasion. */80*

Sir, during that state of things, Parliament was not idle. They attempted to subdue the fierce spirit of the Welsh by all sorts of rigorous laws. They prohibited by statute the sending all sorts of arms into Wales, as you prohibit by proclamation (with something more of doubt on the legality) the sending arms to America. They disarmed the Welsh by statute, as you attempted (but still with more question on the legality) to disarm New England by an instruction. They made an act to drag offenders from Wales into England for trial, as you have done (but with more hardship) with regard to America. By another act, where one of the parties was an Englishman, they ordained that his trial should be always by English. They made acts to restrain trade, as you do; and they prevented the Welsh from the use of fairs and markets, as you do the Americans from fisheries and foreign ports. In short, when the statute book was not quite so much swelled as it is now, you find no less than fifteen acts of penal regulation on the subject of Wales. */81*

Here we rub our hands. A fine body of precedents for the authority of Parliament and the use of it! I admit it fully; and pray add likewise to these precedents that all the while Wales rid this kingdom like an *incubus;* that it was an unprofitable and oppressive burden; and that an Englishman traveling in that country could not go six yards from the highroad without being murdered. */82*

The march of the human mind is slow. Sir, it was not until after two hundred years discovered, that, by an eternal law, Providence had decreed vexation to violence, and poverty to rapine. Your ancestors did, however, at length open their eyes to the ill husbandry of injustice. They found that the tyranny of a free people could of all tyrannies the least be endured, and that laws made against a whole nation were not the most effectual methods for securing its obedience. Accordingly, in the twenty-seventh year of Henry the Eighth the course was entirely altered. With a preamble stating the entire and perfect rights of the Crown of England, it gave to the Welsh all the rights and privileges of English subjects. A political order was established; the military power gave way to the civil; the marches were turned into counties. But that a nation should have a right to English liberties, and yet no share at all in the fundamental security of these liberties—the grant of their own property—seemed a thing so incongruous that eight years after, that is, in the thirty-fifth of that reign, a complete and not ill-proportioned representation by counties and boroughs was bestowed upon Wales by act of Parliament. From that moment, as by a charm, the tumults subsided; obedience was restored; peace, order, and civilization followed in the train of liberty. When the daystar of the English Constitution had arisen in their hearts, all was harmony within and without:

Simul alba nautis
Stella refulsit,
Defluit saxis agitatus humor,
Concidunt venti, fugiuntque nubes,
Et minax (quod sic voluere) ponto
Unda recumbit. */83*

The very same year the County Palatine of Chester received the same relief from its oppressions, and the same remedy to its disorders. Before this time Chester was little less distempered than Wales. The inhabitants, without rights themselves, were the fittest to destroy the rights of others; and from thence Richard the Second drew the standing army of archers with which for a time he oppressed England. The people of Chester applied to Parliament in a petition penned as I shall read to you:

> To the King our sovereign lord, in most humble wise shown unto your most excellent Majesty, the inhabitants of your Grace's

> County Palatine of Chester: That where the said County Palatine of Chester is and hath been alway hitherto exempt, excluded, and separated out and from your high court of Parliament, to have any knights and burgesses within the said court; by reason whereof the said inhabitants have hitherto sustained manifold disherisons, losses, and damages, as well in their lands, goods, and bodies, as in the good, civil, and politic governance and maintenance of the commonwealth of their said country: And forasmuch as the said inhabitants have always hitherto been bound by the acts and statutes made and ordained by your said Highness, and your most noble progenitors, by authority of the said court, as far forth as other counties, cities, and boroughs have been, that have had their knights and burgesses within your said court of Parliament, and yet have had neither knight ne burgess there for the said County Palatine; the said inhabitants, for lack thereof, have been oftentimes touched and grieved with acts and statutes made within the said court, as well derogatory unto the most ancient jurisdictions, liberties, and privileges of your said County Palatine, as prejudicial unto the commonwealth, quietness, rest, and peace of your Grace's most bounden subjects inhabiting within the same. */84*

What did Parliament with this audacious address? Reject it as a libel? Treat it as an affront to government? Spurn it as a derogation from the rights of legislature? Did they toss it over the table? Did they burn it by the hands of the common hangman? They took the petition of grievance, all rugged as it was, without softening or temperament, unpurged of the original bitterness and indignation of complaint; they made it the very preamble to their act of redress, and consecrated its principle to all ages in the sanctuary of legislation. */85*

Here is my third example. It was attended with the success of the two former. Chester, civilized as well as Wales, has demonstrated that freedom, and not servitude, is the cure of anarchy; as religion, and not atheism, is the true remedy for superstition. Sir, this pattern of Chester was followed in the reign of Charles the Second with regard to the County Palatine of Durham, which is my fourth example. This county had long lain out of the pale of free legislation. So scrupulously was the example of Chester followed, that the style of the preamble is nearly the same with that of the Chester act; and, without affecting the abstract extent of the authority of Parliament, it recognizes the equity of not suffering any considerable district, in which the British subjects may act as a body, to be taxed without their own voice in the grant. */86*

Now if the doctrines of policy contained in these preambles, and the force of these examples in the acts of Parliament, avail anything, what can be said against applying them with regard to America? Are not the people of America as much Englishmen as the Welsh? The preamble of the act of Henry the Eighth says the Welsh speak a language no way resembling that of his Majesty's English subjects. Are the Americans not as numerous? If we may trust the learned and accurate Judge Barrington's account of North Wales, and take that as a standard to measure the rest, there is no comparison. The people cannot amount to above 200,000—not a tenth part of the number in the colonies. Is America in rebellion? Wales was hardly ever free from it. Have you attempted to govern America by penal statutes? You made fifteen for Wales. But your legislative authority is perfect with regard to America. Was it less perfect in Wales, Chester, and Durham? But America is virtually represented. What! does the electric force of virtual representation more easily pass over the Atlantic than pervade Wales, which lies in your neighborhood? or than Chester and Durham, surrounded by abundance of representation that is actual and palpable? But, sir, your ancestors thought this sort of virtual representation, however ample, to be totally insufficient for the freedom of the inhabitants of territories that are so near, and comparatively so inconsiderable. How, then, can I think it sufficient for those which are infinitely greater, and infinitely more remote? */87*

You will now, sir, perhaps imagine that I am on the point of proposing to you a scheme for a representation of the colonies in Parliament. Perhaps I might be inclined to entertain some such thought; but a great flood stops me in my course. *Opposuit natura.* I cannot remove the eternal barriers of the creation. The thing, in that mode, I do not know to be possible. As I meddle with no theory, I do not absolutely assert the impracticability of such a representation; but I do not see my way to it; and those who have been more confident have not been more successful. However, the arm of public benevolence is not shortened; and there are often several means to the same end. What nature has disjoined in one way, wisdom may unite in another. When we cannot give the benefit as we would wish, let us not refuse it altogether. If we cannot give the principal, let us find a substitute. But how? where? what substitute? */88*

Fortunately, I am not obliged, for the ways and means of this substitute, to tax my own unproductive invention. I am not even obliged to go to the rich treasury of the fertile framers of imaginary commonwealths: not to the *Republic* of Plato, not to the *Utopia* of More, not to the *Oceana* of Harrington. It is before me, it is at my feet, "And the rude swain/Treads daily on it with his clouted shoon." I only wish you to recognize, for the theory, the ancient constitutional policy of this kingdom with regard to representation, as that policy has been declared in acts of Parliament; and as to the practice, to return to that mode which an uniform experience has marked out to you as best, and in which you walked with security, advantage, and honor, until the year 1763. */89*

My resolutions, therefore, mean to establish the equity and justice of a taxation of America by *grant,* and not by *imposition;* to mark the *legal competency* of the colony assemblies for the support of their government in peace, and for public aids in time of war; to acknowledge that this legal competency has had *a dutiful and beneficial exercise*, and that experience has shown *the benefit of their grants*, and *the futility of parliamentary taxation, as a method of supply.* /90

These solid truths compose six fundamental propositions. There are three more resolutions corollary to these. If you admit the first set, you can hardly reject the others. But if you admit the first, I shall be far from solicitous whether you accept or refuse the last. I think these six massive pillars will be of strength sufficient to support the temple of British concord. I have no more doubt than I entertain of my existence that, if you admitted these, you would command an immediate peace, and, with but tolerable future management, a lasting obedience in America. I am not arrogant in this confident assurance. The propositions are all mere matters of fact; and if they are such facts as draw irresistible conclusions even in the stating, this is the power of truth, and not any management of mine. /91

Sir, I shall open the whole plan to you together, with such observations on the motions as may tend to illustrate them, where they may want explanation. /92

The first is a resolution: "That the colonies and plantations of Great Britain in North America, consisting of fourteen separate governments, and containing two millions and upwards of free inhabitants, have not had the liberty and privilege of electing and sending any knights and burgesses, or others, to represent them in the high court of Parliament." /93

This is a plain matter of fact, necessary to be laid down, and (excepting the description) it is laid down in the language of the Constitution; it is taken nearly *verbatim* from acts of Parliament. /94

The second is like unto the first: "That the said colonies and plantations have been made liable to, and bounden by, several subsidies, payments, rates, and taxes, given and granted by Parliament, though the said colonies and plantations have not their knights and burgesses in the said high court of Parliament, of their own election, to represent the condition of their country; by lack whereof they have been oftentimes touched and grieved by subsidies given, granted, and assented to, in the said court, in a manner prejudicial to the commonwealth, quietness, rest, and peace of the subjects inhabiting within the same." /95

Is this description too hot or too cold, too strong or too weak? Does it arrogate too much to the supreme legislature? Does it lean too much to the claims of the people? If it runs into any of these errors, the fault is not mine. It is the language of your own ancient acts of Parliament. *Non meus hic sermo, sed quae praecepit Ofellus/Rusticus, abnormis sapiens.* It is the genuine produce of the ancient, rustic, manly, homebred sense of this country. I did not dare to rub off a particle of the venerable rust that rather adorns and preserves than destroys the metal. It would be a profanation to touch with a tool the stones which construct the sacred altar of peace. I would not violate with modern polish the ingenuous and noble roughness of these truly constitutional materials. Above all things, I was resolved not to be guilty of tampering, the odious vice of restless and unstable minds. I put my foot in the tracks of our forefathers, where I can neither wander nor stumble. Determining to fix articles of peace, I was resolved not to be wise beyond what was written; I was resolved to use nothing else than the form of sound words, to let others abound in their own sense, and carefully to abstain from all expressions of my own. What the law has said, I say. In all things else I am silent. I have no organ but for her words. This, if it be not ingenious, I am sure is safe. */96*

There are, indeed, words expressive of grievance in this second resolution, which those who are resolved always to be in the right will deny to contain matter of fact, as applied to the present case; although Parliament thought them true with regard to the Counties of Chester and Durham. They will deny that the Americans were ever "touched and grieved" with the taxes. If they consider nothing in taxes but their weight as pecuniary impositions, there might be some pretense for this denial. But men may be sorely touched and deeply grieved in their privileges, as well as in their purses. Men may lose little in property by the act which takes away all their freedom. When a man is robbed of a trifle on the highway, it is not the twopence lost that constitutes the capital outrage. This is not confined to privileges. Even ancient indulgences withdrawn, without offense on the part of those who enjoyed such favors, operate as grievances. But were the Americans, then, not touched and grieved by the taxes, in some measure, merely as taxes? If so, why were they almost all either wholly repealed or exceedingly reduced? Were they not touched and grieved even by the regulating duties of the sixth of George the Second? Else why were the duties first reduced to one third in 1764, and afterwards to a third of that third in the year 1766? Were they not touched and grieved by the Stamp Act? I shall say they were, until that tax is revived. Were they not touched and grieved by the duties of 1767, which were likewise repealed, and which Lord Hillsborough tells you (for the ministry) were laid contrary to the true principle of commerce? Is not the assurance given by that noble person to the colonies of a resolution to lay no more taxes on them an admission that taxes would touch and grieve them? Is not the resolution of the noble lord in the blue riband, now standing on your journals, the strongest of all proofs that parliamentary subsidies really touched and grieved them? Else why all these changes, modifications, repeals, assurances, and resolutions? */97*

The next proposition is: "That, from the distance of the said colonies, and from other circumstances, no method hath hitherto been devised for procuring a representation in Parliament for the said colonies." */98*

This is an assertion of a fact. I go no further on the paper, though, in my private judgment, a useful representation is impossible; I am sure it is not desired by them, nor ought it, perhaps, by us—but I abstain from opinions. */99*

The fourth resolution is: "That each of the said colonies hath within itself a body, chosen, in part or in the whole, by the freemen, freeholders, or other free inhabitants thereof, commonly called the General Assembly, or General Court, with powers legally to raise, levy, and assess, according to the several usages of such colonies, duties and taxes towards defraying all sorts of public services." */100*

This competence in the colony assemblies is certain. It is proved by the whole tenor of their acts of supply in all the assemblies, in which the constant style of granting is "An aid to his Majesty"; and acts granting to the Crown have regularly, for near a century, passed the public offices without dispute. Those who have been pleased paradoxically to deny this right, holding that none but the British Parliament can grant to the Crown, are wished to look to what is done, not only in the colonies, but in Ireland, in one uniform, unbroken tenor, every session. Sir, I am surprised that this doctrine should come from some of the law servants of the Crown. I say that if the Crown could be responsible, his Majesty—but certainly the ministers, and even these law officers themselves, through whose hands the acts pass biennially in Ireland, or annually in the colonies, are in a habitual course of committing impeachable offenses. What habitual offenders have been all presidents of the council, all secretaries of state, all first lords of trade, all attorneys and all solicitors general! However, they are safe, as no one impeaches them; and there is no ground of charge against them, except in their own unfounded theories. */101*

The fifth resolution is also a resolution of fact: "That the said general assemblies, general courts, or other bodies legally qualified as aforesaid, have at sundry times freely granted several large subsidies and public aids for his Majesty's service, according to their abilities, when required thereto by letter from one of his Majesty's principal secretaries of state; and that their right to grant the same, and their cheerfulness and sufficiency in the said grants, have been at sundry times acknowledged by Parliament." */102*

To say nothing of their great expenses in the Indian wars, and not to take their exertion in foreign ones, so high as the supplies in the year 1695, not to go back to their public contributions in the year 1710, I shall begin to travel only where the journals give me light, resolving to deal in nothing but fact authenticated by parliamentary record, and to build myself wholly on that solid basis. */103*

On the 4th of April, 1748, a committee of this House came to the following resolution: "*Resolved,* That it is the opinion of this committee *that it is just and reasonable* that the several provinces and colonies of Massachusetts Bay, New Hampshire, Connecticut, and Rhode Island be reimbursed the expenses they have been at in taking and securing to the Crown of Great Britain the island of Cape Breton and its dependencies." */104*

These expenses were immense for such colonies. They were above £200,000 sterling: money first raised and advanced on their public credit. */105*

On the 28th of January, 1756, a message from the King came to us, to this effect: "His Majesty, being sensible of the zeal and vigor with which his faithful subjects of certain colonies in North America have exerted themselves in defense of his Majesty's just rights and possessions, recommends it to this House to take the same into their consideration, and to enable his Majesty to give them such assistance as may be a *proper reward and encouragement.*" */106*

On the 3d of February, 1756, the House came to a suitable resolution, expressed in words nearly the same as those of the message, but with the further addition that the money then voted was as an *encouragement* to the colonies to exert themselves with vigor. It will not be necessary to go through all the testimonies which your own records have given to the truth of my resolutions. I will only refer you to the places in the journals:

Vol. XXVII – 16th and 19th May, 1757.
Vol. XXVIII – June 1st, 1758; April 26th and 30th, 1759; March 26th and 31st, and April 28th, 1760; Jan. 9th and 20th, 1761.
Vol. XXIX – Jan. 22d and 26th, 1762; March 14th and 17th, 1763. */107*

Sir, here is the repeated acknowledgment of Parliament that the colonies not only gave, but gave to satiety. This nation has formally acknowledged two things: first, that the colonies had gone beyond their abilities, Parliament having thought it necessary to reimburse them; secondly, that they had acted legally and laudably in their grants of money, and their maintenance of troops, since the compensation is expressly given as reward and encouragement. Reward is not bestowed for acts that are unlawful; and encouragement is not held out to things that deserve reprehension. My resolution, therefore, does nothing more than collect into one proposition what is scattered through your journals. I give you nothing but your own; and you cannot refuse in the gross what you have so often acknowledged in detail. The admission of this, which will be so honorable to them and to you, will, indeed, be mortal to all the miserable stories by which the passions of the misguided people have been engaged in an unhappy system. The people heard, indeed, from the beginning of these disputes, one thing continually dinned in their ears: that reason and justice demanded that the Americans, who paid no taxes, should be compelled to contribute. How did that fact, of their paying nothing, stand, when the taxing system began? When Mr. Grenville began to form his system of American revenue, he stated in this House that the colonies were then in debt two million six hundred thousand pounds sterling money, and was of opinion they would discharge that debt in four years. On this state, those untaxed people were actually subject to the payment of taxes to the amount of six hundred and fifty thousand a year. In fact, however, Mr. Grenville was mistaken. The funds given for sinking the debt did not prove quite so ample as both the colonies and he expected. The calculation was too sanguine: the reduction was not completed till some years after, and at different times in different colonies. However, the taxes after the war continued too great to bear any addition with prudence or propriety; and when the burdens imposed in consequence of former requisitions were discharged, our tone became too high to resort again to requisition. No colony, since that time, ever has had any requisition whatsoever made to it. */108*

We see the sense of the Crown, and the sense of Parliament, on the productive nature of a *revenue by grant*. Now search the same journals for the produce of the *revenue by imposition*. Where is it? Let us know the volume and the page. What is the gross, what is the net produce? To what service is it applied? How have you appropriated its surplus? What! can none of the many skillful index-makers that we are now employing find any trace of it? Well, let them and that rest together. But are the journals, which say nothing of the revenue, as silent on the discontent? Oh, no! a child may find it. It is the melancholy burden and blot of every page. */109*

I think, then, I am, from those journals, justified in the sixth and last resolution, which is: "That it hath been found by experience that the manner of granting the said supplies and aids by the said general assemblies hath been more agreeable to the inhabitants of the said colonies, and more beneficial and conducive to the public service, than the mode of giving and granting aids and subsidies in Parliament, to be raised and paid in the said colonies." */110*

This makes the whole of the fundamental part of the plan. The conclusion is irresistible. You cannot say that you were driven by any necessity to an exercise of the utmost rights of legislature. You cannot assert that you took on yourselves the task of imposing colony taxes, from the want of another legal body that is competent to the purpose of supplying the exigencies of the state without wounding the prejudices of the people. Neither is it true that the body so qualified, and having that competence, had neglected the duty. */111*

The question now, on all this accumulated matter, is whether you will choose to abide by a profitable experience or a mischievous theory? whether you choose to build on imagination or fact? whether you prefer enjoyment or hope? satisfaction in your subjects, or discontent? */112*

If these propositions are accepted, everything which has been made to enforce a contrary system must, I take it for granted, fall along with it. On that ground, I have drawn the following resolution, which, when it comes to be moved, will naturally be divided in a proper manner: "That it may be proper to repeal an act, made in the seventh year of the reign of his present Majesty, entitled 'An act for granting certain duties in the British colonies and plantations in America; for allowing a drawback of the duties of customs upon the exportation from this kingdom of coffee and cocoa-nuts of the produce of the said colonies or plantations; for discontinuing the drawbacks payable on China earthenware exported to America; and for more effectually preventing the clandestine running of goods in the said colonies and plantations.' And also that it may be proper to repeal an act, made in the fourteenth year of the reign of his present Majesty, entitled 'An act to discontinue, in such manner and for such time as are therein mentioned, the landing and discharging, lading or shipping, of goods, wares, and merchandise, at the town and within the harbor of Boston, in the province of Massachusetts Bay, in North America.' And also that it may be proper to repeal an act, made in the fourteenth year of the reign of his present Majesty, entitled 'An act for the impartial administration of justice, in the cases of persons questioned for any acts done by them, in the execution of the law, or for the suppression of riots and tumults, in the province of the Massachusetts Bay, in New England.' And also that it may be proper to repeal an act, made in the fourteenth year of the reign of his present Majesty, entitled 'An act for the better regulating the government of the province of the Massachusetts Bay, in New England.' And also that it may be proper to explain and amend an act, made in the thirty-fifth year of the reign of King Henry the Eighth, entitled 'An act for the trial of treasons committed out of the King's dominions.' " */113*

I wish, sir, to repeal the Boston Port Bill, because (independently of the dangerous precedent of suspending the rights of the subject during the King's pleasure) it was passed, as I apprehend, with less regularity, and on more partial principles, than it ought. The corporation of Boston was not heard before it was condemned. Other towns, full as guilty as she was, have not had their ports blocked up. Even the Restraining Bill of the present session does not go to the length of the Boston Port Act. The same ideas of prudence, which induced you not to extend equal punishment to equal guilt, even when you were punishing, induce me, who mean not to chastise, but to reconcile, to be satisfied with the punishment already partially inflicted. */114*

Ideas of prudence and accommodation to circumstances prevent you from taking away the charters of Connecticut and Rhode Island, as you have taken away that of Massachusetts Colony, though the Crown has far less power in the two former provinces than it enjoyed in the latter, and though the abuses have been full as great and as flagrant in the exempted as in the punished. The same reasons of prudence and accommodation have weight with me in restoring the charter of Massachusetts Bay. Besides, sir, the act which changes the charter of Massachusetts is in many particulars so exceptionable that, if I did not wish absolutely to repeal, I would by all means desire to alter it; as several of its provisions tend to the subversion of all public and private justice. Such, among others, is the power in the governor to change the sheriff at his pleasure, and to make a new returning officer for every special cause. It is shameful to behold such a regulation standing among English laws. */115*

The act for bringing persons accused of committing murder under the orders of government to England for trial is but temporary. That act has calculated the probable duration of our quarrel with the colonies, and is accommodated to that supposed duration. I would hasten the happy moment of reconciliation, and therefore must, on my principle, get rid of that most justly obnoxious act. */116*

The act of Henry the Eighth for the trial of treasons I do not mean to take away, but to confine it to its proper bounds and original intention—to make it expressly for trial of treasons (and the greatest treasons may be committed) in places where the jurisdiction of the Crown does not extend. */117*

Having guarded the privileges of local legislature, I would next secure to the colonies a fair and unbiased judicature; for which purpose, sir, I propose the following resolution: "That, from the time when the general assembly, or general court, of any colony or plantation in North America shall have appointed, by act of assembly duly confirmed, a settled salary to the offices of the chief justice and other judges of the superior courts, it may be proper that the said chief justice and other judges of the superior courts of such colony shall hold his and their office and offices during their good behavior; and shall not be removed therefrom but when the said removal shall be adjudged by his Majesty in council, upon a hearing on complaint from the general assembly, or on a complaint from the governor, or the council, or the house of representatives, severally, of the colony in which the said chief justice and other judges have exercised the said offices." */118*

The next resolution relates to the courts of admiralty. It is this: "That it may be proper to regulate the courts of admiralty or vice-admiralty, authorized by the fifteenth chapter of the fourth of George the Third, in such a manner as to make the same more commodious to those who sue or are sued in the said courts, and to provide for the more decent maintenance of the judges of the same." */119*

These courts I do not wish to take away; they are in themselves proper establishments. This court is one of the capital securities of the Act of Navigation. The extent of its jurisdiction, indeed, has been increased; but this is altogether as proper, and is, indeed, on many accounts, more eligible, where new powers were wanted, than a court absolutely new. But courts incommodiously situated, in effect, deny justice; and a court partaking in the fruits of its own condemnation is a robber. The Congress complain, and complain justly, of this grievance. */120*

These are the three consequential propositions. I have thought of two or three more; but they come rather too near detail, and to the province of executive government, which I wish Parliament always to superintend, never to assume. If the first six are granted, congruity will carry the latter three. If not, the things that remain unrepealed will be, I hope, rather unseemly encumbrances on the building than very materially detrimental to its strength and stability. */121*

Here, sir, I should close, but that I plainly perceive some objections remain, which I ought, if possible, to remove. The first will be that in resorting to the doctrine of our ancestors, as contained in the preamble to the Chester act, I prove too much: that the grievance from a want of representation, stated in that preamble, goes to the whole of legislation as well as to taxation; and that the colonies, grounding themselves upon that doctrine, will apply it to all parts of legislative authority. */122*

To this objection, with all possible deference and humility, and wishing as little as any man living to impair the smallest particle of our supreme authority, I answer that *the words are the words of Parliament, and not mine;* and that all false and inconclusive inferences drawn from them are not mine; for I heartily disclaim any such inference. I have chosen the words of an act of Parliament, which Mr. Grenville, surely a tolerably zealous and very judicious advocate for the sovereignty of Parliament, formerly moved to have read at your table in confirmation of his tenets. It is true that Lord Chatham considered these preambles as declaring strongly in favor of his opinions. He was a no less powerful advocate for the privileges of the Americans. Ought I not from hence to presume that these preambles are as favorable as possible to both, when properly understood: favorable both to the rights of Parliament, and to the privilege of the dependencies of this Crown? But, sir, the object of grievance in my resolution I have not taken from the Chester, but from the Durham act, which confines the hardship of want of representation to the case of subsidies, and which therefore falls in exactly with the case of the colonies. But whether the unrepresented counties were *de jure*, or *de facto*, bound, the preambles do not accurately distinguish; nor, indeed, was it necessary; for, whether *de jure* or *de facto*, the legislature thought the exercise of the power of taxing, as of right, or as of fact without right, equally a grievance, and equally oppressive. */123*

I do not know that the colonies have, in any general way, or in any cool hour, gone much beyond the demand of immunity in relation to taxes. It is not fair to judge of the temper or dispositions of any man or any set of men, when they are composed and at rest, from their conduct or their expressions in a state of disturbance and irritation. It is, besides, a very great mistake to imagine that mankind follow up practically any speculative principle, either of government or of freedom, as far as it will go in argument and logical illation. We Englishmen stop very short of the principles upon which we support any given part of our Constitution, or even the whole of it together. I could easily, if I had not already tired you, give you very striking and convincing instances of it. This is nothing but what is natural and proper. All government, indeed every human benefit and enjoyment, every virtue and every prudent act, is founded on compromise and barter. We balance inconveniences; we give and take; we remit some rights, that we may enjoy others; and we choose rather to be happy citizens than subtle disputants. As we must give away some natural liberty to enjoy civil advantages, so we must sacrifice some civil liberties for the advantages to be derived from the communion and fellowship of a great empire. But, in all fair dealings, the thing bought must bear some proportion to the purchase paid. None will barter away the immediate jewel of his soul. Though a great house is apt to make slaves haughty, yet it is purchasing a part of the artificial importance of a great empire too dear to pay for it all essential rights, and all the intrinsic dignity of human nature. None of us who would not risk his life rather than fall under a government purely arbitrary. But although there are some amongst us who think our Constitution wants many improvements to make it a complete system of liberty, perhaps none who are of that opinion would think it right to aim at such improvement by disturbing his country and risking everything that is dear to him. In every arduous enterprise, we consider what we are to lose, as well as what we are to gain; and the more and better stake of liberty every people possess, the less they will hazard in a vain attempt to make it more. These are *the cords of man.* Man acts from adequate motives relative to his interest, and not on metaphysical speculations. Aristotle, the great master of reasoning, cautions us, and with great weight and propriety, against this species of delusive geometrical accuracy in moral arguments, as the most fallacious of all sophistry. */124*

The Americans will have no interest contrary to the grandeur and glory of England, when they are not oppressed by the weight of it; and they will rather be inclined to respect the acts of a superintending legislature, when they see them the acts of that power which is itself the security, not the rival, of their secondary importance. In this assurance my mind most perfectly acquiesces, and I confess I feel not the least alarm from the discontents which are to arise from putting people at their ease; nor do I apprehend the destruction of this empire from giving, by an act of free grace and indulgence, to two millions of my fellow citizens some share of those rights upon which I have always been taught to value myself. */125*

It is said, indeed, that this power of granting, vested in American assemblies, would dissolve the unity of the empire—which was preserved entire, although Wales, and Chester, and Durham were added to it. Truly, Mr. Speaker, I do not know what this unity means; nor has it ever been heard of, that I know, in the constitutional policy of this country. The very idea of subordination of parts excludes this notion of simple and undivided unity. England is the head; but she is not the head and the members too. Ireland has ever had from the beginning a separate, but not an independent, legislature, which, far from distracting, promoted the union of the whole. Everything was sweetly and harmoniously disposed through both islands for the conservation of English dominion and the communication of English liberties. I do not see that the same principles might not be carried into twenty islands, and with the same good effect. This is my model with regard to America, as far as the internal circumstances of the two countries are the same. I know no other unity of this empire than I can draw from its example during these periods, when it seemed to my poor understanding more united than it is now, or than it is likely to be by the present methods. */126*

But since I speak of these methods, I recollect, Mr. Speaker, almost too late, that I promised, before I finished, to say something of the proposition of the noble lord on the floor, which has been so lately received, and stands on your journals. I must be deeply concerned, whenever it is my misfortune to continue a difference with the majority of this House. But as the reasons for that difference are my apology for thus troubling you, suffer me to state them in a very few words. I shall compress them into as small a body as I possibly can, having already debated that matter at large, when the question was before the committee. /127

First, then, I cannot admit that proposition of a ransom by auction, because it is a mere project. It is a thing new, unheard of, supported by no experience, justified by no analogy, without example of our ancestors, or root in the Constitution. It is neither regular parliamentary taxation nor colony grant. *Experimentum in corpore vili* is a good rule, which will ever make me adverse to any trial of experiments on what is certainly the most valuable of all subjects, the peace of this empire. /128

Secondly, it is an experiment which must be fatal in the end to our Constitution. For what is it but a scheme for taxing the colonies in the antechamber of the noble lord and his successors? To settle the quotas and proportions in this House is clearly impossible. You, sir, may flatter yourself you shall sit a state auctioneer, with your hammer in your hand, and knock down to each colony as it bids. But to settle (on the plan laid down by the noble lord) the true proportional payment for four or five and twenty governments, according to the absolute and the relative wealth of each, and according to the British proportion of wealth and burden, is a wild and chimerical notion. This new taxation must therefore come in by the back door of the Constitution. Each quota must be brought to this House ready formed. You can neither add nor alter. You must register it. You can do nothing further. For on what grounds can you deliberate either before or after the proposition? You cannot hear the counsel for all these provinces, quarreling each on its own quantity of payment, and its proportion to others. If you should attempt it, the Committee of Provincial Ways and Means, or by whatever other name it will delight to be called, must swallow up all the time of Parliament. /129

Thirdly, it does not give satisfaction to the complaint of the colonies. They complain that they are taxed without their consent. You answer that you will fix the sum at which they shall be taxed. That is, you give them the very grievance for the remedy. You tell them, indeed, that you will leave the mode to themselves. I really beg pardon; it gives me pain to mention it; but you must be sensible that you will not perform this part of the compact. For suppose the colonies were to lay the duties which furnished their contingent upon the importation of your manufactures; you know you would never suffer such a tax to be laid. You know, too, that you would not suffer many other modes of taxation. So that, when you come to explain yourself, it will be found that you will neither leave to themselves the quantum nor the mode, nor indeed anything. The whole is delusion, from one end to the other. /130

Fourthly, this method of ransom by auction, unless it be *universally* accepted, will plunge you into great and inextricable difficulties. In what year of our Lord are the proportions of payments to be settled? To say nothing of the impossibility that colony agents should have general powers of taxing the colonies at their discretion, consider, I implore you, that the communication by special messages and orders between these agents and their constituents on each variation of the case, when the parties come to contend together and to dispute on their relative proportions, will be a matter of delay, perplexity, and confusion that never can have an end. */131*

If all the colonies do not appear at the outcry, what is the condition of those assemblies who offer, by themselves or their agents, to tax themselves up to your ideas of their proportion? The refractory colonies, who refuse all composition, will remain taxed only to your old impositions, which, however grievous in principle, are trifling as to production. The obedient colonies in this scheme are heavily taxed; the refractory remain unburdened. What will you do? Will you lay new and heavier taxes by Parliament on the disobedient? Pray consider in what way you can do it. You are perfectly convinced that, in the way of taxing, you can do nothing but at the ports. Now suppose it is Virginia that refuses to appear at your auction, while Maryland and North Carolina bid handsomely for their ransom, and are taxed to your quota—how will you put these colonies on a par? Will you tax the tobacco of Virginia? If you do, you give its death-wound to your English revenue at home, and to one of the very greatest articles of your own foreign trade. If you tax the import of that rebellious colony, what do you tax but your own manufactures, or the goods of some other obedient and already well-taxed colony? Who has said one word on this labyrinth of detail, which bewilders you more and more as you enter into it? Who has presented, who can present you, with a clue to lead you out of it? I think, sir, it is impossible that you should not recollect that the colony bounds are so implicated in one another (you know it by your other experiments in the bill for prohibiting the New England fishery) that you can lay no possible restraints on almost any of them which may not be presently eluded, if you do not confound the innocent with the guilty, and burden those whom upon every principle you ought to exonerate. He must be grossly ignorant of America who thinks that, without falling into this confusion of all rules of equity and policy, you can restrain any single colony, especially Virginia and Maryland, the central and most important of them all. */132*

Let it also be considered that either in the present confusion you settle a permanent contingent, which will and must be trifling, and then you have no effectual revenue; or you change the quota at every exigency, and then on every new repartition you will have a new quarrel. */133*

Reflect besides that, when you have fixed a quota for every colony, you have not provided for prompt and punctual payment. Suppose one, two, five, ten years' arrears. You cannot issue a Treasury extent against the failing colony. You must make new Boston Port Bills, new restraining laws, new acts for dragging men to England for trial. You must send out new fleets, new armies. All is to begin again. From this day forward the empire is never to know an hour's tranquillity. An intestine fire will be kept alive in the bowels of the colonies, which one time or other must consume this whole empire. I allow, indeed, that the empire of Germany raises her revenue and her troops by quotas and contingents; but the revenue of the empire and the army of the empire is the worst revenue and the worst army in the world. */134*

Instead of a standing revenue, you will therefore have a perpetual quarrel. Indeed, the noble lord who proposed this project of a ransom by auction seemed himself to be of that opinion. His project was rather designed for breaking the union of the colonies than for establishing a revenue. He confessed he apprehended that his proposal would not be to *their taste*. I say, this scheme of disunion seems to be at the bottom of the project; for I will not suspect that the noble lord meant nothing but merely to delude the nation by an airy phantom which he never intended to realize. But whatever his views may be, as I propose the peace and union of the colonies as the very foundation of my plan, it cannot accord with one whose foundation is perpetual discord. */135*

Compare the two. This I offer to give you is plain and simple; the other full of perplexed and intricate mazes. This is mild; that harsh. This is found by experience effectual for its purposes; the other is a new project. This is universal; the other calculated for certain colonies only. This is immediate in its conciliatory operation; the other remote, contingent, full of hazard. Mine is what becomes the dignity of a ruling people—gratuitous, unconditional, and not held out as matter of bargain and sale. I have done my duty in proposing it to you. I have, indeed, tired you by a long discourse; but this is the misfortune of those to whose influence nothing will be conceded, and who must win every inch of their ground by argument. You have heard me with goodness. May you decide with wisdom! For my part, I feel my mind greatly disburdened by what I have done today. I have been the less fearful of trying your patience, because on this subject I mean to spare it altogether in future. I have this comfort—that, in every stage of the American affairs, I have steadily opposed the measures that have produced the confusion, and may bring on the destruction, of this empire. I now go so far as to risk a proposal of my own. If I cannot give peace to my country, I give it to my conscience. */136*

But what (says the financier) is peace to us without money? Your plan gives us no revenue. No! But it does; for it secures to the subject the power of *refusal*, the first of all revenues. Experience is a cheat, and fact a liar, if this power in the subject, of proportioning his grant, or of not granting at all, has not been found the richest mine of revenue ever discovered by the skill or by the fortune of man. It does not, indeed, vote you £152,750 11*s.* 2¾*d.*, nor any other paltry, limited sum; but it gives the strongbox itself, the fund, the bank, from whence only revenues can arise amongst a people sensible of freedom. *Posita luditur arca.* Cannot you in England, cannot you at this time of day, cannot you, a House of Commons, trust to the principle which has raised so mighty a revenue, and accumulated a debt of near 140 millions in this country? Is this principle to be true in England and false everywhere else? Is it not true in Ireland? Has it not hitherto been true in the colonies? Why should you presume that, in any country, a body duly constituted for any function will neglect to perform its duty, and abdicate its trust? Such a presumption would go against all government in all modes. But, in truth, this dread of penury of supply from a free assembly has no foundation in nature. For first observe that, besides the desire which all men have naturally of supporting the honor of their own government, that sense of dignity, and that security to property, which ever attends freedom, has a tendency to increase the stock of the free community. Most may be taken where most is accumulated. And what is the soil or climate where experience has not uniformly proved that the voluntary flow of heaped-up plenty, bursting from the weight of its own rich luxuriance, has ever run with a more copious stream of revenue than could be squeezed from the dry husks of oppressed indigence by the straining of all the politic machinery in the world? */137*

Next, we know that parties must ever exist in a free country. We know, too, that the emulations of such parties, their contradictions, their reciprocal necessities, their hopes, and their fears, must send them all in their turns to him that holds the balance of the state. The parties are the gamesters; but government keeps the table, and is sure to be the winner in the end. When this game is played, I really think it is more to be feared that the people will be exhausted than that government will not be supplied. Whereas whatever is got by acts of absolute power ill obeyed because odious, or by contracts ill kept because constrained, will be narrow, feeble, uncertain, and precarious. "Ease would retract/Vows made in pain, as violent and void." */138*

I, for one, protest against compounding our demands: I declare against compounding, for a poor limited sum, the immense, ever-growing, eternal debt which is due to generous government from protected freedom. And so may I speed in the great object I propose to you, as I think it would not only be an act of injustice, but would be the worst economy in the world, to compel the colonies to a sum certain, either in the way of ransom, or in the way of compulsory compact. */139*

But to clear up my ideas on this subject—a revenue from America transmitted hither. Do not delude yourselves; you can never receive it; no, not a shilling. We have experience that from remote countries it is not to be expected. If, when you attempted to extract revenue from Bengal, you were obliged to return in loan what you had taken in imposition, what can you expect from North America? For, certainly, if ever there was a country qualified to produce wealth, it is India; or an institution fit for the transmission, it is the East India Company. America has none of these aptitudes. If America gives you taxable objects on which you lay your duties here, and gives you at the same time a surplus by a foreign sale of her commodities to pay the duties on these objects which you tax at home, she has performed her part to the British revenue. But with regard to her own internal establishments, she may, I doubt not she will, contribute in moderation. I say in moderation; for she ought not to be permitted to exhaust herself. She ought to be reserved to a war; the weight of which, with the enemies that we are most likely to have, must be considerable in her quarter of the globe. There she may serve you, and serve you essentially. */140*

For that service, for all service, whether of revenue, trade, or empire, my trust is in her interest in the British Constitution. My hold of the colonies is in the close affection which grows from common names, from kindred blood, from similar privileges, and equal protection. These are ties which, though light as air, are as strong as links of iron. Let the colonies always keep the idea of their civil rights associated with your government—they will cling and grapple to you, and no force under heaven will be of power to tear them from their allegiance. But let it be once understood that your government may be one thing and their privileges another, that these two things may exist without any mutual relation—the cement is gone, the cohesion is loosened, and everything hastens to decay and dissolution. As long as you have the wisdom to keep the sovereign authority of this country as the sanctuary of liberty, the sacred temple consecrated to our common faith, wherever the chosen race and sons of England worship freedom, they will turn their faces towards you. The more they multiply, the more friends you will have; the more ardently they love liberty, the more perfect will be their obedience. Slavery they can have anywhere. It is a weed that grows in every soil. They may have it from Spain, they may have it from Prussia. But, until you become lost to all feeling of your true interest and your natural dignity, freedom they can have from none but you. This is the commodity of price, of which you have the monopoly. This is the true Act of Navigation, which binds to you the commerce of the colonies, and through them secures to you the wealth of the world. Deny them this participation of freedom, and you break that sole bond which originally made, and must still preserve, the unity of the empire. Do not entertain so weak an imagination as that your registers and your bonds, your affidavits and your sufferances, your cockets and your clearances, are what form the great securities of your commerce. Do not dream that your letters of office, and your instructions, and your suspending clauses are the things that hold together the great contexture of this mysterious whole. These things do not make your government. Dead instruments, passive tools as they are, it is the spirit of the English communion that gives all their life and efficacy to them. It is the spirit of the English Constitution, which, infused through the mighty mass, pervades, feeds, unites, invigorates, vivifies every part of the empire, even down to the minutest member. */141*

Is it not the same virtue which does everything for us here in England?

Do you imagine, then, that it is the Land Tax Act which raises your revenue? that it is the annual vote in the Committee of Supply which gives you your army? or that it is the Mutiny Bill which inspires it with bravery and discipline? No! surely, no! It is the love of the people; it is their attachment to their government, from the sense of the deep stake they have in such a glorious institution, which gives you your army and your navy, and infuses into both that liberal obedience without which your army would be a base rabble and your navy nothing but rotten timber. */142*

All this, I know well enough, will sound wild and chimerical to the profane herd of those vulgar and mechanical politicians who have no place among us—a sort of people who think that nothing exists but what is gross and material, and who, therefore, far from being qualified to be directors of the great movement of empire, are not fit to turn a wheel in the machine. But to men truly initiated and rightly taught, these ruling and master principles, which in the opinion of such men as I have mentioned have no substantial existence, are in truth everything, and all in all. Magnanimity in politics is not seldom the truest wisdom; and a great empire and little minds go ill together. If we are conscious of our situation, and glow with zeal to fill our place as becomes our station and ourselves, we ought to auspicate all our public proceedings on America with the old warning of the Church, "*Sursum corda!*" We ought to elevate our minds to the greatness of that trust to which the order of Providence has called us. By adverting to the dignity of this high calling our ancestors have turned a savage wilderness into a glorious empire, and have made the most extensive and the only honorable conquests, not by destroying, but by promoting, the wealth, the number, the happiness of the human race. Let us get an American revenue as we have got an American empire. English privileges have made it all that it is; English privileges alone will make it all it can be. */143*

In full confidence of this unalterable truth, I now (*quod felix faustumque sit!*) lay the first stone of the Temple of Peace; and I move you: "That the colonies and plantations of Great Britain in North America, consisting of fourteen separate governments, and containing two millions and upwards of free inhabitants, have not had the liberty and privilege of electing and sending any knights and burgesses, or others, to represent them in the high court of Parliament." */144*

Burke seems to have believed that a full-scale review of conditions in America might yet win to his side those members of the House uncommitted in the battle between Crown and colonists. He was wrong. In the vote that followed, Burke's first motion was defeated by 270 to 78; his subsequent resolutions were similarly lost. Lexington and Concord were now less than a month away.

"On Conciliation with America" is an expression of the views of a man ahead of his time. Had Burke's advice been followed, the American Revolutionary War might never have been fought. What is now the United States might have become the first self-governing dominion in the British Commonwealth of Nations.

Why study a speech that failed? Because Burke's imagery, his epigrams, and his composition represent quality unsurpassed in political discourse. If speakers spoke only when they were assured of success, the whole process of speaking would become purely ceremonial.

QUESTIONS

1. Whom is Burke addressing at the outset of his speech? Why?

2. Burke indicates in his opening paragraph that the House is now free to adopt a new position in relation to America. Is this the effect Lord North intended when he introduced his bill?

3. Why do you suppose the speaker includes paragraphs 2–8 in this speech? Is he merely full of self-importance, or does this passage serve some significant purpose in speech development?

4. Some critics maintain that Burke has a tendency to be wordy. Is paragraph 9 an example of wordiness? Could another speaker have presented Burke's ideas in this paragraph in shorter space?

5. Why does Burke choose to present a program for colonial government at this time? Isn't that the responsibility of the party in power?

6. Burke has a habit of stating his views in the negative. (For example, see pars. 9–10.) Why do you suppose so experienced a communicator would do this?

7. What reason does Burke give for beginning his analysis with a statement on the population of the colonies? Were the members of the House unaware of this statistic?

8. Is Burke's presentation of the figures on colonial trade persuasive? Or are statistics inherently dull when they appear in a speech?

9. Does Burke's reference to the life of Lord Bathurst (par. 25) help or hinder his purpose? Why?

10. Burke speaks of a policy of "wise and salutary neglect" (par. 30). To what does he refer?

11. Why did Burke think that Protestant sects flourished in America whereas Roman Catholicism and Anglicanism did not (par. 40)? Would Englishmen emigrating in the time of John Pym agree?

12. Why did Burke object to imposing an embargo on the English colonies in America?

13. What specific examples of imagery do you find in Burke's speech? Are Burke's word pictures dated, or do they seem to possess a timeless quality?

14. What are Burke's four objections to force as an instrument of national policy toward American colonists? Do these objections seem valid today? Are they limited in application to colonial powers only?

PROJECTS

1. Prepare a topical outline of Burke's address, relating each section to the numbered paragraphs in your text. What evidence can you cite to demonstrate that Burke was a well-informed speaker?

2. The activities Burke pursued as a college student laid the groundwork for a lifetime of public service. Compose a 500-word essay on the activities of the Trinity Historical Club of Burke's day. Start your investigation by examining *Poole's Index to Periodical Literature.*

3. Prepare a list of the constituencies Burke represented in the House of Commons. How did he become the representative of each?

4. Describe the historical event which made William Lenthall famous as a Speaker of the House of Commons.

5. Compare and contrast the roles of the Speakers of the British House of Commons and of the American House of Representatives: What similarities and differences are there between their offices?

6. Does the term *concession* carry the implication of *surrender*? Define *concession,* first as you think Lord North would have done, then as you think Burke would have. What dictionary definitions of *concession* existed in Burke's day? (Consult *The Oxford English Dictionary.*)

7. Prepare a five-minute oral report on the activities of the Continental Congresses prior to the date of Burke's speech. How soon after the delivery of this speech could a copy have reached the American colonies?

8. Burke describes his six resolutions as "factual." Why then should they have been rejected by the House of Commons? Read W. E. H. Lecky's account of the English scene in 1775 in *A History of England in the Eighteenth Century* (New York: D. Appleton and Co., 1891).

9. Reread the American Declaration of Independence. What similarities in reasoning do you find in Jefferson's document and Burke's speech? What differences?

10. Read Chauncey A. Goodrich's account of Charles James Fox in *Select British Eloquence* (Indianapolis: The Bobbs-Merrill Company, Inc., 1963). How did Burke and Fox differ in their methods of gathering speech material? How did they differ as parliamentary debaters?

11. Burke is often described as the greatest political philosopher that eighteenth-century England produced. List the political maxims you find embedded in this speech. Apply one to the contemporary world scene.

12. Is the British Constitution Burke reveres the same series of precedents Pym knew? What events altered the British system of government in 1688? 1832? 1911?

SPEAKING ON BEHALF OF THE MODERATE CONSCIENCE

The Young Men's Business Club of Birmingham, Alabama, composed of professional men throughout the city, gathered for a weekly meeting in mid-September 1963. On the preceding Sunday morning, a bomb had been thrown into a Negro church within the city. Four young children attending Sunday School were killed in the latest battle for civil rights.

A member of the club rose to introduce a motion condemning the unnamed perpetrators of the Sabbath tragedy. Similar motions by white groups in the South had become regular occurrences during the past ten years. Southern politicians claimed that these crimes were the deeds of a small group of extremists—that the overwhelming majority of Southern whites deplored such lawlessness as much as Northern whites did. Nevertheless, the violence continued. The ferment provided newspapers the world over with almost daily copy.

Seated in the audience was club member Charles Morgan, Jr., a young attorney. As Morgan later described his feelings, "The time had come for someone to place the guilt where it had always belonged—not on the outsiders or the hostile national press or the Negro leaders or even the white supremacists alone." (*A Time to Speak* [New York: Harper & Row, 1964], p. 10.) Morgan rose to speak to the motion on the floor. As you read the speech, note Morgan's indictment of his own society. In light of this indictment, try to decide whether Morgan was speaking on behalf of a group or of his own conscience. Can he have been speaking on behalf of the moderates if he criticized them so severely?

A TIME TO SPEAK

CHARLES MORGAN, JR.

Four little girls were killed in Birmingham yesterday. A mad, remorseful, worried community asks, "Who did it? Who threw that bomb? Was it a Negro or a white?" The answer should be "We all did it." Every last one of us is condemned for that crime and the bombing before it and the ones last month, last year, a decade ago. We all did it. */1*

A short time later, white policemen kill a Negro and wound another. A few hours later two young men on a motorbike shoot and kill a Negro child. Fires break out and, in Montgomery, white youths assault Negroes. */2*

And all across Alabama an angry, guilty people cry out their mocking shouts of indignity and say they wonder "why?" "who?" Everyone then "deplores" the "dastardly" act. /3

But you know the *who* of *Who did it?* is really rather simple. The *who* is every little individual who talks about the "niggers" and spreads the seeds of his hate to his neighbor and his son. The jokester, the crude oaf whose racial jokes rock the party with laughter. The *who* is every governor who ever shouted for lawlessness and became a law violator. It is every senator and every representative who in the halls of Congress stands and with mock humility tells the world that things back home aren't really like they are. It is courts that move ever so slowly and newspapers that timorously defend the law. It is all the Christians and all their ministers who spoke too late in anguished cries against violence. It is the coward in each of us who clucks admonitions. We are ten years of lawless preachments, ten years of criticism of law, of courts, of our fellow man; a decade of telling school children the opposite of what the civics books say. We are a mass of intolerance and bigotry and stand indicted before our young. We are cursed by the failure of each of us to accept responsibility, by our defense of an already dead institution. /4

Yesterday while Birmingham, which prides itself on the number of its churches, was attending worship services, a bomb went off and an all-white police force moved into action, a police force which has been praised by city officials and others at least once a day for a month or so. A police force which has solved no bombings. A police force which many Negroes feel is perpetrating the very evils we decry. And why would Negroes think this? /5

There are no Negro policemen: there are no Negro sheriff's deputies. Few Negroes have served on juries; few have been allowed to vote; few have been allowed to accept responsibility, or granted even a simple part to play in the administration of justice. Do not misunderstand me. It is not that I think that white policemen had anything whatsoever to do with the killing of these children or previous bombings. It's just that Negroes who see an all-white police force must think in terms of its failure to prevent or solve the bombings and think perhaps Negroes would have worked a little bit harder. They throw rocks and bottles and bullets. And we whites don't seem to know why the Negroes are lawless. So we lecture them. /6

Birmingham is the only city in America where the police chief and the sheriff, in the school crisis, had to call our local ministers together to tell them to do their duty. The ministers of Birmingham who have done so little for Christianity call for prayer at high noon in a city of lawlessness and, in the same breath, speak of our city's "image." Did those ministers visit the families of the Negroes in their hour of travail? Did many of them go to the homes of their brothers and express their regrets in person or pray with the crying relatives? Do they admit Negroes into their ranks at the church? /7

Who is guilty? A moderate mayor elected to change things in Birmingham and who moves so slowly and looks elsewhere for leadership? A business community which shrugs its shoulders and looks to the police or perhaps somewhere else for leadership? A newspaper which has tried so hard of late, yet finds it necessary to lecture Negroes every time a Negro home is bombed? A governor who offers a reward but mentions not his own failure to preserve either segregation or law and order? And what of those lawyers and politicians who counsel people as to what the law is not, when they know full well what the law is? */8*

Those four little Negro girls were human beings. They had lived their fourteen years in a leaderless city; a city where no one accepts responsibility, where everyone wants to blame somebody else. A city with a reward fund which grew like Topsy as a sort of sacrificial offering, a balm for the consciences of the "good people," whose ready answer is for those "right-wing extremists" to shut up. People who absolve themselves of guilt. The liberal lawyer who told me this morning, "Me? I'm not guilty," he then proceeding to discuss the guilt of the other lawyers, the ones who told the people that the Supreme Court did not properly interpret the law. And that's the way it is with the southern liberals. They condemn those with whom they disagree for speaking while they sit in fearful silence. */9*

Birmingham is a city in which the major industry, operated from Pittsburgh, never tried to solve the problem. It is a city where four little Negro girls can be born into a second-class school system, live a segregated life, ghettoed into their own little neighborhoods, restricted to Negro churches, destined to ride in Negro ambulances to Negro wards of hospitals or to a Negro cemetery. Local papers, on their front and editorial pages, call for order and then exclude their names from obituary columns. */10*

And who is really guilty? Each of us. Each citizen who has not consciously attempted to bring about peaceful compliance with the decisions of the Supreme Court of the United States, each citizen who has ever said "They ought to kill that nigger," every citizen who votes for the candidate with the bloody flag; every citizen and every school board member and schoolteacher and principal and businessman and judge and lawyer who has corrupted the minds of our youth; every person in this community who has in any way contributed during the past several years to the popularity of hatred is at least as guilty, or more so, than the demented fool who threw that bomb. */11*

What's it like living in Birmingham? No one ever really has and no one will until this city becomes part of the United States. */12*

Birmingham is not a dying city. It is dead. */13*

One can only guess at the impact of Morgan's words upon his listeners. We do know that shortly afterward he moved to Washington, D.C., where he became Counsel for the American Association of University Professors.

QUESTIONS

1. If you had been a southern moderate like Charles Morgan, Jr., would you have waited until 1963 to speak out? Or would you have chosen an earlier day? Or would you have simply remained silent?

2. Morgan's speech is, in a sense, a sermon on self-guilt. Do you think the speaker would have been more persuasive if he had spent more of his time documenting his own inactivity in the civil rights struggle? Why or why not?

3. Could Morgan have exercised greater influence by speaking before a political gathering or a church group instead of the Young Men's Business Club? Explain your answer.

4. What compositional techniques account for the tone of immediacy in this speech? Would the speech have been improved by the use of greater detail in recording earlier disturbances in the community?

5. Morgan's speech was part of the discussion which followed a motion to condemn the bombing. What alternative courses would have been open to a club member who wanted to protest more strongly?

6. In physics we learn about the principle of inertia—the tendency of an object to remain at rest once in a motionless state and, conversely, to keep moving once set in motion. Could such a principle exist in human affairs as well? That is, does an individual or a community tend to resist change? Once change begins, do individuals or the community feel a sense of momentum pushing them onward? Is such a principle important in the teen-ager's desire for independence? Can resistance to equality for the American Negro be partially explained on this basis?

PROJECTS

1. Examine four or five printed works by and about Harry Golden. Prepare a five-minute oral report on the topic "Harry Golden's Fight for Southern Integration." How does Golden's approach to this problem differ from Morgan's?

2. Define *satire*. Explain why Harry Golden's writings on segregation are or are not good examples of satire.

3. Read any three speeches of Dr. Martin Luther King. What factors account for King's leadership among American Negroes? What use does King make of personal experience in the speeches you examined?

4. Read the Senate debate on the 1964 Civil Rights Bill in the *Congressional Record.* What seem to be the principal arguments of southern senators opposed to the bill?

5. Study articles treating Negro-white relations in *Life* and *Ebony* for one month. Examine reports of a particular event in each source. What similarities and what differences do you find?

6. What is it like to be a Negro in the South? Read the account of John Howard Griffin in *Black Like Me* (Boston: Houghton Mifflin Company 1961). Prepare a five-minute oral report on what Griffin found.

SPEAKING ON BEHALF OF A NATION IN TIME OF WAR

Sir Winston Churchill's speeches became models of eloquence in his own lifetime. They are the works of a well-informed speaker, a man who knew his audience, a man who had an acute awareness of time and place. In addition, Churchill's speeches are characterized by an elevated style. His ability to phrase an idea so that it stayed in the minds of his listeners was virtually his trademark: "I have nothing to offer but blood, toil, tears, and sweat"; "Never in the field of human conflict have so many owed so much to so few"; ". . . an iron curtain has descended across the continent."

The speech that follows is unusual, to begin with, in that the target audience was not British but American. The United States, which had tried to remain neutral during World War II while assisting the Western democracies through the Lend-Lease program, had just declared war on Japan; Italy and Germany, in turn, declared war on us. The war had suddenly become our business on December 7, 1941, when Japanese bombers attacked the Pacific fleet at Pearl Harbor.

The speech was presented nineteen days after the United States' entrance into the war. Churchill was asked to speak before a joint session of Congress. To Americans it seemed fitting that the leader of their ally of nineteen days should come to address Congress and, through radio, themselves. Churchill was more than the political leader of Great Britain; he had become identified with his people in much the same way that Napoleon was identified with imperial France. Personifying Britain, Churchill was also a wartime symbol of optimism and determination. As you read his speech, notice his humorous use of understatement, his vigorous phrasing, his simple language, and his adaptation to the audience before him.

ADDRESS TO THE CONGRESS

WINSTON CHURCHILL

Members of the Senate and of the House of Representatives of the United States, I feel gratefully honored that you should have thus invited me to enter the United States Senate chamber and address the representatives of both branches of Congress. */1*

The fact that my American forebears have for so many generations played their part in the life of the United States and that here I am, an

Text from **The New York Times**, December 27, 1941.

Englishman, welcomed in your midst makes this experience one of the most moving and thrilling in my life, which is already long and has not been entirely uneventful. /2

I wish indeed that my mother, whose memory I cherish across the veil of years, could have been here to see me. By the way, I cannot help reflecting that if my father had been American and my mother British, instead of the other way around, I might have got here on my own. /3

In that case, this would not have been the first time you would have heard my voice. In that case I would not have needed any invitation, but if I had it is hardly likely that it would have been unanimous. So, perhaps, things are better as they are. I may confess, however, that I do not feel quite like a fish out of water in a legislative assembly where English is spoken. /4

CHILD OF THE HOUSE OF COMMONS

I am a child of the House of Commons. I was brought up in my father's house to believe in democracy; trust the people, that was his message. I used to see him cheered at meetings and in the streets by crowds of workingmen way back in those aristocratic Victorian days when Disraeli said, "The world was for the few and for the very few." Therefore, I have been in full harmony with the tides which have flowed on both sides of the Atlantic against privileges and monopoly and I have steered confidently towards the Gettysburg ideal of government of the people, by the people, for the people. /5

I owe my advancement entirely to the House of Commons, whose servant I am. In my country, as in yours, public men are proud to be the servants of the state and would be ashamed to be its masters. On any day, if they thought the people wanted it, the House of Commons could, by a simple vote, remove me from my office. But I am not worrying about it at all. /6

As a matter of fact, I am sure they will approve very highly of my journey here, for which I obtained the King's permission, in order to meet the President of the United States, and to arrange with him for all that mapping of our military plans and for all those intimate meetings of the high officers of both countries, which are indispensable for the successful prosecution of the war. /7

IMPRESSED BY FORTITUDE HERE

I should like to say, first of all, how much I have been impressed and encouraged by the breadth of view and sense of proportion which I have found in all quarters over here to which I have had access. Anyone who did not understand the size and solidarity of the foundation of the United States might easily have expected to find an excited, disturbed, self-centered atmosphere, with all minds fixed upon the novel, startling, and painful episodes of sudden war as it hit America. /8

After all, the United States has been attacked and set upon by three most powerfully armed dictator states, the greatest military power in Europe, the greatest military power in Asia—Japan, Germany, and Italy have all declared and are making war upon you, and the quarrel is opened, which can only end in their overthrow or yours. */9*

But, here in Washington in these memorable days, I have found an Olympian fortitude which, far from being based upon complacency, is only the mask of an inflexible purpose and the proof of a sure, well-grounded confidence in the final outcome. */10*

We in Britain had the same feeling in our darkest days. We, too, were sure that in the end all would be well. You do not, I am certain, underrate the severity of the ordeal to which you and we have still to be subjected. The forces ranged against us are enormous. They are bitter. They are ruthless. The wicked men and their factions, who have launched their peoples on the path of war and conquest, know that they will be called to terrible account if they cannot beat down by force of arms the peoples they have assailed. */11*

"OUR RESOURCES FAR GREATER"

They will stop at nothing. They have a vast accumulation of war weapons of all kinds. They have highly trained and disciplined armies, navies, and air services. They have plans and designs which have long been contrived and matured. They will stop at nothing that violence or treachery can suggest. It is quite true that on our side our resources in man power and materials are far greater than theirs. But only a portion of your resources are as yet mobilized and developed, and we both of us have much to learn in the cruel art of war. */12*

We have, therefore, without doubt, a time of tribulation before us. In this same time some ground will be lost which it will be hard and costly to regain. Many disappointments and unpleasant surprises await us. Many of them will afflict us before the full marshaling of our latent and total power can be accomplished. */13*

For the best part of twenty years the youth of Britain and America have been taught that war was evil, which is true, and that it would never come again, which has been proved false. For the best part of twenty years the youth of Germany, of Japan, and Italy have been taught that aggressive war is the noblest duty of the citizen and that it should be begun as soon as the necessary weapons and organization have been made. We have performed the duties and tasks of peace. They have plotted and planned for war. This naturally has placed us, in Britain, and now places you, in the United States, at a disadvantage which only time, courage, and untiring exertion can correct. */14*

We have indeed to be thankful that so much time has been granted to us. If Germany had tried to invade the British Isles after the French collapse in June 1940, and if Japan had declared war on the British Empire and the United States at about the same date, no one can say what disasters and agonies might not have been our lot. But now at the end of December 1941, our transformation from easygoing peace to total war efficiency has made very great progress. */15*

HAILS STRIDES IN PRODUCTION

The broad flow of munitions in Great Britain has already begun. Immense strides have been made in the conversion of American industry to military purposes, and now that the United States is at war, it is possible for orders to be given every day which in a year or eighteen months hence will produce results in war power beyond anything which has been seen or foreseen in the dictator states. */16*

Provided that every effort is made, that nothing is kept back, that the whole man power, brain power, virility, valor, and civic virtue of the English-speaking world, with all its galaxy of loyal, friendly, or associated communities and states, provided that it is bent unremittingly to the simple but supreme task, I think it would be reasonable to hope that the end of 1942 will see us quite definitely in a better position than we are now. And that the year 1943 will enable us to assume the initiative upon an ample scale. Some people may be startled or momentarily depressed when, like your President, I speak of a long and a hard war. */17*

''DELIVERANCE'' IN ITS PLACE

Our peoples would rather know the truth, somber though it be. And after all, when we are doing the noblest work in the world, not only defending our hearths and homes but the cause of freedom in every land, the question of whether deliverance comes in 1942 or 1943 or 1944 falls into its proper place in the grand proportions in human history. */18*

Sure I am that this day now we are masters of our fate, that the task which has been set us is not above our strength, that its pangs and toils are not beyond our endurance. As long as we have faith in our cause and unconquerable will power, salvation will not be denied us. */19*

In the words of the Psalmist: "He shall not be afraid of evil tidings, his heart is fixed, trusting in the Lord." */20*

Not all the tidings will be evil. On the contrary, mighty strokes of war have already been dealt against the enemy—the glorious defense of their native soil by the Russian armies and people. Wounds have been inflicted upon the Nazi tyranny and system which have bitten deep and will fester and inflame not only in the Nazi body but in the Nazi mind. */21*

The boastful Mussolini has crumpled already. He is now but a lackey and a serf, the merest utensil of his master's will. He has inflicted great suffering and wrong upon his own industrious people. He has been stripped of all his African empire, Abyssinia has been liberated. Our armies of the East, which were so weak and ill-equipped at the moment of French desertion, now control all the regions from Teheran to Bengazi and from Aleppo and Cyprus to the sources of the Nile. */22*

For many months we devoted ourselves to preparing to take the offensive in Libya. The very considerable battle which has been proceeding there for the last six weeks in the desert has been most fiercely fought on both sides. Owing to the difficulties of supply upon the desert flank we were never able to bring numerically equal forces to bear upon the enemy. Therefore we had to rely upon a superiority in the numbers and qualities of tanks and aircraft, British and American. */23*

For the first time, aided by these—for the first time we have fought the enemy with equal weapons. For the first time we have made the Hun feel the sharp edge of those tools with which he has enslaved Europe. The armed forces of the enemy in Cyrenaica amounted to about 150,000 men, of whom a third were Germans. General Auchinleck set out to destroy totally that armed force, and I have every reason to believe that his aim will be fully accomplished. */24*

I am so glad to be able to place before you, members of the Senate and of the House of Representatives, at this moment when you are entering the war, the proof that, with proper weapons and proper organization, we are able to beat the life out of the savage Nazi. What Hitlerism is suffering in Libya is only a sample and a foretaste of what we have got to give him and his accomplices wherever this war should lead us in every quarter of the globe. */25*

THE LIFELINE OF THE ATLANTIC

There are good tidings also from blue water. The lifeline of supplies which joins our two nations across the ocean, without which all would fail—that lifeline is flowing steadily and freely in spite of all that the enemy can do. It is a fact that the British Empire, which many thought eighteen months ago was broken and ruined, is now incomparably stronger and is growing stronger with every month. */26*

Lastly, if you will forgive me for saying it, to me the best tidings of all, the United States, united as never before, has drawn the sword for freedom and cast away the scabbard. */27*

All these tremendous steps have led the subjugated peoples of Europe to lift up their heads again in hope. They have put aside forever the shameful temptation of resigning themselves to the conqueror's will. Hope has returned to the hearts of scores of millions of men and women, and with that hope there burns a flame of anger against the brutal, corrupt invader. And still more fiercely burn the fires of hatred and contempt for the filthy quislings whom he has suborned. */28*

WAITING FOR THE DAWN TO COME

In a dozen famous ancient states, now prostrate under the Nazi yoke, the masses of the people—all classes and creeds—await the hour of liberation when they, too, will once again be able to play their part and strike their blows like men. That hour will strike and its solemn peal will proclaim that night is past and that the dawn has come. */29*

The onslaught upon us, so long and so secretly planned by Japan, has presented both our countries with grievous problems for which we could not be fully prepared. If people ask me, as they have a right to ask me in England, "Why is it that you have not got an ample equipment of modern aircraft and army weapons of all kinds in Malaya and in the East Indies?" I can only point to the victory General Auchinleck has gained in the Libyan campaign. Had we diverted and dispersed our gradually growing resources between Libya and Malaya, we should have been found wanting in both theaters. */30*

If the United States has been found at a disadvantage at various points in the Pacific Ocean, we know well that that is to no small extent because of the aid which you have been giving to us in munitions for the defense of the British Isles, and for the Libyan campaign, and above all, because of your help in the Battle of the Atlantic, upon which all depends and which has in consequence been successfully and prosperously maintained. */31*

Of course, it would have been much better, I freely admit, if we had had enough resources of all kinds to be at full strength at all threatened points, but considering how slowly and reluctantly we brought ourselves to large-scale preparations, and how long these preparations take, we had no right to expect to be in such a fortunate position. */32*

A CHOICE OF USING RESOURCES

The choice of how to dispose of our hitherto limited resources had to be made by Britain in time of war and by the United States in time of peace. And I believe that history will pronounce that upon the whole, and it is upon the whole that these matters must be judged, that the choice made was right. */33*

Now that we are together, now that we are linked in a righteous comradeship of arms, now that our two considerable nations, each in perfect unity, have joined all their life energies in a common resolve, a new scene opens upon which a steady light will glow and brighten. */34*

Many people have been astonished that Japan should, in a single day, have plunged into war against the United States and the British Empire. We all wonder why, if this dark design, with its laborious and intricate preparations, had been so long filling their secret minds, they did not choose our moment of weakness eighteen months ago. */35*

Viewed quite dispassionately, in spite of the losses we have suffered and the further punishment we shall have to take, it certainly appears an irrational act. It is, of course, only prudent to assume that they have made very careful calculations, and think they see their way through. */36*

Nevertheless, there may be another explanation. We know that for many years past the policy of Japan has been dominated by secret societies of subalterns and junior officers of the army and navy who have enforced their will upon successive Japanese Cabinets and Parliaments by the assassination of any Japanese statesman who opposed or who did not sufficiently further their aggressive policies. It may be that these societies, dazzled and dizzy with their own schemes of aggression and the prospect of early victory, have forced their country against its better judgment into war. They have certainly embarked upon a very considerable undertaking. /37

After the outrages they have committed upon us at Pearl Harbor, in the Pacific Islands, in the Philippines, in Malaya, and the Dutch East Indies, they must now know that the stakes for which they have decided to play are mortal. When we look at the resources of the United States and the British Empire, compared to those of Japan, when we remember those of China, which have so long valiantly withstood invasion and tyranny, and when also we observe the Russian menace which hangs over Japan, it becomes still more difficult to reconcile Japanese action with prudence or even with sanity. /38

What kind of a people do they think we are? Is it possible that they do not realize that we shall never cease to persevere against them until they have been taught a lesson which they and the world will never forget? /39

"HERE WE ARE TOGETHER"

Members of the Senate and members of the House of Representatives, I will turn for one moment more from the turmoil and convulsions of the present to the broader spaces of the future. /40

Here we are together facing a group of mighty foes who seek our ruin. Here we are together defending all that to free men is dear. /41

Twice in a single generation the catastrophe of world war has fallen upon us. Twice in our lifetime has the long arm of fate reached out across the oceans to bring the United States into the forefront of the battle. If we had kept together after the last war, if we had taken common measures for our safety, this renewal of the curse need never have fallen upon us. /42

Do we not owe it to ourselves, to our children, to tormented mankind, to make sure that these catastrophes do not engulf us for the third time? It has been proved that pestilences may break out in the Old World which carry their destructive ravages into the New World from which, once they are afoot, the New World cannot escape. /43

Duty and prudence alike command, first, that the germ centers of hatred and revenge should be constantly and vigilantly curbed and treated in good time and that an adequate organization should be set up to make sure that the pestilence can be controlled at its earliest beginning before it spreads and rages throughout the entire earth. /44

Five or six years ago it would have been easy without shedding a drop of blood for the United States and Great Britain to have insisted on the fulfillment of the disarmament clauses of the treaties which Germany signed after the Great War. /45

And that also would have been the opportunity for assuring to the Germans those materials, those raw materials, which we declared in the Atlantic Charter should not be denied to any nation, victor or vanquished. /46

The chance has passed. It is gone. Prodigious hammer strokes have been needed to bring us together today. */47*

If you will allow me to use other language I will say that he must indeed have a blind soul who cannot see that some great purpose and design is being worked out here below, of which we have the honor to be the faithful servants. */48*

It is not given to us to peer into the mysteries of the future. Still I avow my hope and faith, sure and inviolate, that in the days to come the British and American people will for their own safety and for the good of all walk together in majesty, in justice, and in peace. */49*

According to *The New York Times*, "the crowded Senate chamber rose as one in tribute" to Churchill as he ended his speech. When Churchill received the Nobel Prize for Literature after the war, equal credit was given in the citation to his speeches and his books.

QUESTIONS

1. What proportion of Churchill's speech is devoted to an introduction? What specific functions does he seek to perform in this section? Could the opening have been improved? If so, how?

2. One of the hallmarks of Churchill's style is his choice of simple, concrete words. Are there any words in this address which are new to you? Does this speaker ever use an abstract word when a concrete one would be preferable?

3. Speaking, more than writing, must be instantly intelligible if it is to be effective. Are there any sentences in Churchill's speech which you find hard to grasp on first exposure?

4. Borrow a recording of Churchill's speeches from a library and listen to the speech you have just read. What qualities in the speaker's oral presentation aid him in communicating his message? From your viewpoint, what qualities of delivery make Churchill more difficult to listen to than, say, the President of the United States?

5. How many instances of parallel construction can you detect in Churchill's speech? Is this device effective? Why or why not?

6. What evidence of Churchill's realism do you find in this speech to Congress? Do you think he should have omitted references to hardship in favor of a more optimistic approach to the war?

7. Churchill says he is glad to be able to present the proof that "we are able to beat the life out of the savage Nazi" (par. 25). What proof does he present? Is it convincing? Why or why not?

8. What proportion of Churchill's speech is devoted to his conclusion? What functions does he seek to perform here? Could the conclusion have been improved, and if so, how?

9. Are Churchill's references to the Bible and to God effective in this speech? Or is this merely the politician's time-tested technique for winning over a segment of his audience?

10. The great speech, like the great painting, is the product of an art which conceals itself. What speaking techniques, if any, were you aware of as you read Churchill's address?

PROJECTS

1. Examine three biographical accounts of Winston Churchill. Prepare a five-minute oral report on the highlights of his career.

2. Discuss the career of Churchill's father as it is presented in the *Dictionary of National Biography.* In what ways were the careers of father and son alike?

3. When did Churchill first warn the House of Commons of the threat of war in Europe? Discuss why he was not listened to then.

4. Investigate and report on the following: How is the British Prime Minister chosen? Was Churchill the leader of a political party in 1940 or something of a political maverick? How did he become Prime Minister?

5. Compare Churchill's first address as Prime Minister with Franklin D. Roosevelt's first wartime address to Congress, December 8, 1941. In these two instances, which speaker seems to you to have a better command of language? Defend your answer.

6. Shortly after the war, Churchill was removed from office. Describe the reasons for this and explain the process by which it was done. Did this event indicate that the British people were ungrateful to him?

7. Read Churchill's "Iron Curtain" speech, delivered at Fulton, Missouri, March 5, 1946. To what extent has Churchill's desire for a closer relationship between the United States and Great Britain become a reality? If a serious proposal were made that this country join the British Commonwealth of Nations, would you be in favor or opposed? Why?

PART THREE

THE PROBLEM OF PRESENTING SPECIALIZED MATERIAL

America is fast becoming a nation of specialists, not only in the medical profession, but in most other areas as well. Students flock to our vocational schools, colleges, and universities in search of the skills and specialized knowledge that will ensure them a prosperous future. One of the most difficult communication obstacles such specialists face is an audience of laymen. Securing the understanding of other specialists is relatively easy, as Andrew T. Weaver points out in his speech in Part I. But when *common structure* and *common environment* are lacking, the speaker's challenge is much greater.

Have you ever had the experience of hearing a doctor diagnose an illness, using medical terminology? Or of hearing a mechanic explain to the average motorist why his car will not run? On such occasions a layman is apt to be mystified by the language used. And yet specialized terminology enables specialists of like background to communicate with one another. The problem is simply stated: Too many specialists fail to address lay listeners in terms they will understand.

A DOCTOR EXPLAINS PSYCHOSOMATIC ILLNESS

Dr. John A. Schindler (1903–1957) was a medical doctor from Monroe, Wisconsin. He had been asked to talk to a group of Wisconsin farmers and their families, the address to be part of the University of Wisconsin's Farm and Home Week program. Schindler's speech, presented on February 3, 1949, was broadcast "live" by the state FM network and Madison station WHA—the oldest radio station in the nation in continuous operation. Therefore, rural listeners anywhere in the state, as well as the immediate audience, could hear Schindler at the time of his presentation.

As you read this speech, notice the speaker's conversational style, his concrete examples, his avoidance of technical terminology.

HOW TO LIVE A HUNDRED YEARS HAPPILY

JOHN A. SCHINDLER

Friends of the Wisconsin farmland: My inclusion in the program is to provide a sort of atmosphere. Anybody that has heard me before always turns to the one next to him and says, "Just sit back; Schindler talks for a hundred years." /1

The centennial title, "How To Live a Hundred Years Happily," was, so to speak, thrown into my lap. As a matter of fact, it has been coming down around my head, like the roof falling in. It worried me; I lost many a night's sleep; till finally I went to a lawyer friend of mine, a very brilliant man—he might have been a Philadelphia lawyer if he'd wanted to—and I put the question up to him. He studied it for some time, and then he said, "Ah! there's a loophole. There's a loophole in this title. You don't have to tell those people how to live a hundred years. The title infers that *if*, if they live to be a hundred, here's how they can do it happily. That, after all, is the important thing, because nobody wants to live to be a hundred unless he's happy. A hundred years is a powerful long time to be unhappy. As a matter of fact," he said, "there's no point in wanting to live to be sixty unless you're happy. And that's all you've got to tell them." /2

I thought just one moment, and then I said to him, "But—I'm just a country doctor. All I see from one year's end to the other is about six thousand sick people—all of them with a bellyache! And they're not happy. Who am I to tell these people how to stay happy? Aristotle wrote a book on it, and he didn't get any place." /3

"I'm just a lawyer," my friend said, "and from one year's end to the

Text used was distributed by the speaker; printed with the permission of Mrs. John A. Schindler.

other I see people who are in a mess. They're not happy! Even if you change this title to 'How To Live a Hundred Years Honestly,' I can't help you because none of the people that I see are honest. But," he said, "Doc, why don't you start out telling those people what it is that makes all your patients unhappy? Maybe in the course of the gabfest you'll come to some positive point on how to be happy." /4

So, rather than waste my fee to the lawyer, I'm going to start that way! /5

Looking at this thing purely from a physician's point of view, we'll ask the rhetorical question: On your centennial course toward a hundred, what is most apt to upset your happiness? Any physician's answer, of course, would be, "My dear centennial friends, the thing that would be most apt to take the props out from under your happiness would be a long period of illness." And when you think of that, it becomes a little bit frightening, because in the textbooks there are a thousand different diseases that this human clay is heir to. Looking at that fact from a slightly different angle, there's one consolation, and that is that in my seventeen years of practice—as a matter of fact, probably in all medical history—there has not been one individual who has had all 1000 of the diseases at one time. A possible exception to that, of course, is Job, but our scientific data on him isn't sufficient to make him the one exception. /6

But, looking at it from still a different angle, there's another more startling feature, and that is that there is one disease that is as common as the other 999 put together. In other words, if you on your way to one hundred get sick, the chances are 50 per cent right off the bat that it's this one disease that you're going to be sick from. In still other words, 50 per cent of all the people who are going to doctors in the United States today are sick with this one disease. So we better know a little about that. Now, that figure isn't an exaggeration. Many men would put the figure higher. As a matter of fact, at the Ochsner Clinic in New Orleans a couple of years ago they published a paper reviewing five hundred consecutive patient admissions to that institution, and of those five hundred, 386, or 76 per cent, were sick with this one disease. That is terrific! It excepts no one. Anybody of any age can get this disease. Anybody in any walk of life can get this disease. If you put that into money figures, if the Murray-Wagner-Dingle bill, or some similar bill, were passed, it would cost the country about four billion dollars a year in medical expense. Of that amount, two billion dollars would be expended for the care and diagnosis of this one disease! In fact, probably a little more, because this is a terrifically expensive disease to diagnose, and it's a terrifically expensive disease to treat. /7

I hate to give the name of it, because immediately I give you the name you'll get a lot of misconceptions as to what this thing is. And the first misconception that you will get when I tell you the name is that it's not a real disease. But, don't kid yourself. This is a terrifically real thing. The name that it used to go by is psychoneurosis. The name that it has now is *psychosomatic illness.* And it is *not* a disease in which the patient just *thinks* that he is sick. I want to dispel that idea first and foremost, because this is a terrifically real disease. The pain that you get with this disease is just as hard, very often, as the pain you get with a gallbladder colic. The suffering that you can endure in this disease is just as great as the suffering there is with any disease you want to name. /8

Now, this disease isn't produced by a bacterium. It isn't produced by a new growth. It's produced by a certain situation, a certain condition in our lives—your life, my life, everybody's life. If you wanted to name the feature, the characteristic feature, that colors human living more than any other feature, I don't think there'd be any question as to what it would be. I've tried to find one word for it, but it takes three, each one of them meaning about the same thing, but different degrees of the same thing. And those three words that describe the most characteristic thing about human living as we know it are: *cares, difficulties,* and *troubles.* You take cares, difficulties, and troubles out of the lives of some people that you and I know, and there's nothing left to talk about! Now the thing that brings on a psychosomatic illness is this layer of c.d.t. that everybody has in his life. And whenever one has such a thick, impenetrable layer of c.d.t. that he can't get up above it into a realm of joy and pleasure occasionally, he gets a psychosomatic illness. Now, naturally conditions vary with individuals as to the thickness, the impenetrability of this layer of c.d.t. that they live in. People also differ in their ability to bounce up above this layer occasionally. /9

As regards the layer of c.d.t. that people have in their lives, there are three divisions. There is the first division, and nobody here tonight belongs in this first division, but I'll mention it to you anyway. Those are the people who are habitually crabby. They get up in the morning grumpy; they're mean all day; they don't crack a joke; they don't have a smile; and they go to bed the same way. I have a friend who illustrates that group. He has a farm, a beautiful farm, and a couple years ago in our country we had a wonderful crop of oats. I drove past his farm one week early in July and I saw this field of oats and I thought to myself, "This ought to make Sam happy." Now, I had inquired among his relatives and friends as to whether they had ever heard Sam say a happy, pleasant word. None of them ever had, excepting his wife, who thought that he had the first year they were married, but that was so long ago that she wasn't sure. So I drove into Sam's yard and saw Sam, and I said, "Sam, that's a wonderful field of oats," and Sam came back with this, "Yes, but the wind will blow it down before I get it cut." But I watched his field. He got it out all right, he got it threshed, and I know he got a good price for it—'twas the year before last. Well, I saw him one day and I thought, "Now I've got Sam where he just can't get out of this!" So I said, "Sam, how did the oats turn out?" And he said, "Oh, it was a good crop, and I guess the price was all right, but you know a crop of oats like that sure takes a lot out of the soil." Some time later in October—it was a beautiful

October—on a nice, warm afternoon I saw him on the street and I said, "Sam, it's a wonderful day, isn't it?" I said it real enthusiastically, to try to make it contagious. But not Sam, he didn't catch. He just said, "Yes, but when we get it we'll get it hard." */10*

Now, people like Sam invariably get a psychosomatic illness before they get to be a hundred. Usually it's in the late 50's or the 60's or the 70's, and when they get it they get it hard. As a rule, they're invalids for the rest of their lives. They're cares to their families, and there is nothing that you can do about it. */11*

The second group is the group that most of us belong in. These are the people whose layer of c.d.t. isn't too thick. Financially they're well enough off; they don't have any domestic troubles; things are going along well enough; but they make their own c.d.t. All day long they manage to be concerned, to be dissatisfied, to be anxious, to be worrying about something. If there's nothing around home or the business, then they begin to worry about Mrs. Smith down the street. Why doesn't she get her daughter in before eleven o'clock at night? Something is going to happen to her! That's the group most of us belong in. */12*

The third group is made up of those who really have a layer of c.d.t. Maybe a couple of armies have marched back and forth across their farms. Maybe they've gotten themselves into some kind of a mess—financial ruin, domestic trouble, everything in the courts. They've really got a mess. Those people are usually easier to treat than those in the second group. And those in the second group are certainly easier to treat than those in the first group. */13*

Now, how does this c.d.t. bring on this disease? In order to understand that, we have to stop just a moment to consider what thinking is and what an emotion is. Thinking, we ordinarily suppose, is something that goes on solely in the brain, but that is quite wrong. Whenever we think, we use our entire body in one way or another, in a series of correlated nerve impulses that center in the brain. Particularly is that true when an emotion enters our thinking, and practically all of our thinking is colored, in one way or another, by an emotion. If we understand what an emotion is, we'll understand how thinking does things to our bodies. The best definition of an emotion comes from our own William James, who took the work of the physiologist Lange about 1888 and formed a definition that's still the best we have. Nobody has improved on it. Occasionally somebody tries but doesn't succeed. William James said that an emotion is the state of mind that manifests itself by a sensible change in the body. */14*

In a moment we'll consider a few emotions and show you how a state of mind produces changes in the body. I want to read you the names of just a few emotions. We have so many emotions that you could write them in a line from here to Chicago and you wouldn't list all of them. Emotions are terrifically numerous things, things that we're throwing off all the time. We can divide them roughly into two groups: the pleasant emotion and the unpleasant emotion. Here is a very fractional list of unpleasant emotions: anger, dissatisfaction, fear, distrust, disappointment, hatred, sorrow, grief, anxiety, remorse, and disgust. You could add to that ad infinitum. Here are a few of the pleasant emotions that all of us have felt: satisfaction, assurance, hopefulness, approval, love, joy, pleasure, cheerfulness, contentment, humor, and so on. You could add to that. But I want to show you some examples so that you can understand just what an emotion is. For instance, there is anger. A state of mind presents itself to an individual which results in anger. You can see that; you don't have to be told by somebody else that the man must be angry. He either gets white in the face or he gets red; his eyes get wider; his muscles tighten up so that he trembles. That is the state of mind manifesting itself by a sensible change in the body. Got it? */15*

Another emotion that all of you are more or less acquainted with is that which brings about blushing. Now, a person who blushes doesn't have a disease of the skin that makes him blush. In such a person, anything that's embarrassing, sometimes even just slightly embarrassing, produces a dilatation of the blood vessels in the skin of the face that brings on the blush. That is part of the emotion of embarrassment in that person. Others display the emotion of embarrassment in a different way. */16*

Another emotion that you are all acquainted with is exhibited by people who can look at a toad or blood and faint or vomit. Such a person doesn't have a disease of the stomach that makes him vomit or disease of the heart that makes him faint. In such a person the sight of blood or a toad is so disgusting—leads to such painfully disagreeable thinking—that the stomach does the things that result in vomiting. Or the heart and the blood vessels leading to the brain do the things that result in fainting. That is the emotion. */17*

There's another example that all of you have probably experienced. During a period of acute mourning when some loved member of the family has died, you feel extremely weak. You don't feel like working. You've lost your appetite. That is part of the emotion of grief, in which muscles become utterly relaxed. The deeper the grief, the greater the relaxation. That's grief. That's a sensible change in the body manifesting a state of mind. */18*

One more example. We had a man carried into the hospital one morning about nine o'clock. He was carried in because he couldn't have stood up. He'd have fallen over. He was faint; his heart was going 180 times a minute; he was vomiting; he couldn't control his bowels; he couldn't control his urine. And he stayed in that state for about three months! Up until eight o'clock that morning, he was a perfectly healthy man. He was a cheese-maker—strong, able to work every day, never sick. At eight o'clock he walked into his wife's bedroom, and found that his wife had killed their only girl and committed suicide. Now, he didn't at that moment develop heart disease or cancer or tuberculosis. His thinking became acutely disagreeable. He had a terrific emotional upset, which produced the bodily changes that put him in the hospital. */19*

Now, those are examples of the disagreeable emotions. One thing that every disagreeable emotion does, excepting grief: It produces muscle tightness, tension of muscles. The happy emotions on the other side produce a relaxation of muscles to just an optimal degree, not the relaxation that you get in grief, but an optimal relaxation. They're in optimal tone. If you want them to do something they're ready to do it, and very quickly. You can feel that. Some afternoon you take the kids out on a picnic and everything goes along well, everybody's behaving, and you stop suddenly, and you ask yourself, "How do I feel?" You feel good. What is it? It's that relaxation, that optimal tone that all your muscles have assumed because of the emotion of pleasure. */20*

Now, many of the happy emotions you can see. If you think of something funny, the muscles of your face do a certain thing which you call a *smile.* If it's a little funnier than that, then the muscles of the diaphragm and the intercostal muscles and the muscles of your larynx help to do certain things, and you laugh. You don't have to say to yourself, "Well, this emotion that I'm smiling about is getting to be second degree; now I've got to laugh." It does that all by itself because that is the emotion. See? */21*

Now, how does this business bring about a disease? Very simply. Suppose that all day long your thinking is acutely disagreeable. You're tightening up muscles. You take your fist and hold it loosely; it doesn't hurt; but you hold it tight for a long time and it begins to hurt. If you squeeze your fist very tight, it hurts right away. Either squeeze produces pain. One of the first places that you feel that tension is in the muscles in the back of the neck. About 85 per cent of all our patients that complain of a pain in the back of the neck going down the cords of the neck have this disease. To demonstrate that tightness, just sit in an easy chair some night—the easiest chair that you have, to be sure that it isn't the chair that's doing it—and worry hard about something for an hour. When you get up, you stretch and twist, and you find that the muscles of your neck are stiff. That's one of the first groups of muscles to show tension. */22*

There's also another group that comes into play very early, and those are the muscles of the upper end of the esophagus. When they squeeze down, it feels like a lump. About 90 per cent of all the people complaining of a lump here have this disease. Now, if they try to swallow while that esophagus is narrowed down, there's a moment's hesitation before it opens up and they feel as though they can't swallow. If the muscles in the lower esophagus are the ones that contract, then it's a more serious thing. Such a person can't get anything through into his stomach. And that spasm will stay tight like that day after day, week after week. Fortunately it doesn't occur nearly as often in the lower end of the esophagus as it does in the upper. Much more commonly is the stomach involved in this thing. And when the muscles of the stomach begin to squeeze down, it feels like a pressure inside, a disagreeable feeling. When the muscles squeeze down real hard, then it hurts. And it hurts just as bad as any ulcer. In fact, 50 per cent of all the people that we see, who have a pain exactly like that of an ulcer, don't have an ulcer. They've got that kind of stomach. Now, even if the pain in an individual is coming from an ulcer, it isn't the ulcer that hurts. It's a spasm of the muscle in the stomach adjacent to that ulcer that causes the pain. When something gets into the stomach, the stomach muscles relax and the pain stops. When the stomach empties, the muscle squeezes down again, and the pain starts. Now, whether that spasm of muscle is occurring because there's an ulcer there or because there's a nervous system there doesn't make any difference as far as the type of pain is concerned. We had a grocer who had that kind of pain all the time. He was in competition, of course, with the chain stores, which isn't easy, and he had a wife who—well, I believe if I'd have had his wife, I'd have had his pain. And as if that wasn't enough c.d.t. for anybody, he had a son who was always getting into trouble. Not just a little trouble, but a whole lot of trouble! And between the three—his business, his wife, and his son—he had this pain in the stomach most all of the time. Every once in a while, somebody would tell him, "Yes, you have an ulcer," and of course that made it worse. But whenever he went some place where they knew what they were talking about, they assured him that "you have no ulcer." He finally began to believe himself that he didn't have, because every time he went up north fishing, which was twice a year, all his pain stopped. And it didn't come back again until he got to Round Grove Hill on the way home where he could see the courthouse tower, and right there his pain started. Up at the Mayo Clinic in Rochester, there is a doctor who has the same kind of pain. A very famous doctor—if I gave you his name you'd all have heard it. He has the same kind of pain. He says, "I know there's nothing there, but I can't help it. Here in Rochester I'm driven; I've got things to do; I've got a hundred things on my mind all the time; and that thing keeps hurting me. The only way I can get rid of it is to get on the train. When the train gets to Winona, the pain stops; when the train comes back into the station, the pain starts." */23*

Now, the same kind of spasm in muscle can happen in the rest of the twenty-eight feet of bowel, particularly in the colon. Some wag in Philadelphia said not long ago that the colon is the mirror of the mind—that when the mind gets tight, the colon gets tight. And that's about the way it works. Usually in the same individual it's the same muscle that squeezes down. In some individuals it's the muscles in the back of the neck that squeeze down every time they get anxious, every time they get dissatisfied. In others it may be a three-inch section of the colon. If it happens to be in a certain place, it looks for all the world like gallbladder disease, and it can hurt just as hard as a gallbladder spasm. Fifty per cent of all the people that we see complaining of a pain exactly like gallbladder pain don't have gallbladder pain at all. They've got this disease. If the pain happens to be lower down in the colon, it will seem just like appendicitis. And then it takes a very smart doctor not to open that abdomen. In other people the pain can occur throughout the entire length of the colon. And believe me, they are uncomfortable, and their suffering is real. */24*

Now, we've considered mainly just the muscles of the intestinal tract; but it can be the muscles in any part of the body, particularly the muscles of the blood vessels. They respond very readily to emotional stimuli. I've already mentioned blushing. But 80 per cent of the people that we see with headaches—terrific headaches, severe enough to cause them to go to the doctor—have a headache because some blood vessel inside or outside of the skull is squeezing down so hard from nervous excitation that it produces the pain. We had, for instance, a lady who got a terrifically sick headache that put her to bed for two days every time she got ready to go to town, because going to town for her meant getting the house ready, getting the children ready, thinking about what she was going to get in town, and hating to meet the people that she was going to meet there, for she was very shy. The only way she could keep from getting a headache was just not to go to town. */25*

Other blood vessels come into this thing; for instance, the blood vessels in the skin. And 30 per cent of all the skin diseases that dermatologists see over the country are produced by blood vessels in the skin reacting this way to anxiety, worry, disgust, and so on. Every time such an individual becomes upset or irritated or peeved, these particular blood vessels in some sections of the skin—usually it's on the back of the neck, but it can be any place—squeeze down and actually squeeze serum out through the wall of the blood vessel into the skin. And if that keeps happening, the tissue becomes thickened with serum. It becomes reddish; finally the serum is actually pushed up through the surface of the skin where it becomes scaly, crusty, and itchy, and they have a neurodermatitis. */26*

Muscles anywhere in the body can react, and 30 per cent of all the rheumatism that we see is produced by a muscle group some place hurting because it is constantly kept tight by nervous tension. One very favorite place is the muscles in the left upper part of the thorax. Never over on the right side. People never come in because they have a pain on the right. Or almost never; it's always on the left. The reason for that is that they watch for it on the left side. Almost everybody will get a pain on his left side or his right. If it's on the right—pshaw!—it doesn't amount to anything. If it's on the left—ah!—could be heart trouble! Then they watch for it. The next day it comes again. "Now, I must have heart trouble!" And then when it happens again—"Yes, I'm afraid it is heart trouble!" Then they watch it. And all you have to do to bring on a pain is to watch something. If you stop any time of the day and ask yourself, "Where do I hurt? Where am I uncomfortable right now?" and if you're under tension, you're going to hurt some place. Then if you begin to pay attention to that, pretty soon it hurts more often and it hurts harder. */27*

Now, muscle tension is just one way in which the symptoms are produced in a psychosomatic illness. One of the other ways is the effect that the emotion has on the endocrine system. I'll give you just two examples of that. All of you have driven down a street in an automobile too fast, and suddenly somebody has backed out from a side road and you've just barely missed them. Now, you had to miss them in order to see what comes next! Things you noticed were these: You started to breathe deeply, your heart started to pound, and you got just a little faint. Maybe the one next to you fainted. You daren't because you're at the wheel. The reason those things happen is that the acute fear that's presented to your mind produces these bodily changes. An impulse is sent to the adrenal glands. The adrenals squeeze adrenaline into the blood stream which is immediately carried through the body. When that adrenaline hits the heart, the heart starts to thump. When it hits the respiratory center in the brain, you start to gasp. When it hits the blood vessels going into the brain, they narrow down and you feel just a little woozy. */28*

Another example of how an emotional upset affects the endocrine system is illustrated by girls going away to college, for the first time especially. About 30 per cent of them miss from three to four months' menstrual periods, simply because of the strange newness and tenseness of their lives. Most of the menstrual irregularities in women are produced by the same mechanism. */29*

There's one more way that's very important in producing the symptoms of a psychosomatic illness. Some doctors say that it's the most important—I don't think so, so I always put it last in my list—and that is by hyperventilation. By *hyperventilation* we simply mean "overbreathing." There are some people who are so continually excited, so continually up in the air, that they're overbreathing all the time. All of us overbreathe some of the time. And the symptoms that are produced are very noticeable. The reason they are produced by overbreathing is that as we breathe out [we remove] carbon dioxide, which comes from the blood and has to be replaced in the blood at the rate that it's removed. If we remove it faster by overbreathing, it goes down in the blood and the blood becomes a little alkaline, and when it reaches a certain degree of alkalinity things begin to happen. The first thing that usually happens is a tingling numbness of your hands or feet. About the same time, you feel a quivering in your abdomen which is due to the muscles of the intestines going into action. About the same time, your heart usually starts to beat fast, and you get dizzy; you have a kind of sudden light-headedness. All of that comes very quickly. And then if you keep on overbreathing, you begin to get cramps in the arms and legs until by persistence you can bring on such a cramp that it will double you up in what we call *tetany*. */30*

We had a man who was having his teeth pulled. Every time he had a date with the dentist, he became apprehensive about two hours before he had to go and he started to overbreathe. By the time he got into the dentist's chair, he was in tetany. He fell out of the chair, and the dentist called up and said, "Come right down and see Mr. So-and-so; he's having a fit!"

But he wasn't having a fit: he was just overbreathing. And he did that every time he had to go to the dental chair. /31

Now, all of us hyperventilate much of the time, particularly at night. If you watch people asleep, you'll find as a rule, particularly after a hard day, that they're very restless. They move around, they assume awkward positions, and they breathe funny. Ever watch them? They'll breathe fast for a while: and if, at a time like that, they wake up, they'll often find that they have a cramp. In fact, the cramp will wake them up. During sleep we think about the same things we did during the day, and if Mr. So-and-so down the street said something nasty to us during the day, he may be shooting at us in our sleep. And we react emotionally, the same as though he really were shooting at us. And it produces changes in the body just as terrific. That is one of the reasons that that restlessness, that tenseness we go through at night, makes us so tired in the morning. /32

In this disease that I'm talking about, one of the characteristic things is that people get up in the morning more tired than when they went to bed the night before. This is the only disease that does that. We used to think that that was the only explanation for the tiredness. Another explanation, of course, is that in many of these states there is a measure of grief mixed up in it, and the relaxation of muscles is so terrific in grief that it gives you a very tired feeling. But more recently, in the last few years, Dr. Hans Selye, a professor of medicine at Toronto University, has given us a new and very startling idea of what this tiredness comes from that these people have. Tiredness is always a feature of it. In fact, when they get so tired that they can't walk across the room anymore, we call it a nervous breakdown. Doctor Selye took some rats and kept them worried. Just how he did that I won't describe to you, but it didn't hurt the rats, except that he kept them worried. He had them look for food and had a dog look through a glass into their cage to frighten them. And although these rats did not have to move around very much, they became very tired. When he took the blood from a tired rat and put it into a normal rat, that rat was immediately tired. When he took the blood from a person who was in a nervous breakdown and put that into a normal rat, that rat became tired. And then he isolated a substance from the blood of these animals that would produce the tiredness. He followed its action through the body, and he knew just what mechanism produces that tiredness. Now that, of course, is an organic effect from inner psychosomatic disease. /33

We have other such organic effects. For instance, if it happens to be the blood vessels on your heart that squeeze down every time you get excited, every time you get angry, it's a very serious thing. You then have a disease called *angina pectoris* that can put you into the happy hunting grounds almost any moment. John Hunter, one of the greatest physiologists in England, had that kind of heart, and he always said, "The first scoundrel that gets me angry will kill me." And that's exactly what happened. He got up in the medical meeting one time to refute something that he didn't like, and in a fit of anger produced such a contraction of the blood vessels on his heart that he fell dead. /34

There are other organic effects of the psychosomatic illness that I could go into, but you get the idea. You see what we mean when we talk about a psychosomatic illness. Many of the people that have such an illness are up and around. Many of them are in hospitals. Thousands of them have been in bed at home for years. The illness can have all degrees of severity. And you don't want to get it, because when you get it, you're unhappy. Now, it's easy to keep from getting it. And it's easy to get over it if you've got it. It's so easy that it's hard to believe. All you have to do not to get a psychosomatic illness is to make use of this key thought: *I'm going to make my attitude and my thinking as cheerful and as pleasant as possible.* Say it over and over to yourself, "I'm going to make my attitude and my thinking as cheerful and as pleasant as possible." /35

Now, it would be idiotic to stand up here and tell this centennial audience that you can be pleasant and cheerful all the time. Of course, you can't. But you can be pleasant and cheerful part of the time. And it's easy to use this key thought if you learn to do eight things. By the way, there ought to be a course in the university called "The Art of Human Living," where you could learn all eight of them. I remember that I learned some of them in Benny Snow's Physics I-A and in Max Otto's "Man and Nature" and in William Kiekhofer's Economics I-A, but the whole thing wasn't integrated. I had to go all over the university to get it. But here are the eight things: /36

The *first* thing that you want to learn is: *Quit looking for a knock in your human motor.* Don't be analyzing your feelings all the time, looking for trouble. That habit will certainly land you in a psychosomatic illness. /37

The *second* thing is: *Learn to like to work.* In this world, to get any place you've got to work. There have been a few that have devised some other methods, but they lead either to the penitentiary or to a political job. But you can learn to like work so much that it becomes as invigorating as dancing. And it pays better! One of the things that you will escape if you learn to like to work is work-tension, the tension that many people get under, with the idea that "I've got to get this done," and "I've got to get that done," or "How am I going to do this?" That's usually because they don't like to work. When you get up in the morning, you want to pound on your chest and say: "Come on, work! Where is it?" /38

Then the *third* thing is: *Learn to have a hobby.* A hobby is a very important element for getting your mind off work-tension. During the day when you're hurrying, speeding, and you've got things on your mind, just relax for thirty seconds by getting your mind on that thing that you're making in the basement or that fishing trip that you're going to take next Sunday. Then, when you get home, drop your business, go down in the basement, and work on that thing. Or get your fishing tackle out and get ready for Sunday. I had an elderly patient who had alienated her friends and her children. They didn't want to come to see her, and they didn't invite her to see them, because all she ever talked about was how miserable she was, all the pains and feelings she had. They didn't want to hear about her troubles anymore. Of course, when they had alienated her, she had that to add to her troubles. So I said to her one afternoon, "Why don't you get a hobby?" I didn't think she was even listening to me, but a week later, to my surprise, she called up and said, "Well, I've got a hobby!" I said, "Good! What is it?" She said, "Button collecting." I thought to myself, "My goodness, button collecting!" But since I've seen her collect buttons, I think that some day when I have time, I'm going to collect buttons myself, because it has done her a tremendous amount of good. Now, instead of spending an afternoon telling her friends how awful she feels, she goes out looking for a button she has heard about. Or she puts several of them on a card, and when people come in she tells them about these buttons. One afternoon she came up to see good old Governor Goodland. She got into his office, and she explained to him that she would like a button for her collection off his vest. He laughed and said, "I'd give you one, but I haven't got anything to cut it off with," and she took her scissors out of her purse and handed them to him. He cut off three buttons from his vest and one from his coat! And she has those up on one card all by itself. /39

The *fourth* thing is: *Learn to like people.* You'd be surprised how many individuals there are who hate everybody, who carry a dissatisfaction around. We had a man in the hospital—he was that sick—who got there because he had to work in an office with another man whom he didn't like. He was assistant superintendent of a plant that hired five thousand people. He had a good job; he didn't want to leave it; and he had to be in this office with this one other man. He said, "The first time I saw him I didn't like him. I didn't like the way he combed his hair; I didn't like the way he whistled through his teeth; I didn't like the way he always started a sentence with 'Listen!'" On questioning the patient, I found that he never liked anybody. He didn't like his mother or his father or any of his family. His wife always came in with him, so I never dared to ask him whether he liked her! But you have to meet people. You've got to live with them all the time, so learn to like them. /40

Now, the *fifth* thing is: *Learn to be satisfied.* I mean by that, of course, to be satisfied when the situation is such that you can't easily change it, or when you're in a situation in which dissatisfaction isn't going to be of some use. For example, you all know of the person who becomes very distressed because he is violently dissatisfied with the weather. Obviously you can't change the weather. So the best thing to do is to like it, or if you can't like it, at least don't get violently dissatisfied with it. Another example is that of the young lady who was sick in a hospital with a psychosomatic illness because she had become violently dissatisfied with her life. She had been educated to be a secretary in a fine school and had a wonderful job in Washington when the war came along. That brought army officers to Washington, and she married an army captain, which was very good—until after the war she found herself living in a trailer, raising three children. She did not like to live in a trailer and didn't like to raise children in a trailer, and she wasn't sure anymore that she liked to live with her husband in a trailer. All the time she wanted to be a secretary back in Washington, which was obviously impossible. I didn't tell her what her trouble was; I just advised her to send to the library and get the four Pollyanna books—four perfectly silly books—and to read them. When she had read them she volunteered her therapy herself. She said, "I know what you want me to do. You want me to like to live in a trailer. And I guess I do, after all. Keeping house in a trailer is easy. There's not much to it, and when you don't like the view out of the trailer you can move and get another view. And raising children in a trailer is nice because there's a lot of room outside to run around in; and I certainly don't want to be a secretary back in Washington." She had learned her lesson. She learned to be satisfied and she's been getting along fine. But she didn't let her satisfaction stand in the way of moving into a nice home which they just recently built and completed. So that's the trick. Just learn to be satisfied. It's just as easy under most conditions to be satisfied as it is to be dissatisfied, and it's much more pleasurable. */41*

Next, the *sixth* thing is: *Learn to accept adversity.* In this life you're going to have some adversity. You may have a lot; you may have a little; but don't let it bowl you over. I had a man who hadn't worked for a year. Three months before he got sick, his wife died. A month later his son was killed, and from that moment on he sat around thinking, "How unfortunate I am; why did this have to happen to me? Why can't my wife be here? Why did my son have to go?" He carried on in that vein until he became very sick. He hadn't learned to accept adversity. A lot of people start out a psychosomatic illness after an adversity. */42*

The *seventh* thing is: *Learn to say the cheerful, humorous thing.* Be like George Briggs. Get in the habit of saying the pleasant thing, and get out of the habit of saying anything mean. Never say the mean thing, even if you feel you have to. Get up in the morning, look at your wife or your husband, and even if it isn't so, say, "My dear, you look good this morning." It'll make her feel better, and it'll make you feel better. Then look out the window and say, "Boy! what a beautiful day." If it's raining, "My, isn't that good for the soil?" And get in that habit. */43*

Finally, the *eighth* thing is: *Learn to meet your problems with decision.* About the worst thing to do is to have a problem and to mull it over and over in your mind. If you've got a problem, decide what you're going to do about it and then quit thinking about it. If you've got a problem that you can't solve, tell yourself, "That's insoluble," and then you've got to quit thinking about it. Like one lady I knew who had a husband who'd been drunk for twenty-five years. That used to bother her. She worried about it. Then one day she said to herself, "It doesn't do any good to think about it; that's insoluble. I'm going to make my life and my children's lives as happy as I can under the circumstances." And she quit thinking about her problem, to her great advantage. /44

Well, those are the eight things that you have to learn. Then the key will work easily. And the key is again: *I'm going to keep my attitude and my thinking as pleasant and as cheerful as possible.* And that's it, folks. That's happiness. There isn't any better definition for happiness than "the state of being in which your thinking is cheerful and pleasant most of the time." If you can think of a better definition, I wish you'd write to me. And so that's it. That's the way to be happy while you live to be a hundred. /45

Requests for copies of Schindler's speech poured in—over ten thousand were distributed throughout the United States and Canada.

QUESTIONS

1. What mood is the speaker trying to create in his first five paragraphs? Does this approach strike you as appropriate for a professional man? Why do you suppose he includes the first paragraph?

2. What evidence of audience adaptation do you find in this speech? Does the speaker seem to be talking down to his listeners at any time?

3. Frequently Schindler resorts to direct address in this speech, using such questions as "Got it?" or "See?" Are these devices effective, in your opinion? Can you conceive of any situation where they might be inappropriate?

4. Do you think Schindler's eight steps to happiness are easy to understand? Are they easy to follow? If so, why do you suppose they are followed so infrequently in American society?

5. Would Schindler have been more effective with a farm audience if he had mastered some agricultural terminology and used it liberally throughout his speech? Why or why not?

PROJECTS

1. Do you know an individual who might profit from reading Schindler's speech? Ask him to do so in your presence and observe his reactions. Is Schindler effective in communicating with your subject?

2. Listen to the conversational behavior of a friend or relative for a week. What words and phrases does your subject use most frequently? Do others seem to understand the speaker or do they seem confused by his characteristic expressions?

3. Secure a medical dictionary and look up the definitions of ten terms at random. From these definitions, would you infer that the dictionary was compiled for a specialist or a layman? Does your conclusion agree with that of the editor in his preface?

4. How did William James define *emotion?* List ten emotions and their physical manifestations which you have observed in yourself or others in the past week.

5. Read an article on some phase of medicine in the *Scientific American*. Is the article meaningful to you? If not, what special training does the author seem to assume that you possess?

6. Choose any three articles from a recent issue of the *Reader's Digest* which have been abstracted from other sources. Then locate the original version of each. Compare each shortened form with the longer one. What sorts of material have the *Digest* editors omitted? Could such omissions lead readers to misconstrue the authors' meaning?

7. Schindler defines *happiness* as "the state of being in which your thinking is cheerful and pleasant most of the time" (par. 45). Examine five other definitions of *happiness*. Can you locate a more satisfying definition than Schindler's?

8. One of Schindler's recommendations for happiness is that we "learn to accept adversity." Read Helen Keller's autobiography, *The Story of My Life* (New York: Doubleday & Company, Inc., 1954). What setbacks did Miss Keller experience in addition to her lack of sight and hearing? How did she overcome them?

A CLERGYMAN TALKS SENSE ABOUT DEATH

As we indicated earlier, technical language often constitutes an important barrier to understanding. Another barrier is emotional in nature. Some subjects are evocative of such deep human feeling that objective, meaningful discussion of them is very difficult. Such a subject is death.

Undeniably, death is mysterious. Since none of us really know what happens after the end of mortal life, many persons fear death. For these reasons, and because of the emotional reaction we associate with bereavement, death is a theme we are prone to treat euphemistically. "To soften the blow," newspapers commonly resort to word substitutes, and morticians employ coined expressions together with the latest expensive techniques of their profession.

Because of our cultural disinclination to speak frankly about death, the following sermon, delivered by the Reverend Earle C. Page of the Holy Trinity Episcopal Church, Gainesville, Florida, is both unique and revealing. The audience was his regular congregation, meeting on a Sunday in January 1963.

As you read the sermon, notice the personal, straightforward approach, the outline of practical steps to be taken, and the omission of various customs associated with death and burial.

ARRANGEMENTS ON THIS SIDE

EARLE C. PAGE

Many of you have read *O Ye Jigs and Juleps* (published by Macmillan in 1962) and know Virginia Hudson's remarkable theological statement on everlasting life. She says:

> Most of the things you get somebody dies so you can get it, but you have to die your own self to get Everlasting Life.
>
> When you are dead as a doornail, God gives it to you, and you can't get rid of it. You can't buy it, or sell it, or trade it. You have to keep it whether it suits you or not. When you take it to Heaven with you, that's good, but when you have to take it along with you to Hell, that's different.
>
> I sure am glad that Jesus is going to be in Heaven because if I get in trouble he will be there to help me out. When my mother sews on her new Wilcox and Gibbs, she sings, "What a friend we have in Jesus." I sure hope she knows what she is singing about. */1*

Text supplied by the speaker and used with permission.

That's as straightforward a statement of the Christian hope as I know, and in something of the spirit of Virginia's realism about her future, I want to share with you this morning some thoughts about mine. */2*

Most sermons on this subject are about everlasting life itself. This one is about the practical arrangements to be made on this side when my everlasting life begins. */3*

Sooner or later, all of us are going to be, as Virginia says, dead as a doornail, and I'm thinking about this in advance before there's any issue. Since God put me here to enjoy his world and to love the people here, I hope I can stay here and do that for a good long time to come. */4*

But I was also made to love him, and to be with him in a fuller, more direct way than is possible here. I'm glad to be getting older and older every year, and closer to the time when I can leave behind me the problems of being in the flesh. The satisfactions won't be left behind. They will be fulfilled, just as my relationships with people I love won't be left behind, but fulfilled. */5*

When the time comes I may be anxious about dying, for I expect my flesh to be reluctant to give up its domination. But I also hope that I'll be glad to take the next step. After all, that's also what I'm here for. */6*

This doesn't mean that the people who love me necessarily ought to feel glad as soon as it happens. I hope my family and friends will have the confidence of the Christian faith, and will eventually be able to rejoice in the fulfillment of my destiny, but at the time they will feel grief and loss. */7*

They won't feel it all the time, for their life here will be going on. So I hope that the friends who come to be with them during those difficult days will be able to accept their grief, when that's what they are feeling, and able to accept their sense of ongoing life, if that feeling is uppermost at the moment. They may want to weep about the frustrations and losses that have been part of our life together, but if they want to remember private jokes and laugh about the good times we have shared, that will be fine with me. */8*

You see, I hope they will keep on seeing me as me: no better and no worse than they see me now, the bad with the good, the foolish vanities and ridiculous little pretensions as well as the things they can be proud of. */9*

And if anyone starts blaming me, or praising me in an overly generous way, I hope my family has the theological good sense to remember that God is my judge, and he will judge me with truth and with love. */10*

There are some very definite things I want them to do if they can, some because I am a Christian, and others because I am opinionated. If these things are inconvenient or impossible, then I certainly don't want them to fret. After all, they will be the ones to be concerned about when I die, not me, and whatever arrangements are best for them are what I want. */11*

The first thing for them to do is to call a clergyman. If it's in the middle of the night, or inconvenient for him to come, they should still call him.

When he gets there, I want them all to take the time from whatever else is going on and do what the Prayer Book provides on page 319. /12
The priest will say,

> Depart, O Christian soul, out of this world,
> In the Name of God the Father Almighty who created thee.
> In the Name of Jesus Christ who redeemed thee.
> In the Name of the Holy Ghost who sanctifieth thee.
> May thy rest be this day in peace, and thy dwelling-place in the Paradise of God.

And then he will say,

> Into thy hands, O merciful Saviour, we commend the soul of thy servant, now departed from the body. Acknowledge, we humbly beseech thee, a sheep of thine own fold, a lamb of thine own flock, a sinner of thine own redeeming. Receive him into the arms of thy mercy, into the blessed rest of everlasting peace, and into the glorious company of the saints in light. Amen. /13

This is what you call a clergyman for when a Christian dies, and it's tremendously helpful for the family to have that final moment lifted up to God. If there is no priest around to do this, then I hope one of my family or friends will use this commendation and prayer. /14

After they call their pastor, then will be the time to call the funeral director. Since my family has also loved this body which I now inhabit, it may be hard for them to remember that what the undertaker is taking care of is not me, but only my remains. For all its imperfections, this body has served me well. If it, or any part of it, can serve the good work of medicine, that will be fitting. /15

My family won't have to plan the service. The Prayer Book provides a burial office, and the more funerals I attend the more grateful I am that the Prayer Book office will be used when I die. It's brief, dignified, and it helps people do what they are there to do: to bury the dead in sure and certain hope of the Resurrection, and to commit the body to the ground. /16

Symbolically, the body came from the ground, and to the ground it returns, and the sooner the better as far as I am concerned. My family will not be burying me, and I hope they can keep that straight. They will be returning earth to earth, ashes to ashes, and dust to dust. Cremation is merely a hastening of that return, and for that reason is appealing. At any rate, my family is not to interfere with good natural processes by buying a vault to protect my remains. /17

My preference is to be laid away in a simple wooden box. I have always loved wood and it disintegrates fairly quickly. We have gotten so far from reality in our funeral customs—with things like artificial grass to hide the grave—that it might cause more trouble to get a wooden casket than it would to buy a manufactured one, so the family will have to use their judgment at the time. */18*

When my remains are placed in the casket it will be for disposal, not for display. At no time is the casket to be left open for people to pay their respects, and this includes the members of the family. I want my body to be left looking as plain or as pretty as the Lord and the passing of time have made it, with no last-minute improvements. */19*

There are situations in which there are adequate reasons for having the service in a funeral home chapel, but you can't have the full Prayer Book service there, and the congregation can't participate. */20*

Since I was not only ordained, but baptized, confirmed, and married in the church, and have been prepared for everlasting life week after week at the altar of the church, I want the burial office to be read from the church. */21*

No sermon; no eulogy; no special poetry or prayers: just the straight Prayer Book, with the congregation taking part. It won't cost any more to be buried from the church, and it certainly shouldn't be decided by whether there will be a big congregation or not. In the presence of God, the angels and archangels, and with all the company of heaven, it won't matter how many people are in the pews. */22*

If it's possible on the day of the burial, I hope my family will come together sometime beforehand for a celebration of the Holy Communion in the church. My wife and I did this before our wedding, and I hope she and others can do this before the burial. This is another thing the Prayer Book provides. But if that's too much for them at the time, there will be other times. */23*

The only flowers at the church will be on the altar, just as for other services of worship. I think it's a good idea for people who feel like doing something to make a small donation to some good cause rather than send flowers, but I know from experience that sending and receiving flowers can be a way of witnessing to the Resurrection. But no flowers on the casket. */24*

As a veteran, I'm entitled to have the American Flag used as a covering for the casket. But as a Christian, I prefer for the casket to be covered by a pall: a kind of cloak or mantle. This custom is so old that from it we get the word *pallbearer.* */25*

In the Episcopal Church we use a pall for much the same reason we use vestments for the choir and clergy and altar. Vestments not only look beautiful, but they cover up any distinction between rich and poor. When the casket is brought into the church, it will be covered with this symbol of the Christian faith. The pall will be removed at the door after the service, and you can just leave my plain wooden box looking like a plain wooden box when you take it to the cemetery for the final prayers. */26*

While we're talking about the cemetery, it doesn't matter to me where my remaining earth is returned to the earth. I won't be at that place, either then or any other time. I'll be at home. If it's the custom of that cemetery to have some sort of marker for identification, then that's all right, but I have no desire to have any monuments erected to my name. */27*

People will remember any real good I have done in this world, and they'll know me for a while, but God will know me through eternity. */28*

I hope the cemetery will be one that cares for the plot so my family won't have to. If they ever want to visit that place, that's all right, but I hope they remember that I am closer to them in their prayers and in their Communion and in their love for one another than I am out at the cemetery. */29*

It will be important for my family and those who love me to face the fact of my death as directly and as thoroughly as possible. That's the only way their grief can be healed, and the only way they can see that my death day is my birth day into eternity. */30*

The words of the Bible and the Prayer Book will help them see that, and I hope the music will also. */31*

One of the things I have the strongest opinion about is the music at the service. Don't you dare have mournful hymns that sound like death is the worst thing that could happen to me. Let the organ be strong and firm, with the sound of trumpets, not sad and sentimental. */32*

If it's possible to have a choir, let them go down the aisle leading the congregation in singing, "Jesus Christ is risen today; Alleluia." I want people to know that in the midst of their grief my family is celebrating the fact that I am at the moment sharing in the victory of Jesus Christ over the final power of death—and I want the music to sound like our side has won. */33*

If all this sounds like a very simple burial, you are right. It will be as unpretentious and, quite literally, as inexpensive as possible. */34*

But it will also be glorious—and I hope it will help people know that this life is only the beginning. */35*

Thank God, there's a lot more life to come. */36*

When one of his parishioners requested a copy of the sermon that morning, Page was sure he could provide one. He was not prepared, however, for the many other requests for copies in the ensuing week. The demand for "Arrangements on This Side" was so great that a pile of copies was placed near the door the Sunday following.

QUESTIONS

1. What expressions or constructions impart a personal tone to Page's remarks? Ending a sentence with a preposition and using contractions in written prose are frowned upon by grammarians. Should the speaker have avoided these in his sermon? Why or why not?

2. What widely accepted customs does Page ignore in outlining the type of funeral he wants?

3. Page recommends the use of victorious music at his funeral service. Why do you suppose the funeral dirge is so much more common?

4. What reasons do funeral directors give for recommending the following: airtight vaults, embalming, the erection of monuments in cemeteries? Why would Page be likely to ignore the recommendations?

5. Do you think Page would approve of the traditional burial of sailors at sea? Why or why not?

6. What speaking qualities do you normally associate with pulpit oratory? Do these traits help or hinder the speaker in communicating with his listeners?

PROJECTS

1. According to Page (par. 28), "People will remember any real good I have done in this world." This conclusion is in direct contrast with that voiced in *Julius Caesar* when Shakespeare has Mark Antony say, "The evil that men do lives after them; The good is oft interred with their bones." Defend one of these two positions.

2. Investigate the topic of medical uses of the human body after death. Which parts of the body are most frequently transplanted to a living being? What procedure is followed in arranging for the medical use of a corpse? What position do antivivisectionists take on this topic?

3. Write a 500-word essay on the history of cremation. What position does the Hindu religion take on the subject of cremation? Compare the expense of cremation in America with that of an average-priced burial.

4. Describe an old-fashioned Irish wake. What function, if any, did the festivities play in this custom?

5. Read Jessica Mitford's *The American Way of Death* (New York: Simon and Schuster, Inc., 1963). How does this author account for the expensive burial customs Americans often observe?

6. Read a sermon by each of the following: a Protestant minister, a Catholic priest, a Jewish rabbi. Do you detect any significant similarity in the rhetorical style of the three? What differences do you find, aside from differences in subject matter?

A DIPLOMATIC ADVISER DISCUSSES FOREIGN POLICY

Foreign policy is a topic which affects every American, yet many of us are hesitant to discuss it. We know that the variables are many when a problem is international in scope. We know, too, that the State Department spends much time, money, and energy training experts to represent this nation abroad. So many new countries and new personalities have emerged since the Second World War that keeping up with the times requires a major effort on our part. The temptation is strong to let others do our thinking for us. At the root of our apparent indifference, in addition to a sense of hopelessness about getting all the facts, is an unfamiliarity with other peoples and distant lands, or a lack of *common structure*, as Andrew T. Weaver would put it.

One specialist who firmly believes we ought to know where the nation is going and why is Robert T. Oliver, Professor and Head of the Department of Speech, The Pennsylvania State University. In addition to being a professor of speech, Oliver has served for over a dozen years as both a speech writer and adviser on international affairs for the Republic of South Korea. He also has written half a dozen books on Korea, two of which were cited by *The New York Times* for excellence in nonfiction. *Syngman Rhee: The Man Behind the Myth* (New York: Dodd, Mead & Company, Inc., 1954) is his analysis of the founder of the Korean Republic.

The following speech was delivered at the annual convention of the Pennsylvania Nurses Association at Pittsburgh, October 24, 1961. Notice that three main ideas form the structure of this speech. Notice, too, that the speech moves at a fast pace, for the speaker has considerable ground to cover.

AMERICAN FOREIGN POLICY IN THE MIDST OF THE WORLD REVOLUTION

ROBERT T. OLIVER

Two different ways occurred to me of adapting my remarks for this evening, particularly to this audience. One way was to discuss the sick world—and no one can doubt it is highly feverish—in terms of diagnosis and treatment. This was tempting, because as nurses you know that laymen commonly are concerned with symptoms rather than with causes of disease, which often gives a ludicrously false notion of what is wrong and what needs to be done about it. I think it would not be difficult to

Text supplied by the speaker and used with permission.

demonstrate that laymen also make the same error in thinking about international relations. /1

The second method of adaptation that also seemed appealing for a time was to select those particular aspects of the world situation that might be of special interest to your profession—the growth of population, the prevalence of hunger, the lengthening of the life span through public health measures, the problems of the rapidly developing underdeveloped nations. This method also had some appeal, for what we all are primarily concerned about is the welfare of individuals, regardless of national boundary lines and ideologies. /2

What I have decided to do, however, is to talk to you simply and straightforwardly about how we ordinary American citizens can set about analyzing the world situation in an effort to make sense of it—to see where we are going, and why, and what our future is likely to be. This is the kind of problem that concerns all of us, not as nurses or as professors, but as men and women with our own lives to live and with the future of our children to think about. /3

In the first place, when we read the newspapers and when we get together to talk about American foreign policy, it seems to me there are five simple but valuable guidelines by which we should try to govern our thinking. /4

First, we should try to think in terms of practicalities, not of impossible ideals. It does no good, and it simply confuses the issues, for us to retreat from reality into the never-never land of dreams and fantasies. What good does it do to indulge in such wishful evasions as: "Why can't we human beings act like rational creatures?" "Why don't the Russians and the Allies just get together and talk things over like sensible people?" Or "If everyone would be truly Christian, or intelligent, or pure of heart, we could settle all these problems in a hurry." People are people, and governments are governments. We must deal with problems and possibilities as they are, not as we wish they were. /5

Second, we have to deal with the situation as it exists today. We cannot turn back the clock and eliminate errors that have been made. Germany and Korea, and Vietnam ought not to have been divided. Castro should not have been allowed to seize power in Cuba. The African colonies should have been much better prepared for self-government during the past several decades. We should have insisted on some fundamental settlements while the United States had a monopoly on the atomic bomb and while we were the only nation in the world with a sound economy. All these things are true, but we can't wipe the slate clean and start all over again. Every decision we now can make is already largely predetermined by past events—just as every action we now may take will shape and determine our possibilities in the future. /6

Third, when we criticize what our government is now doing, it should be done in terms of constructive suggestions for better policies or wiser methods. Partisan sniping seems peculiarly unproductive in the realm of international affairs. Many of us criticized Truman and Acheson; then we found the same kinds of fault with Eisenhower and Dulles; and now it appears that Kennedy and Rusk are not doing any better. Criticizing our leadership has very little value except as a release for our emotional frustration. A good test for each of us to keep in mind is this question: "What would I do if I were the Secretary of State?" This is the best prescription I know of for encouraging a realistic approach to American foreign policy. /7

Fourth, we cannot evade our responsibility as citizens on the assumption that we do not have available the facts on which decisions should be based. Of course President Kennedy gets some detailed information on Berlin, and Cuba, and Vietnam that we ordinary citizens do not have. The precise timing of actions and the determination of some of the tactics to pursue do surely depend on secret data known only to the Executive. On the whole, however, the significant facts concerning all the major international issues are completely available to anyone who takes the trouble to keep up with the news. For more than twelve years I served in a very intimate capacity in the inner councils of the Korean government, dealing with foreign policy matters; and from this experience I am convinced that we should not shrug off our own responsibility on the theory that our leaders somehow have insights and knowledge that we are unable to share. The very theory of democracy rests on the dominance of public opinion—and we have a duty to help form it. /8

The fifth of these suggested guidelines for thinking about international problems is that we learn to look beneath the surface of contemporary crises, to try to fix our attention on the basic trends that persist over a long period of time. Events flow rapidly, but the basic factors that affect human affairs remain relatively stable. We can avoid a lot of fuzzy thinking and emotional turmoil by developing the habit of historical thinking. This does not mean that we should wave aside concern about urgent problems with the airy assurance that "it will be all the same a thousand years from now." It does mean that nations, like individuals, should learn from experience. In other words, if we refuse to profit from mistakes of the past, we shall be condemned to repeat them. /9

As we try to look through the booming, buzzing, confused mass of world problems to the solid realities that underlie them, I think the major fact that emerges is that changes occur with dizzying speed, but that on the whole the changes are in a predictable direction. The huge and overriding fact that needs to dominate our thinking is that *we are living in an Age of Obsolescence.* /10

Mankind has always lived in the midst of change—but never before in such a tornado of rearrangements and development as that which besets our own generation. We human beings are creatures of habit. Our minds get set into patterns. We long to be left alone, to do as we have done, to think as we have thought, to live as we are used to living. But this hope is vain. We live in a period of tremendously rapid transition. The values we have clung to have to be reassessed. Old methods no longer work. New ones must be tried. The way of life into which we were born is not yet obsolete—but it definitely is obsolescent. */11*

As we try to peer into the whirlwind to see where it is heading, it seems to me there are four types of change to which we need to be alert. */12*

The first of these is that the cultural context of each one of us has become world-wide. The comfortable isolationism of the past is gone forever. The United States is no longer a psychological island in the midst of the Atlantic community. Whether we like it or not, we have to try to understand Asia, Africa, the Middle East, and Latin America. Global news is fed into our homes several times a day. Military rockets with a range of six thousand miles are forcing us to plan and build bomb shelters in our own homes. Our own sons are liable for military service—and many of us are right now getting letters from them addressed from Germany or Okinawa. */13*

The world, every part of it, affects us, every day of our lives. Similarly, what we do, day by day, is no longer our own business but is a matter of global interest. What we teach in our schools is determined in part by Moscow and Peiping. How we treat our American Negroes is front-page news around the world. The rise and fall of our stock market and what we do about our five million unemployed are fever charts that help determine the policies of nations we never even have heard of. The view that every religion except our own is paganism or idolatry is a luxury we no longer can afford. The world may not yet be one family, but it certainly is one community. In much that matters, Asia and Africa are just as much a part of our environment today as are Mississippi and Massachusetts. */14*

The second basic factor that underlies the whirl of rapid change grows directly out of the first—the comfortable compartmentalization of nations is rapidly ending. We do not have and may not soon get world government, but nevertheless the old privileges and special benefits of independent sovereignty are visibly vanishing. We have realized for a generation that peace is indivisible—that war anywhere threatens war everywhere. Now we are gradually learning that human welfare is also indivisible—that poverty anywhere threatens our own welfare, even in the midst of our wealth. Every day we are suffering consequences because two thirds of humanity are undernourished, undereducated, and underprivileged. The old safeguards of tariff walls, immigration quotas, and exclusive national currencies are already outmoded—not yet, of course, discarded, but obsolescent crudities that are manifestly unsuited to deal with the needs of our age. */15*

Let us glance at just one illustration of the intimacy with which all peoples are now bound together, for better or for worse. Many Americans are puzzled because the peoples and governments of the Afro-Asian bloc, the so-called neutralists, insist still on condemning us for "colonialism," even after we (meaning the Western democratic powers) have actually set free more than six hundred million people since 1945, with the result that the United Nations has grown from fifty members to one hundred. How in the world, we wonder, can they still think of us as colonial? The answer, I think, lies not in policies, but in attitudes. We are the white minority in a colored world. Our racist attitudes, our feeling that there inevitably is a line of distinction that separates the white people from those who are black, or yellow, or brown, brands us around the world as being still colonial-minded. This world is not going to persist as one-fifth white and four-fifths colored. We can't afford to consider it an achievement because thirteen Negro children were admitted to white schools in Memphis, Tennessee, without a riot. So long as we remain colonial-minded—so long, that is, as we are racist in our thinking—we shall continue to be denounced as a colonial power. This is one of the facts of the twentieth century which we shall be forced to accept. */16*

The third fact of consequence is that conditions will continue to get worse before there is any hope of their being better. The complexities are going to become greater, the problems even more urgent than they now are. The trend into increasing difficulty is easily discernible. */17*

The population of the world, for one thing, is multiplying with amazing speed. One tenth of the whole human race that has ever lived is alive today. The United States will have a population of four hundred million within another forty years. Red China's population is already close to seven hundred million and is increasing at the rate of forty-five to fifty millions a year. The "Lebensraum" which Hitler made a slogan for Nazi expansion has ceased to be an excuse for imperialism by nations and has become a genuine need for the human race. */18*

Natural resources—coal, iron, timber, the topsoil of our farmlands—are being used up and wasted so rapidly that an observer in space might be pardoned if he mistook humanity for a kind of cancer eating away the earth's surface. Of course, human ingenuity is hard at work developing synthetic substitutes—plastics for wood and steel, atomic energy for coal and oil, fresh water from the oceans for use in irrigation, vitamin pills to supplement our foods. One result is that a higher and higher premium is being placed on ability and on education. An economist whom I respect forecasts that by 1970 the United States will be in a major depression—but that there will be an urgent demand for scientists and workers with technical skills. What this means is that life is going to become very much harder for the uneducated masses of the world—and they are and will remain the great majority of mankind. */19*

Moreover, despite everything we can do, individualism, individuality, and civil liberties are going to become increasingly harder to defend. The sheer size and complexity of the modern world demand ever-increasing numbers of rules and regulations. Critical international issues demand centralized power to make decisions and to enforce them. Already Thomas Jefferson-style democracy has been largely swallowed up by the welfare state. And regardless of which party is in power, the movement toward bureaucracy and control is growing and expanding. */20*

Democratic and totalitarian governments are becoming more and more alike in their methods of governing—through the manipulation of public opinion by control of secrecy and publicity. On the one hand, high government officials create news and focus public attention where they wish by means of their public statements—as witness the dominance of the front pages of our newspapers by stories flowing out of presidential and cabinet-level news conferences. On the other hand, every two weeks, in the Pentagon alone, the stamp of secrecy is placed on a stack of documents higher than the Empire State Building. The situation is not one we like. But in a world of tensions, dangers, and complexity of relationships, it is one we cannot avoid. */21*

The growing complexity and urgency of problems is still further illustrated as we look at a map of the world and read recent history. Nine hundred million people have been gathered under Communist dominance since 1945, and the menace is increasingly sharp right now in Southeast Asia, in Africa, and in Latin America. Many of the democratic governments established in new nations after World War II have been replaced by military dictatorships. Government controls are expanding, everywhere, over production, distribution, and income. Much of this is bad; some of it is good; but all of it emphasizes the tremendously growing need for more and more education for the whole mass of the world's population. */22*

And this brings me directly to the fourth basic factor in the world situation—which is that in many parts of the world, education is already and inevitably outrunning economic and social developments. To put the matter simply, people are getting educated faster than jobs are being created in which they can utilize their new skills and knowledge. This is happening especially in the rapidly developing underdeveloped nations—and it is creating an explosive sense of mass frustration. */23*

I can discuss this with real feeling in connection with the Republic of Korea. For eighteen years, ever since 1942, I have maintained a close friendship with Dr. Syngman Rhee, the first President of Korea—and it was naturally a sad disappointment when his government was overturned. It is also a satisfaction that history has hastened to justify Dr. Rhee's record in Korea. He was accused of dominating the government too thoroughly, but Dr. Chang Myun, who succeeded him, failed utterly because he was not strong enough. Dr. Rhee was also accused in some quarters of being dictatorial—but now, under the present military dictatorship in Korea, we are seeing by contrast how free and liberal Dr. Rhee's government actually was. The reason why it was overthrown is, I think, rather simple. In a real sense, it was a victim of its own success—or perhaps I should say, of its partial success. */24*

To realize what happened in Korea—and what is happening in many parts of the world—we need to look at two sets of facts and to understand their very close relationship. In the first place, when Korea was freed from Japan, 78 per cent of the population was illiterate. Dr. Rhee's government, with American help, did a magnificent job of correcting this sad deficiency. Within a dozen years, illiteracy was reduced to 5 per cent; more than half a million young people were enrolled in senior high schools; and there were eighty thousand students enrolled in more than seventy colleges. This was achievement of a high order. However, the second fact is that the Korean standard of living was and still is among the lowest in the world, with a per-capita income of about $105—in contrast to the $2,500-per-capita income in the United States. The Korean government could educate its people, but it had no magic with which to create wealth or to multiply high-level jobs. */25*

The dilemma lies in the fact that you can't educate the sons and daughters of rice paddy farmers, and then send them back to the rice paddy farms. Yet this is what happened in Korea. It is virtually what happened in Cuba, and what is now happening in Africa and in many other underdeveloped parts of the world. The problem is that progress cannot be achieved uniformly in education, in social conditions, and in economics. People can and do develop knowledge and aspirations for self-improvement. They do attain to equality and a new sense of personal dignity. After that, they can't be restrained in unemployment, underemployment, and in the lower echelons of labor. Yet this is precisely the situation that confronts us in many parts of the world—and it is rapidly becoming a serious threat to stability in many areas. */26*

As we view the various factors I have briefly discussed, the question of principal import is: What shall we do about them? How and in what ways should American foreign policy be reoriented to deal with these fundamental facts in our Age of Obsolescence? */27*

First and perhaps most important, I think we should emphasize, far more than we commonly do, our feeling of unity with the other peoples of the world. Our Declaration of Independence stated very well the faith upon which our democracy rests—that "all men are created free and equal." Talk of our national rights, or slogans such as "America First" hurt us a great deal in the world community. The principal appeal of Communism, I believe, is that it at least pretends to be world-wide in its sympathies and in its concern. For selfish reasons, Soviet Russia refuses to recognize the sanctity of national boundary lines. For unselfish reasons, we Americans should always stress that the brotherhood of man is of more consequence to us than purely national goals. */28*

Secondly, and closely connected with this first principle, in my opinion we should devote not less, but more, of our resources to foreign aid. The time is past when we can build a wall around our prosperity. We cannot live in either physical or spiritual comfort in a hungry world. The best protection we can possibly devise for the American standard of living is to do everything in our power to make it universal. This sounds as though I am advising that Americans should be taxed for the benefit of African natives and South American peons—and this is exactly right. I know the point of view is not popular; but there never was a time in all history when there was more force behind the saying of Jesus that whosoever would save his life must lose it. We can serve ourselves best by serving others better. We cannot expect the understanding and support of the rest of the world while their problem is how to survive, and our problem is how to reduce. Our program of foreign aid rests solidly upon two foundations—one of which is humanitarian service and the other self-interest. Those of us who believe in this principle can do our bit by helping to elect politicians who will vote for more, not less, foreign aid. */29*

Thirdly, I wish that somehow we could become as evangelistic for democracy as the Communists are for Communism. Personally, I don't believe in ethical neutralism. I don't believe our foreign aid should be given without any strings. I do believe we should help the people who are doing their level best to develop democracy and to maintain the decencies of international relations. In my view we should do everything in our power to keep Red China out of the United Nations. I can see very little reason for giving two billions of dollars to Yugoslavia, as we have done since 1948. My own preference is for channeling our aid largely to people who are doing their best to live in freedom and who cherish the ideal of international cooperation. */30*

Finally, under existing conditions it is my conviction that we should maintain the strongest military force in the world—while, at the same time, we continue to do everything we can to establish a workable system of disarmament with a dependable system of inspection. I can never forget what Lenin is reported to have said in 1922, and which has been operative ever since as the guiding principle of Communism: "First we shall take Eastern Europe, then the masses of Asia. After that we shall surround and undermine the United States, which will fall into our laps like overripe fruit, without a struggle." This is the measure of the danger that confronts us—and we must do everything we can, including the building of bomb shelters and facing the threat of war, to defend not only ourselves but the future of freedom and democracy everywhere. */31*

In conclusion, it seems to me that a gigantic world revolution is now in process which parallels, but is different from the French Revolution that occurred between 1791 and 1840. You will recall that John Locke developed the theory that all men are created equal—that the first benefits of political freedom, based on his theory, came to England and the United States. Then the masses of France arose to claim that same freedom for themselves. The tragedy is that Napoleon Buonaparte intervened to try to funnel that perfectly legitimate yearning into the form of French imperialism. Because of this misuse of the political aspirations of the French, Napoleon had to be defeated by a European alliance led by England. After that, the normal and proper yearning for political equality was brought to fruition not only in France but also throughout most of western Europe. */32*

Then, a hundred years after Locke, Adam Smith in one way and Karl Marx in another confronted the exploitative evils of the Industrial Revolution and developed a theory that there can and should be a degree of economic equality. The tragedy is that first Lenin, then Stalin, and now Khrushchev and Mao Tse-tung have tried and are trying to convert this reasonable hope into Russian and Chinese imperialism. Because of their misuse of the ideal of economic fairness, the United States is destined to lead a world-wide federation to defeat their goal of nationalistic conquest. I am confident that this can and will be accomplished. */33*

But our goal will not be to defend a system in which a few benefit at the cost of the many. Just as we have proved that free enterprise can help elevate living conditions for everyone in the United States, so we must cooperate to bring this same result for the masses of the world. The revolution that is sweeping the world in our time will not end until there is both bread and freedom—democracy and opportunity—for all men, everywhere. */34*

This is the size of the challenge that confronts our foreign policy. The task is appalling. But failure would be so utterly disastrous that we have no choice except to do whatever is demanded to make sure that it succeeds. */35*

After examining this speech, you should not be surprised to learn that Oliver's addresses frequently find their way into *Vital Speeches of the Day*.

QUESTIONS

1. At the outset of his talk, Oliver mentions two approaches to his topic which would have been appropriate for an audience of nurses. Do you think the audience would have grasped his meaning more easily if he had used one of them, instead of the approach he does follow? Why or why not?

2. Are Americans colonial-minded, as Oliver contends (par. 16)? How does he define *colonial-minded?*

3. Oliver says (par. 26) that "you can't educate the sons and daughters of rice paddy farmers, and then send them back to the rice paddy farms." Will this same principle hold true for the American Negro? If so, do you foresee any imminent changes in the American economy?

4. Do you agree or disagree with Oliver that America cannot build a wall around her prosperity (par. 29)?

5. Would Oliver have been more effective if he had chosen to speak about what his listeners could do about foreign policy? Or does he answer this question by implication?

PROJECTS

1. Oliver says (par. 8), "The significant facts concerning all the major international issues are completely available to anyone who takes the trouble to keep up with the

news." Choose a recent development of world-wide importance. Then read Section 4—"The News of the Week in Review"—of *The New York Times* for four Sundays preceding the event. Would the facts in these reports have enabled you to foresee the development?

2. Oliver maintains (par. 13) that the days of America's isolationism are gone forever. Read Herbert Hoover's *Addresses upon the American Road, 1948–1950* (Stanford, Calif.: Stanford University Press, 1951). What does Hoover mean when he advocates that America become "the Gibraltar of Western Civilization"?

3. Discuss differences that exist between "Thomas Jefferson-style democracy" and "the welfare state" (par. 20). How did "the welfare state" get started in America? Read Arthur Schlesinger, Jr.'s, *The Coming of the New Deal,* Vol. II of *The Age of Roosevelt* (Boston: Houghton Mifflin Company, 1959) as a guide to answering this question.

4. What does Oliver mean when he maintains that "what we teach in our schools is determined in part by Moscow and Peiping" (par. 14)? Do the writings of James Conant and Hyman Rickover bear out his contention? Explain.

5. Read Stewart Udall's *The Quiet Crisis* (New York: Holt, Rinehart & Winston, Inc., 1963). Does this author think that our development of synthetic substitutes will offset the depletion of our natural resources? Why does Udall insist that the federal government, rather than governments of the various states, take the lead in conservation of our natural resources?

6. Read C. N. Parkinson's *Parkinson's Law, and Other Studies in Administration* (Boston: Houghton Mifflin Company, 1957). What is "Parkinson's Law"? Does this principle apply equally well to the United States and Britain? Defend your answer.

7. Compose a 500-word essay on the federal government's control and release of information. What security and publicity techniques are currently in use?

8. Investigate U.S. expenditures for foreign aid since 1945. Has the annual amount increased or decreased over the years? Do you consider these funds to be well spent? Explain.

9. Read Barry Goldwater's *Conscience of a Conservative* (Shepherdsville, Ky.: Victor Publishing Company, 1960). Where and on what grounds does Goldwater disagree with the positions taken by Oliver?

10. What reasons have been advanced for giving aid to Yugoslavia since 1948? Do you agree with Oliver that we ought to help only those nations favorable to the West? Why or why not?

11. Compare the economic theories of Adam Smith and Karl Marx. In what ways have the Communists altered Marx's doctrine?

12. Secure some Russian publications written in English for American readers. Compare Russian reports of a particular racial disturbance in the United States with the report in *The New York Times.* What differences do you find? Is there evidence of slanted reporting in *either* source?

PART FOUR

THE PROBLEM OF ADDRESSING VARIED AUDIENCES SIMULTANEOUSLY

What is an audience? To most of us this term denotes a large group of people brought together in one place at one particular time. But *audience,* like many words, has several meanings. In Plato's *Dialogues,* for example, Socrates addressed an audience of one or two. The development of printing and advances in public literacy made speeches readily available to a *reading audience.* For example, since the time of John Pym, important speeches have been circulated in pamphlet form or in the press after delivery. Public-address systems, radio, and television have given rise to *unseen audiences,* sometimes more important in a speaker's thinking than the group seated before him.

In all of these references, we may tend to forget that an audience is composed of one or more *individuals.* An individual never listens in a vacuum; he brings with him his background experiences, his language structure, his beliefs, prejudices, needs, and feelings, all of which affect his response. Of course, these individuals may be loosely grouped together in so far as they share common needs, feelings, values, etc. To the extent that differences exist among these individuals and among audience subgroups, a speaker addresses varied audiences in a single speech.

AN APPEAL FOR NATIONAL UNITY

On the eve of the American Civil War, Abraham Lincoln was elected sixteenth President of the United States. From the steps of the unfinished Capitol in Washington on March 4, 1861, Lincoln delivered his first inaugural address. The Confederacy was already a reality. As Carl Sandburg reports in *Abraham Lincoln: The War Years, 1861-1864,* Vol. II (New York: Dell Publishing Co., Inc., 1959), 9, "In the changing chaos of the American scene, people were dilating with a thousand different interpretations. Lincoln was to be, if he could manage it, the supreme interpreter of the violent and contradictory motives swaying the country, the labor pains of the nation." Beyond the assemblage in Washington for the ceremony, Sandburg noted, ". . . was the vast unseen audience that would read the address in cold print. . . . In its week of delivery it was the most widely read and closely scrutinized utterance that had ever come from an American President." (Sandburg, p. 34)

Notice how the President treats the question of southern dissension. What evidence does he offer that the property, peace, and personal security of southerners is not in danger? How would you phrase his main theme in a single sentence?

FIRST INAUGURAL ADDRESS

ABRAHAM LINCOLN

Fellow citizens of the United States: In compliance with a custom as old as the government itself, I appear before you to address you briefly and to take in your presence the oath prescribed by the Constitution of the United States to be taken by the President "before he enters on the execution of this office." */1*

I do not consider it necessary at present for me to discuss those matters of administration about which there is no special anxiety or excitement. */2*

Apprehension seems to exist among the people of the southern states that by the accession of a Republican administration their property and their peace and personal security are to be endangered. There has never been any reasonable cause for such apprehension. Indeed, the most ample evidence to the contrary has all the while existed and been open to their inspection. It is found in nearly all the published speeches of him who now addresses you. I do but quote from one of those speeches when I declare that—I have no purpose, directly or indirectly, to interfere with

Text from Inaugural Addresses of the Presidents of the United States from George Washington, 1789, to Harry S Truman, 1949 (Washington: United States Government Printing Office, 1952), pp. 109–116.

the institution of slavery in the states where it exists. I believe I have no lawful right to do so, and I have no inclination to do so. /3

Those who nominated and elected me did so with full knowledge that I had made this and many similar declarations and had never recanted them; and more than this, they placed in the platform for my acceptance, and as a law to themselves and to me, the clear and emphatic resolution which I now read:

> *Resolved*, That the maintenance inviolate of the rights of the states, and especially the right of each state to order and control its own domestic institutions according to its own judgment exclusively, is essential to that balance of power on which the perfection and endurance of our political fabric depend; and we denounce the lawless invasion by armed force of the soil of any state or territory, no matter what pretext, as among the gravest of crimes. /4

I now reiterate these sentiments, and in doing so I only press upon the public attention the most conclusive evidence of which the case is susceptible that the property, peace, and security of no section are to be in any wise endangered by the now incoming administration. I add, too, that all the protection which, consistently with the Constitution and the laws, can be given will be cheerfully given to all the states when lawfully demanded, for whatever cause—as cheerfully to one section as to another. /5

There is much controversy about the delivering up of fugitives from service or labor. The clause I now read is as plainly written in the Constitution as any other of its provisions:

> No person held to service or labor in one state, under the laws thereof, escaping into another, shall in consequence of any law or regulation therein be discharged from such service or labor, but shall be delivered up on claim of the party to whom such service or labor may be due. /6

It is scarcely questioned that this provision was intended by those who made it for the reclaiming of what we call fugitive slaves; and the intention of the lawgiver is the law. All members of Congress swear their support to the whole Constitution—to this provision as much as to any other. To the proposition, then, that slaves whose cases come within the terms of this clause "shall be delivered up" their oaths are unanimous. Now, if they would make the effort in good temper, could they not with nearly equal unanimity frame and pass a law by means of which to keep good that unanimous oath? /7

There is some difference of opinion whether this clause should be enforced by national or by state authority, but surely that difference is not a very material one. If the slave is to be surrendered, it can be of but little consequence to him or to others by which authority it is done. And should anyone in any case be content that his oath shall go unkept on a merely unsubstantial controversy as to *how* it shall be kept? */8*

Again: In any law upon this subject ought not all the safeguards of liberty known in civilized and humane jurisprudence to be introduced, so that a free man be not in any case surrendered as a slave? And might it not be well at the same time to provide by law for the enforcement of that clause in the Constitution which guarantees that "the citizens of each state shall be entitled to all privileges and immunities of citizens in the several states"? */9*

I take the official oath today with no mental reservations and with no purpose to construe the Constitution or laws by any hypercritical rules; and while I do not choose now to specify particular acts of Congress as proper to be enforced, I do suggest that it will be much safer for all, both in official and private stations, to conform to and abide by all those acts which stand unrepealed than to violate any of them trusting to find impunity in having them held to be unconstitutional. */10*

It is seventy-two years since the first inauguration of a President under our national Constitution. During that period fifteen different and greatly distinguished citizens have in succession administered the executive branch of the government. They have conducted it through many perils, and generally with great success. Yet, with all this scope of precedent, I now enter upon the same task for the brief constitutional term of four years under great and peculiar difficulty. A disruption of the Federal Union, heretofore only menaced, is now formidably attempted. */11*

I hold that in contemplation of universal law and of the Constitution the union of these states is perpetual. Perpetuity is implied, if not expressed, in the fundamental law of all national governments. It is safe to assert that no government proper ever had a provision in its organic law for its own termination. Continue to execute all the express provisions of our national Constitution, and the Union will endure forever, it being impossible to destroy it except by some action not provided for in the instrument itself. */12*

Again: If the United States be not a government proper, but an association of states in the nature of contract merely, can it, as a contract, be peaceably unmade by less than all the parties who made it? One party to a contract may violate it—break it, so to speak—but does it not require all to lawfully rescind it? */13*

Descending from these general principles, we find the proposition that in legal contemplation the Union is perpetual confirmed by the history of the Union itself. The Union is much older than the Constitution. It was formed, in fact, by the Articles of Association in 1774. It was matured and continued by the Declaration of Independence in 1776. It was further matured, and the faith of all the then thirteen states expressly plighted and engaged that it should be perpetual, by the Articles of Confederation in 1778. And finally, in 1787, one of the declared objects for ordaining and establishing the Constitution was "*to form a more perfect Union.*" /14

But if destruction of the Union by one or by a part only of the states be lawfully possible, the Union is *less* perfect than before the Constitution, having lost the vital element of perpetuity. /15

It follows from these views that no state upon its own mere motion can lawfully get out of the Union; that *resolves* and *ordinances* to that effect are legally void, and that acts of violence within any state or states against the authority of the United States are insurrectionary or revolutionary, according to circumstances. /16

I therefore consider that in view of the Constitution and the laws the Union is unbroken, and to the extent of my ability, I shall take care, as the Constitution itself expressly enjoins upon me, that the laws of the Union be faithfully executed in all the states. Doing this I deem to be only a simple duty on my part, and I shall perform it so far as practicable unless my rightful masters, the American people, shall withhold the requisite means or in some authoritative manner direct the contrary. I trust this will not be regarded as a menace, but only as the declared purpose of the Union that it *will* constitutionally defend and maintain itself. /17

In doing this there needs to be no bloodshed or violence, and there shall be none unless it be forced upon the national authority. The power confided to me will be used to hold, occupy, and possess the property and places belonging to the government and to collect the duties and imposts; but beyond what may be necessary for these objects, there will be no invasion, no using of force against or among the people anywhere. Where hostility to the United States in any interior locality shall be so great and universal as to prevent competent resident citizens from holding the federal offices, there will be no attempt to force obnoxious strangers among the people for that object. While the strict legal right may exist in the government to enforce the exercise of these offices, the attempt to do so would be so irritating and so nearly impracticable withal that I deem it better to forego for the time the uses of such offices. /18

The mails, unless repelled, will continue to be furnished in all parts of the Union. So far as possible the people everywhere shall have that sense of perfect security which is most favorable to calm thought and reflection. The course here indicated will be followed unless current events and experience shall show a modification or change to be proper, and in every case and exigency my best discretion will be exercised, according to circumstances actually existing and with a view and a hope of a peaceful solution of the national troubles and the restoration of fraternal sympathies and affections. /19

That there are persons in one section or another who seek to destroy the Union at all events and are glad of any pretext to do it I will neither affirm nor deny; but if there be such, I need address no word to them. To those, however, who really love the Union may I not speak? /20

Before entering upon so grave a matter as the destruction of our national fabric, with all its benefits, its memories, and its hopes, would it not be wise to ascertain precisely why we do it? Will you hazard so desperate a step while there is any possibility that any portion of the ills you fly from have no real existence? Will you, while the certain ills you fly to are greater than all the real ones you fly from, will you risk the commission of so fearful a mistake? /21

All profess to be content in the Union if all constitutional rights can be maintained. Is it true, then, that any right plainly written in the Constitution has been denied? I think not. Happily, the human mind is so constituted that no party can reach to the audacity of doing this. Think, if you can, of a single instance in which a plainly written provision of the Constitution has ever been denied. If by the mere force of numbers a majority should deprive a minority of any clearly written constitutional right, it might in a moral point of view justify revolution; certainly would if such right were a vital one. But such is not our case. All the vital rights of minorities and of individuals are so plainly assured to them by affirmations and negations, guaranties and prohibitions, in the Constitution that controversies never arise concerning them. But no organic law can ever be framed with a provision specifically applicable to every question which may occur in practical administration. No foresight can anticipate nor any document of reasonable length contain express provisions for all possible questions. Shall fugitives from labor be surrendered by national or by state authority? The Constitution does not expressly say. *May* Congress prohibit slavery in the territories? The Constitution does not expressly say. *Must* Congress protect slavery in the territories? The Constitution does not expressly say. /22

From questions of this class spring all our constitutional controversies, and we divide upon them into majorities and minorities. If the minority will not acquiesce, the majority must, or the government must cease. There is no other alternative, for continuing the government is acquiescence on one side or the other. If a minority in such case will secede rather than acquiesce, they make a precedent which in turn will divide and ruin them, for a minority of their own will secede from them whenever a majority refuses to be controlled by such minority. For instance, why may not any portion of a new confederacy a year or two hence arbitrarily secede again, precisely as portions of the present Union now claim to secede from it? All who cherish disunion sentiments are now being educated to the exact temper of doing this. /23

Is there such perfect identity of interests among the states to compose a new union as to produce harmony only and prevent renewed secession? /24

Plainly the central idea of secession is the essence of anarchy. A majority held in restraint by constitutional checks and limitations, and always changing easily with deliberate changes of popular opinions and sentiments, is the only true sovereign of a free people. Whoever rejects it does of necessity fly to anarchy or to despotism. Unanimity is impossible. The rule of a minority, as a permanent arrangement, is wholly inadmissible; so that, rejecting the majority principle, anarchy or despotism in some form is all that is left. /25

I do not forget the position assumed by some that constitutional questions are to be decided by the Supreme Court, nor do I deny that such decisions must be binding in any case upon the parties to a suit as to the object of that suit, while they are also entitled to very high respect and consideration in all parallel cases by all other departments of the government. And while it is obviously possible that such decision may be erroneous in any given case, still the evil effect following it, being limited to that particular case, with the chance that it may be overruled and never become a precedent for other cases, can better be borne than could the evils of a different practice. At the same time, the candid citizen must confess that if the policy of the government upon vital questions affecting the whole people is to be irrevocably fixed by decisions of the Supreme Court, the instant they are made in ordinary litigation between parties in personal actions the people will have ceased to be their own rulers, having to that extent practically resigned their government into the hands of that eminent tribunal. Nor is there in this view any assault upon the court or the judges. It is a duty from which they may not shrink to decide cases properly brought before them, and it is no fault of theirs if others seek to turn their decisions to political purposes. /26

One section of our country believes slavery is *right* and ought to be extended, while the other believes it is *wrong* and ought not to be extended. This is the only substantial dispute. The fugitive-slave clause of the Constitution and the law for the suppression of the foreign slave trade are each as well enforced, perhaps, as any law can ever be in a community where the moral sense of the people imperfectly supports the law itself. The great body of the people abide by the dry legal obligation in both cases, and a few break over in each. This, I think, cannot be perfectly cured, and it would be worse in both cases *after* the separation of the sections than before. The foreign slave trade, now imperfectly suppressed, would be ultimately revived without restriction in one section, while fugitive slaves, now only partially surrendered, would not be surrendered at all by the other. /27

Physically speaking, we cannot separate. We cannot remove our respective sections from each other nor build an impassable wall between them. A husband and wife may be divorced and go out of the presence and beyond the reach of each other, but the different parts of our country cannot do this. They cannot but remain face to face, and intercourse, either amicable or hostile, must continue between them. Is it possible, then, to make that intercourse more advantageous or more satisfactory *after* separation than *before?* Can aliens make treaties easier than friends can make laws? Can treaties be more faithfully enforced between aliens than laws can among friends? Suppose you go to war, you cannot fight always; and when, after much loss on both sides and no gain on either, you cease fighting, the identical old questions, as to terms of intercourse, are again upon you. */28*

This country, with its institutions, belongs to the people who inhabit it. Whenever they shall grow weary of the existing government, they can exercise their *constitutional* right of amending it or their *revolutionary* right to dismember or overthrow it. I cannot be ignorant of the fact that many worthy and patriotic citizens are desirous of having the national Constitution amended. While I make no recommendation of amendments, I fully recognize the rightful authority of the people over the whole subject, to be exercised in either of the modes prescribed in the instrument itself; and I should, under existing circumstances, favor rather than oppose a fair opportunity being afforded the people to act upon it. I will venture to add that to me the convention mode seems preferable, in that it allows amendments to originate with the people themselves, instead of only permitting them to take or reject propositions originated by others, not especially chosen for the purpose, and which might not be precisely such as they would wish to either accept or refuse. I understand a proposed amendment to the Constitution—which amendment, however, I have not seen—has passed Congress, to the effect that the federal government shall never interfere with the domestic institutions of the states, including that of persons held to service. To avoid misconstruction of what I have said, I depart from my purpose not to speak of particular amendments so far as to say that, holding such a provision to now be implied constitutional law, I have no objection to its being made express and irrevocable. */29*

The Chief Magistrate derives all his authority from the people, and they have conferred none upon him to fix terms for the separation of the states. The people themselves can do this if also they choose, but the Executive as such has nothing to do with it. His duty is to administer the present government as it came to his hands and to transmit it unimpaired by him to his successor. */30*

Why should there not be a patient confidence in the ultimate justice of the people? Is there any better or equal hope in the world? In our present differences, is either party without faith of being in the right? If the Almighty Ruler of nations, with his eternal truth and justice, be on your side of the North, or on yours of the South, that truth and that justice will surely prevail by the judgment of this great tribunal of the American people. */31*

By the frame of the government under which we live this same people have wisely given their public servants but little power for mischief, and have with equal wisdom provided for the return of that little to their own hands at very short intervals. While the people retain their virtue and vigilance no administration by any extreme of wickedness or folly can very seriously injure the government in the short space of four years. */32*

My countrymen, one and all, think calmly and *well* upon this whole subject. Nothing valuable can be lost by taking time. If there be an object to *hurry* any of you in hot haste to a step which you would never take *deliberately*, that object will be frustrated by taking time; but no good object can be frustrated by it. Such of you as are now dissatisfied still have the old Constitution unimpaired, and, on the sensitive point, the laws of your own framing under it; while the new administration will have no immediate power, if it would, to change either. If it were admitted that you who are dissatisfied hold the right side in the dispute, there still is no single good reason for precipitate action. Intelligence, patriotism, Christianity, and a firm reliance on Him who has never yet forsaken this favored land are still competent to adjust in the best way all our present difficulty. */33*

In *your* hands, my dissatisfied fellow countrymen, and not in *mine*, is the momentous issue of civil war. The government will not assail *you*. You can have no conflict without being yourselves the aggressors. *You* have no oath registered in heaven to destroy the government, while I shall have the most solemn one to "preserve, protect, and defend it." /34

I am loath to close. We are not enemies, but friends. We must not be enemies. Though passion may have strained it must not break our bonds of affection. The mystic chords of memory, stretching from every battlefield and patriot grave to every living heart and hearthstone all over this broad land, will yet swell the chorus of the Union, when again touched, as surely they will be, by the better angels of our nature. */35*

Those who heard and read Lincoln's remarks did so within the context of their own beliefs. Northern moderates thought the speech temperate. For example, Stephen A. Douglas, Lincoln's Democratic opponent in the presidential election but his supporter in the struggle to preserve the Union, thought the speech discouraged war. (Sandburg, p. 40) Abolitionists, who demanded an end to slavery in America, were disappointed by the President's refusal to interfere with statutes permitting slavery. Secessionists, by contrast, viewed the speech as a statement designed to provoke war.

A reporter from the Boston *Transcript* wrote, "The language is level to the popular mind, the plain, homespun language of a man accustomed to talk with the 'folks' and the 'neighbors,' whose words fit his facts and thoughts." (Sandburg, p. 39) Divergent audience response was less the result of the speech's content than of the crisis of the hour and the varied disposition of the American people. By the middle of April, the Civil War was a reality.

QUESTIONS

1. How many times in the first eight paragraphs does Lincoln indicate that he will not interfere with slavery? What reasons does he give, and on what authority does he base them? Do you find this accumulation of data persuasive?

2. If you had been the speaker, would you have mentioned the Confederacy by name? Why or why not?

3. What arguments does Lincoln offer against the dissolution of the Union?

4. Why does Lincoln view the secession of any state as a dangerous precedent both for the Union and the Confederacy?

5. What does Lincoln mean when he says (par. 25) that "the central idea of secession is the essence of anarchy"? Is complete freedom of individual action an essential aspect of a democratic society?

PROJECTS

1. According to Earl Wiley in his essay on Lincoln in Vol. II of *The History and Criticism of American Public Address,* ed. W. N. Brigance (New York: McGraw-Hill Book Company, Inc., 1943), p. 859, "It takes a great experience to make a great speech." Defend or refute this position, keeping in mind the speeches you have heard and read.

2. Prepare an oral report on either of the two essays on Lincoln as a speaker in the volume of *The History and Criticism of American Public Address* cited in Project 1.

3. Lincoln maintains (par. 18) that bloodshed or violence can be avoided. What event marked the start of the American Civil War? Describe the circumstances.

4. Investigate the history of the Confederacy's relations with foreign nations. Which European states recognized the new government? Why did recognition pose a particular problem for Great Britain?

5. How did the Supreme Court become the arbiter of constitutionality in the United States? Investigate this topic and the role John Marshall played in making judicial review a regular Court function.

6. Lincoln mentions our "*revolutionary* right to dismember or overthrow" government (par. 29). Read the writings of John Locke and Thomas Jefferson to discover what justification for revolution is given in them.

7. Investigate and report on the following: How many amendments to the United States Constitution were passed prior to 1860? What did they provide for?

8. Read *Antislavery and Disunion, 1858-1861,* ed. J. Jeffery Auer (New York: Harper and Row, 1963). What rhetorical efforts toward compromise occurred in this three-year period? Why were these efforts unsuccessful in preventing war?

THE "PEACEFUL" PRONOUNCEMENT OF A MILITARIST

An address to varied audiences assumed considerably different dimensions on February 20, 1938. Now the speaker was Adolf Hitler, Chancellor and unquestioned master of the German people. His speech was delivered in Berlin before the Reichstag, Germany's national parliament. As leader of the majority National Socialist party, Hitler was surrounded by followers. His remarks were broadcast by radio to the German people.

Hitler knew others would be listening, too. Leaders in Austria to the east and Czechoslovakia to the south were openly worried about his plans, for each of these states had a sizable population of German nationals clamoring for union with the Fatherland. International experts in Great Britain and France would be looking anxiously for reassurance of peaceful intent, because the strongly armed German state had withdrawn from the League of Nations. Imperialists in Italy and Japan shared German views on "overpopulation" and Bolshevism; they would be listening sympathetically. Potential enemies, neutrals, and allies, then, as well as the German people, were audiences for the pronouncements of "the Fuehrer," and each listener would interpret Hitler's speech according to his own frame of reference.

The occasion of this speech was the fifth anniversary of the founding of the Third Reich. Notice how this speech could have affected listeners or readers in different ways: (1) to feel alarm about the peace of Europe, (2) to regard it as just another speech by the leader of a European state, and (3) to believe and even to respect the speaker as one who resents foreign interference and who is committed to the cause of his people's welfare. Would an American acting on Robert T. Oliver's advice (see his speech in Part III) have been able to detect the full significance of Hitler's speech at the time of delivery?

GERMANY'S CLAIMS

ADOLF HITLER

I know you and the German people expected to be called together on the fifth anniversary of the National Socialist state. */1*

The selection of this date is due to two considerations: First, I thought it right to make certain personal changes beforehand, and second, it was necessary to bring about a clarification in one specific sphere of foreign

From **The New York Times**, February 21, 1938. Text includes the chief passages of Hitler's address before the Reichstag.

politics, because such a speech of mine not only deals with the past but also with the future. /2

Despite the really exemplary discipline, strength, and restraint which National Socialists preserved in their revolution, we have seen that a certain portion of the foreign press inundated the new Reich with a virtual flood of lies and calumnies. It was a remarkable mixture of arrogance and deplorable ignorance which led them to act as the judges of a people who should be presented as models to these democratic apostles. /3

The best proof for showing up these lies is success. For if we had acted during these five years like the democratic world citizens of Soviet Russia, that is, like those of the Jewish race, we would not have succeeded in making out of a Germany, which was in the deepest material collapse, a country of material order. For this very reason we claim the right to surround our work with that protection which renders it impossible for criminal elements or for the insane to disturb it. /4

CRITICS ARE CALLED "ENEMIES OF PEOPLE"

Whoever disturbs this mission is the enemy of the people, whether he pursues his aim as a Bolshevist democrat, a revolutionary terrorist, or a reactionary dreamer. In such a time of necessity those who act in the name of God are not those who, citing Bible quotations, wander idly about the country and spend the day partly doing nothing and partly criticizing the work of others; but those whose prayers take the higher form of uniting man with his God, that is, the form of work. /5

I had a right to turn against everyone who, instead of helping, thought his mission was to criticize our work. Foreign nations contributed nothing apart from this spirit, for their rejection was tinged by hate or a spirit of knowing better than we know. /6

It was the ABC of our creed to find help in our own strength. The standard of living of the nation is the outcome of its total production; in other words, the value of every wage and salary corresponds to the volume of goods produced as a result of the work performed. This is a very unpopular doctrine in a time resounding with cries such as "higher wages and less work." /7

Next to the United States, Germany today has become the greatest steel country in the world. I could give many more examples. They are documentary proof of the work such as our people never before achieved. To these successes will be added in a few years the gigantic results of the Four-Year Plan. Is it not a joke of history when those very countries which themselves have only crises think they can criticize us and give us advice? /8

We have given the German nation that weapon of steel which presents a wall at our frontiers against the intentions of the malicious international press campaign. /9

FOREIGN OFFICE NOT CONQUERED ON FEBRUARY 4

At the conclusion of the next decade the German people will bear in mind the success of their efficiency and will be filled with a supreme pride. One of these achievements is the construction of a national leadership which is [as] far removed from parliamentary democracy as it is from military dictatorship. */10*

National Socialism did not conquer Germany's Foreign Office on February 4 as some small international quill drivers perhaps believed, but it has owned the whole of Germany since the day I stepped out of my house onto the Wilhelmplatz as German Chancellor five years ago. */11*

The Reich's protection against the outer world, however, is in the hands of the new National Socialist armed forces. The German army of peace has now a vast air force to protect our homes, and a new power on the sea protects our coasts. */12*

There exists in Germany no problem between the National Socialist state and the National Socialist party, no problem between the National Socialist party and the National Socialist armed forces. In this Reich everyone who holds a responsible position is a National Socialist. */13*

I had to respect the wish of Blomberg [Field Marshal Werner von Blomberg] to spare his health, which had been undermined by his first-rate work. In this connection I should like to express the thanks of myself and the German people for the faithful and loyal work of this soldier of the new Reich and its armed forces. */14*

The same applies to the activity and surpassing achievements of Fritsch [General Werner von Fritsch] and all those who gave up their places in the most noble spirit for the sake of having younger men in the ranks of our political and military leaders. */15*

If ever international agitation or poisoning of opinion should attempt to rupture the peace of the Reich, then steel and iron would take the German people and German homesteads under their protection. The world would then see, as quick as lightning, to what extent this Reich, people, party and these armed forces are fanatically inspired with one spirit, one will. */16*

CRITICIZES THE METHODS
OF INTERNATIONAL JOURNALISTS

Furthermore, it is not my intention to protect the honorable corps of officers from the slander of international journalism. That is not necessary, for, although there are two kinds of journalists—those who prove the truth and those who are miserable swindlers and war agitators—there is only one kind of German officer. */17*

If Great Britain should suddenly dissolve today and England become dependent solely on her own territory, then the people there would, perhaps, have more understanding of the seriousness of the economic tasks which confront us. If a nation which commands no gold reserves, no foreign exchange—not because National Socialism reigns but because a parliamentary, democratic state was exploited for fifteen years by a world hungry after loot, in other words, if a nation which must feed 140 people to the square kilometer and has no colonies, if a nation which lacks numerous raw materials and is not willing to live an illusory life through credits, reduces the number of its unemployed in five years to nil and improves its standard of living, then all those should remain silent who, despite great economic advantages, scarcely succeed in solving their own unemployment problems. *|18*

The claim for German colonial possessions, therefore, will be voiced from year to year with increasing vigor. These possessions, which Germany did not take away from other countries and which today are practically of no value to these powers, are indispensable for our own people. *|19*

I should like to refute here the hope that such claims can be averted by granting credits. Above all, we do not wish for naive assurances that we shall be permitted to buy what we need. We reject such statements once and for all. *|20*

You will not expect me to discuss in detail the individual international plans which appear to arouse the varied interests of the various governments. They are too uncertain and they lack the clarity necessary for me to be able to express myself on these questions. Above all, however, take note of my deep-seated distrust of all so-called conferences which may provide interesting hours of conversation for those taking part in them, but generally lead to the disappointment of hopeful mankind. *|21*

PEACE TREATY FORCED UPON SOME NATIONS

I cannot allow our natural claims to be coupled with political business. Recently rumors have been cropping up, rumors that Germany was about to revise her opinion concerning her return to the League of Nations. I should like again to declare that in 1919 the peace treaty was forced upon some countries. This treaty brought in its train far-reaching inroads upon the lives of the peoples involved. The rape of national and economic destinies and of the communal lives of the nations took place under a cloud of moralizing phrases which, perhaps, tended to salve the uneasy conscience of those who instituted the affair. *|22*

After the revision of the map of the world and of territorial and racial spheres, which was as thorough as it was fundamental, had been effected by means of force, a League of Nations was founded whose task it was to crystallize these crazy, unreasonable proceedings and to coordinate its results into an everlasting and unalterable basis of life. *|23*

I notice very often that English politicians would be glad to give back to us our colonies if they were not so disturbed by the thought of the wrong and violence which would thus be done to the native inhabitants. *|24*

All those colonial empires have not come into being through plebiscites. They are today naturally integral parts of the states in question and form, as such, part of that world order which always has been designated to us, especially by democratic policies, as the "world order of right." /25

That right the League of Nations now has been ordered to protect. I cannot understand why a nation which itself has been robbed by force should join such illustrious company and I cannot permit the conclusion to be drawn that we should not be prepared to fight for the principles of justice just because we are not in the League of Nations. On the contrary, we do not belong to the League of Nations because we believe that it is not an institution of justice but an institution for defending the interests of Versailles. /26

CITES REASONS FOR LEAVING THE LEAGUE OF NATIONS

A number of material considerations must, however, be added. /27

First, we left the League of Nations because—loyal to its origin and obligations—it refused us the right to equal armament and just as equal security. /28

Second, we will never re-enter it because we do not intend to allow ourselves to be used anywhere in the world by a majority vote of the League of Nations for the defense of an injustice. /29

Third, we believe we will please all those nations who are misled by misfortune to rely on and trust the League of Nations as a factor of genuine help. We should have regarded it as more correct, for instance, in the case of the Ethiopian war, for the League to have shown more understanding for vital Italian needs and less disposition to help the Ethiopians with promises. This would, perhaps, have enabled a more simple and reasonable solution for the whole problem. /30

Fourth, on no account will we allow the German nation to become entangled in conflicts in which the nation itself is not interested. We are not willing to stand up for the territorial or economic interests of others without the slightest benefits to Germans being visible. Moreover, we ourselves do not expect such support from others. Germany is determined to impose upon herself wise moderation in her interests and demands. But if German interests should be seriously at stake we shall not expect to receive support from the League of Nations but we shall assume the right from the beginning to shoulder our task ourselves. /31

Fifth, we do not intend to allow our attitude to be determined in the future by any international institution which, while excluding official recognition of indisputable facts, resembles less the acts of a man of considered judgment than the habits of a certain type of large bird [evidently the ostrich]. The interests of nations, in so far as their existence or nonexistence are ultimately concerned, are stronger than formalistic considerations. For in the year 2038 it is possible that new states may have arisen or others disappeared without this new state of affairs having been registered at Geneva. /32

Germany will not take part in such unreasonable proceedings by being a member of the League of Nations. /33

Germany will recognize Manchukuo. I have decided on this step in order to draw the line of finality between the policy of fantastic lack of understanding and the policy of sober respect for the facts of reality. To sum up, I want to explain that Germany no longer thinks of returning to this institution and certainly not since Italy's departure from it. */34*

That does not mean the refusal to collaborate with other nations. On the contrary it only means the rejection of obligations which in most cases are impossible of fulfillment. */35*

With one country alone have we scorned to enter into relations. That state is Soviet Russia. We see in Bolshevism more now than before the incarnation of human destructive forces. We do not blame the Russian people as such for this gruesome ideology of destruction. We know it is a small Jewish intellectual group which led a great nation into this position of madness. If this doctrine would confine itself territorially to Russia maybe one could put up with it. Alas, Jewish international Bolshevism attempts to hollow out the nations of the world from its Soviet center. */36*

DIFFERS WITH EDEN ON BOLSHEVIST ISSUE

Any introduction of Bolshevism into a European country means a changing of conditions. For those territories under Bolshevik leadership are no longer sovereign nations having a national life but sections of the revolutionary center of Moscow. */37*

I know Eden [British Foreign Secretary] does not share this view. Stalin shares it and admits it openly, and in my opinion Stalin himself is a more trustworthy expert and interpreter of Bolshevik views and intentions than the British Minister. We, therefore, oppose any attempt at spreading Bolshevism, wherever it may take place, with disdain and wherever it threatens us with hostility. */38*

From this arises our relationship with Japan. I cannot agree with those politicians who believe they are rendering the European world a service by harming Japan. I believe a Japanese defeat in the Far East would never be any good to Europe or America, but would exclusively benefit Bolshevist Soviet Russia. */39*

I do not consider China mentally or materially strong enough to resist any Bolshevik attack on it, but I believe even the greatest victory for Japan would be infinitely less dangerous to the culture and general peace of the world than a Bolshevik victory would be. Germany has a treaty with Japan to combat Comintern aspirations. It has always been on friendly terms with China. I believe we may be considered most genuinely as neutral observers of this drama. */40*

I do not need to emphasize that we all wished and still wish that relations between those two great Eastern nations will again calm down and become peaceful. We believe that there might have been a peaceful solution in the Far East long ago if certain powers had not, as in the case of Ethiopia, thrown into one scales their advice and, perhaps, promise their moral support. */41*

But a drowning man clutches at any straw. It would have been better to have called China's attention to the full seriousness of her position instead, as usual, of quoting the League of Nations as a sure guarantee of peace. */42*

No matter when and how events in the Far East find their final solution, Germany will always consider and value Japan as an element of security in its stand against Communism and in its assurance of human culture. */43*

Germany has no territorial interest in East Asia. She has an understandable desire for trade and business. This does not bind us to take sides for one party or the other. It does, however, bind us to the recognition that victory for Bolshevism would destroy the last possibility in this sphere. Moreover, Germany once had possessions herself in East Asia. This did not prevent certain nations from combining with yellow races to drive out the Germans. We no longer want an invitation to return there. */44*

Nor have we any territorial interests connected in any way with the terrible civil war now raging in Spain. There is a situation there similar to one Germany once experienced. An attack on an independent national state carried out with men and materials furnished by Moscow leads to the defense by the national population not willing to be slaughtered. Exactly as in the case of Germany, the democratic international is on the side of the incendiaries. */45*

The German government would see the introduction of Bolshevism into Spain as not only an element of unrest in Europe but also as upsetting the European balance of power, for if this country were to become a section of the Moscow center there would arise the danger of the further spread of this plague of destruction to which we should under no circumstances be indifferent. */46*

ITALY ALSO SHARES ANTI-BOLSHEVIST VIEW

But we are happy that our anti-Bolshevist attitude is shared by a third state. */47*

The condition in which Italy finds herself is somewhat similar to that of Germany. It was, therefore, only natural that we who suffer from the same overpopulation showed understanding for the actions of a man and a regime not willing to let a nation perish to please the fantastic ideals of the League of Nations but were determined to save it. Also in the Spanish conflict Germany and Italy have adopted the same views and, therefore, the same attitude. It is their goal to secure for national Spain complete independence. German and Italian friendship has gradually developed from certain causes into an element of stabilization for European peace. */48*

In this connection the two states with Japan represent the most formidable obstacle against the further advance of the Russian Bolshevik force. */49*

As I have more than once stated, Germany has in Europe no more territorial demands to make of France. With the return of the Saar we trust the period of Franco-German territorial differences is finally closed. */50*

Germany also has no quarrel with England, apart from her colonial wishes. However, there is no cause for any conceivable conflict. The only thing that has poisoned and thus injured the common life of these two countries is the utterly unendurable press campaign which in these two countries has existed under the motto "freedom of personal opinion." */51*

I do not understand it when I am told by foreign statesmen and diplomats that there is no legal possibility in these countries of putting an end to the lies, for private matters are not at stake. It concerns the problems of the common lives of the peoples and states. We cannot shut our eyes to the consequences of these campaigns, for it could so easily come to pass that in certain countries contemptible international lie manufacturers could generate such violent hatred against our country that gradually hostile public opinion would be created against us which the German people would not be able to resist. This is a danger to peace. I am no longer prepared to tolerate unanswered this unbridled slander. From now on we shall answer back and do so with National Socialist thoroughness. */52*

CITES "OUTRAGEOUS" STORIES OF THE LAST FEW WEEKS

What has occurred in the last few weeks in the way of utterly mad, stupid, and imprudent statements about Germany is simply unendurable. */53*

What can we reply when Reuters [British News Agency] discovers attacks on my life? When English newspapers publish outrageous stories of the number of arrests in Germany and the closing of the German frontiers on the Swiss, Belgian, and French sides? When other newspapers say that the Crown Prince had fled Germany, that there had been a military putsch in Germany, that German generals had been imprisoned, that German generals had marched with their regiments to the Reich chancellery, that a quarrel over the Jewish question had broken out between Hitler and Goering and that I, myself, was in a difficult position, that a German general through intermediaries had contacted with Daladier [French Defense Minister], that a regiment had mutinied in Skolp, that two thousand officers had been dismissed from the army, that the entire German industry had received mobilization orders for war, that between the government and private industry violent differences had arisen, that twenty German officers and three generals had fled to Salzburg, that fourteen generals with the body of Ludendorff had fled to Prague; also that I had lost my voice and that my voice would be imitated by someone else so that I could in the future speak from gramophone records. */54*

In a recent speech Eden referred warmly to various forms of freedom in his country. There was one very special freedom which had been forgotten, namely, that of allowing journalists to insult other countries, their institutions, their public men, and their government. All this is too stupid to be taken seriously. But in the long run this will prove to be a serious strain on international relations. I gladly state that a section of the foreign press has not taken part in these infamous attacks against the honor of other nations. */55*

Nevertheless, the damage wrought by such a press campaign is so great that henceforth we will no longer be willing to tolerate it without stern objections. This crime becomes especially evil when it obviously pursues the goal of driving nations into war. */56*

I need only to point to a few facts. I remind you of how in the past year the lie was suddenly spread that Germany had landed twenty thousand men on the Spanish Moroccan coast. It was fortunate that this most infamous falsification could be put right immediately. What, however, would happen if such a rectification could not be brought about in the necessarily short space of time? */57*

To the series of these felonies belongs also the assertion that Germany and Italy had come to an agreement to divide Spain between themselves, or the very recent infamous falsehood that Germany and Japan had arrived at an agreement to acquire jointly the Dutch colonial possessions. */58*

The British government desires the limitation of armaments or the prohibition of bombing. I myself proposed this some time ago. However, I also suggested at the time that the most important thing was to prevent the poisoning of the world's public opinion by infamous press articles. That which strengthened our sympathy with Italy, if this were possible, is the fact that in that country, state policy and press policy tread the same road. */59*

CITES DANGERS TO RELATIONS BETWEEN TWO COUNTRIES

To this chapter of disturbance of international relations belongs the arrogance of writing letters to the head of a foreign state with the request for information about court judgments. I recommend that the British House of Commons worry themselves about the verdicts of the British court-martial in Jerusalem and not about the verdicts of the German peoples' court. */60*

Interest in German cases we can, perhaps, understand. But it certainly does not contribute to the improvement of relations between Great Britain and Germany. Moreover, let nobody imagine he can exert any influence by such tactless interferences in German courts or on the execution of German verdicts. I should never allow members of the German Reichstag to interfere in matters of English justice. */61*

The interests of the British Empire certainly are very great and they are recognized by us. Concerning the interests of the German people the

German Reichstag decides and as its delegate it is I who decide and not a delegation of British letter writers. /62

I think it would not only be useful work to prevent the international dropping of poison, incendiary, and explosive bombs upon populations but above all to abolish the selling of newspapers which have a worse effect upon populations than bombs could ever have. /63

Since this press campaign must be considered as an element of danger to the peace of the people, I have decided to carry through that strengthening of the German army which will give us the assurance that these threats of war against Germany will not one day be translated into bloody force. /64

These measures have been under way since February 4 and will be carried out rapidly and with determination. /65

Under these circumstances it cannot be seen what use there is in conferences and meetings as long as governments in general are not in a position to take decisive steps irrespective of public opinion. /66

TEN MILLION GERMANS IN REICH BORDER STATES

I believe, therefore, that for the present the procedure of diplomatic exchanges of notes is the only one that can be adopted in order to remove the possibility of excessive misinterpretation on the part of the international press. /67

There are more than ten million Germans in states adjoining Germany which before 1866 were joined to the bulk of the German nation by a national link. Until 1918 they fought in the Great War shoulder to shoulder with the German soldiers of the Reich. Against their own free will they were prevented by peace treaties from uniting with the Reich. /68

This was painful enough, but there must be no doubt about one thing: Political separation from the Reich may not lead to deprivation of rights, that is, the general rights of racial self-determination which were solemnly promised to us in Wilson's Fourteen Points as a condition for the armistice. We cannot disregard it just because this is a case concerning Germans. /69

In the long run it is unbearable for a world power, conscious of herself, to know there are citizens at her side who are constantly being inflicted with the severest sufferings for their sympathy or unity with the total nation, its faith and philosophy. /70

We well know there can scarcely be a frontier line in Europe which satisfies all. It should be all the more important to avoid the torture of national minorities in order not to add to the suffering of political separation, the suffering of persecution on account of their belonging to a certain people. /71

That it is possible to find ways leading to the lessening of tension has been proved. But he who tries to prevent by force such lessening of tension through creating an equilibrium in Europe will some day inevitably conjure up force among the nations themselves. It cannot be denied that

Germany herself, as long as she was powerless and defenseless, was compelled to tolerate many of these continual persecutions of the German people on our frontier. */72*

But just as England stands up for her interests all over the globe, present-day Germany will know how to guard its more restricted interests. To these interests of the German Reich belong also the protection of those German peoples who are not in a position to secure along our frontiers their political and philosophical freedom by their own efforts. */73*

LEAGUE ABANDONED EFFORTS IN DANZIG

I may say that since the League of Nations has abandoned its continuous attempts at disturbance in Danzig and since the advent of the new Commissioner, this most dangerous place for European peace has entirely lost its menace. */74*

Poland respects the national conditions in the Free City of Danzig and Germany respects Polish rights. */75*

Now I turn to Austria. It is not only the same people but above all a long communal history and culture which bind together the Reich and Austria. */76*

Difficulties which emerged in the carrying out of the agreement of July 11, 1936, made essential an attempt to remove misunderstandings and obstacles to final reconciliation. It is clear that whether we wished it or not an intolerable position might have developed that would have contained the seeds of catastrophe. It does not lie in the power of man to stop the rolling stone of fate which through neglect or lack of wisdom has been set moving. */77*

I am happy to say that these ideas correspond with the viewpoint of the Austrian Chancellor [Kurt von Schuschnigg], whom I invited to visit me. The underlying intention was to bring about a *détente* in our relations which would guarantee to National Socialist sympathizers in Austria within the limits of the law the same rights enjoyed by other citizens. */78*

In connection with it there was to be an act of conciliation in the form of a general amnesty and better understanding between the two states through closer and friendlier relations in the various spheres of cultural, political, and economic cooperation. All this is a development within the framework of the treaty of July 11. */79*

I wish to pay tribute to the Austrian Chancellor for his efforts to find together with me a way which is just as much in the interests of both countries as in that of the entire German people whose sons we all are regardless of where we came from. I believe we have thus made a contribution to European peace. */80*

Our satisfactory relations with other countries are known to all. Above all it is to be mentioned our cooperation with those two great powers which, like Germany, have recognized Bolshevism as a world danger and are therefore determined to resist the Comintern with a common defense.

It is my earnest wish to see this cooperation with Italy and Japan more and more extended. */81*

HOPES FOR IMPROVEMENT IN THE GENERAL SITUATION

We welcome any *détente* which may arise in the general political situation. For, however great the achievements of our people may be, we do not doubt that all would benefit by an improvement in international cooperation. */82*

The German people is no warlike nation. It is a soldierly one, which means it does not want a war but does not fear it. It loves peace but it also loves its honor and freedom. */83*

The new Reich shall belong to no class, no profession but to the German people. It shall help the people find an easier road in this world. It shall help them in making their lot a happier one. Party, state, armed forces, economics are institutions and functions which can only be estimated as a means toward an end. They will be judged by history according to the services they render toward this goal. Their purpose, however, is to serve the people. */84*

To serve you with all my heart was and is the happiness of my life. It is my happy duty to thank my numerous eminent colleagues without whom this work could not have been performed. */85*

I now pray to God that he will bless in the years to come our work, our deeds, our foresight, our resolve, that the Almighty may protect us from both arrogance and cowardly servility, that he may help us find the right way which he has laid down for the German people, and that he may always give us courage to do the right thing and never to falter or weaken before any power or any danger. */86*

Long live Germany and the German people. */87*

Germany "loves its honor and freedom," Hitler declared. He said this again seven months later as Nazi troops marched into Czechoslovakia. In retrospect, we may see that Hitler's rationale for future aggression had been clearly stated. But in February 1938 men failed to understand. What they perceived was an egocentric apologist, an insecure nationalist given to *ad hominem* attacks on foreign newsmen. Most foreigners simply did not take Hitler seriously . . . until it was too late.

QUESTIONS

1. Hitler's speeches are usually characterized by strong emotion. Make a list of all the words you can find in this speech which connote feeling. What proportion of the emotionally colored language is directed against others? What proportion is used in praise of Germany and her people?

2. In your opinion, what is the most striking sentence in this speech? Why?

3. In this speech Hitler makes a number of references to Germany's strength. Do these boasts seem to you to be in good form? Why do you suppose the German people applauded such references?

4. What references does Hitler make to himself in this speech? Assuming you had been listening to him speak, would such references have enhanced or diminished his reputation in your thinking?

5. Hitler complains about the freedom of foreign newsmen to print what they wish about him. Are there situations in which an abridgment of freedom of the press is desirable in a democratic society? If so, what are they?

6. One of the criticisms frequently leveled against Hitler's speeches is that they ramble. Do you agree with this criticism?

7. If you were describing Hitler's purpose in giving this speech, would you agree or disagree with the notion that he is primarily engaged in impressing upon Germany and the world his uncompromising ideas? Why or why not?

PROJECTS

1. Prepare a five-minute oral report on Hitler's speeches as factors in his rise to power, using Konrad Heiden's *Der Fuehrer* (Boston: Houghton Mifflin Company, 1944) as a reference.

2. Read Churchill's wartime speeches to find expressions he used in referring to Hitler. Try to discover what effect, if any, Churchill's speeches had on Hitler.

3. Read Ross Scanlan's "The Nazi Party Speaker System" and "The Nazi Party Speaker System, II," *Speech Monographs* (August 1949), 82–97, and *Speech Monographs* (June 1950), 134–148; also Scanlan's "The Nazi Rhetorician," *The Quarterly Journal of Speech* (December 1951), 430–440. What advice did Nazi leaders give their followers about public speaking? What directions did Hitler give his cohorts for brainwashing the German people, according to Scanlan in "Hitler and Mass Brainwashing," *The Rhetorical Idiom, ed.* Donald C. Bryant (Ithaca, N.Y.: Cornell University Press, 1958)?

4. In a paragraph or two, summarize the principal characteristics of Hitler's rhetoric as evidenced in his address, "Germany's Claims." Then procure an English translation of one of the speeches of Benito Mussolini. Compare and contrast it with Hitler's. What similarities and differences do you find?

5. Define *argumentum ad hominem*. Do you approve or disapprove of the use of this technique: (1) by a dictator? (2) by American politicians campaigning for elective office? (3) by the President of the United States in a public address? (4) by anyone, under any circumstances? Discuss.

6. Investigate the principal developments in Hitler's life prior to 1938. What was his early life like? How did he achieve control of the German government? Why did the German people accept his leadership?

7. Review the provisions of the Versailles Treaty of 1919. What changes were made

in the nations of Europe? What reparations was Germany required to pay? Did she pay them? Why or why not?

8. Read an account of the period to discover what action, if any, the League of Nations took when Japan invaded Manchuria and Italy conquered Ethiopia.

9. What events preceding 1938 account for the hostility of Germany, Italy, and Japan toward the Soviet Union? How, then, did a Russian-German alliance come about in 1939? When did this alliance end, and why? Discuss.

10. Read William L. Shirer's account of the three months preceding Hitler's speech of February 20, 1938, in *The Rise and Fall of the Third Reich* (New York: Simon and Schuster, Inc., 1960). What position does Shirer take on "the outrageous stories of the past few weeks"?

11. What steps did Hitler take between 1933 and 1938 to silence critics in his own country? Investigate and report.

12. To what extent did Hitler's blueprint for Germany's future in *Mein Kampf* (New York: Reynal and Hitchcock, 1939) correspond with the actual history of the Nazi regime in Germany? Discuss.

13. Did the Nazi regime have an explicit policy to follow toward the Jewish people? Toward Negroes? Toward conquered peoples? Discuss.

14. Examine five reviews of *The Diary of Anne Frank* and Leon Uris' *Exodus*. In the reviewers' judgment, how accurate are these accounts of German wartime behavior?

15. If you have access to several textbooks on public speaking or speech fundamentals, examine five of them on the topic of listening. Define the term *critical listening*. Do most of us usually engage in this practice? Why or why not?

16. Some critics of speech as an academic subject maintain that the study of persuasion should be discouraged because it may provide demagogs tools to use for evil ends. How does Gordon F. Hostettler view this argument in his essay at this end of this book? (See Appendix.) Do you think Hostettler would endorse the study of Hitler as a speaker? Explain.

A DISCUSSION OF ISSUES BY OPPOSING CANDIDATES

One of the most stimulating forms of public discourse in America is the political debate. Although the tone and format of political debating have undergone considerable change since pre-Civil War days and the Lincoln-Douglas debates of 1858, the confrontation of rival candidates for office—local, state, or national—continues to fascinate the American voters. Many listeners attend debates because they want to know more about the candidates' viewpoints or personalities. Seeing candidates together and hearing them talk, voters can more readily compare and assess them. They also listen because conflict in the political sphere intrigues them in much the same way as does conflict in the sports arena. Followers of both candidates recognize that their man will receive more publicity by appearing with his rival on the same platform or in the same room than he would in a solo performance. Perhaps the most significant evidence of the importance of this form of public discourse was John F. Kennedy's admission in November 1960 that the television debates with Richard M. Nixon were the determining factor in his narrow election victory.

So interesting has this form of address proven to be that within the past quarter century candidates of the same party have debated in primaries. When candidates of the same party are vying for a nomination, each is usually cautious in speaking about his opponent, for after all his opponent could win the primary election and go on to represent the party. Moreover, the debaters realize that members of the opposition party are listening, hoping to glean ammunition that they can use later in the campaign.

Time allotted to each speaker in the contemporary political debate is sharply limited, not only because of the disinclination of Americans to listen to long addresses, but also because of the high cost of radio and television time. Frequently a panel of newsmen is on the scene to question each participant in turn. In a sense, these journalists replace the responding audience of earlier years, for modern political debates are often conducted in small studios accommodating less than a dozen spectators. Because radio and television coverage makes possible a mass audience and the candidates do not willingly alienate a large segment of the electorate, debaters talk in generalities much of the time. As a result, viewers may perceive more striking differences in candidates' personalities than in their political viewpoints.

The debate chosen for inclusion here pitted Senator John F. Kennedy of Massachusetts against Senator Hubert H. Humphrey of Minnesota. It was televised "live" in Charleston, West Virginia, May 3, 1960, and a tape was later broadcast by regional radio stations. At stake for both candidates was more than a victory in West Virginia. For Kennedy, a victory was essential. The junior senator from Massachusetts had chosen to enter his name in seven state primary elections preceding the Los Angeles convention. If he won all of these primaries, a steamroller effect could result. A loss anywhere along the way could seriously jeopardize his chances for the Democratic presidential nomination. For Humphrey, a defeat in West Virginia would be decisive; he needed a victory to keep his hopes alive.

The number of listeners to the two Democratic politicians far exceeded the number of citizens who could vote for either of them the following Tuesday. The audience included registered Republicans, independents, and a large out-of-state audience—whose votes might be won for a future contest.

As you read the text of this debate, notice the marked difference in approach taken by the two speakers. To whom does Humphrey appeal for support? What issues does he discuss? What sort of image does he convey to you? How does Kennedy fare when his remarks are examined in the same manner? If you were a debater and were given the same complex circumstances, would you pattern your words after either of these speakers?

THE KENNEDY-HUMPHREY TELEVISION DEBATE

JOHN F. KENNEDY—HUBERT H. HUMPHREY

Announcer: The following political debate between Senator John F. Kennedy and Senator Hubert H. Humphrey is being presented by WCHS-TV, *The Charleston Gazette*, and the participating stations as a public service. Now, here is the moderator for the debate, WCHS-TV News Director, Bill Ames. */1*

Ames: Good evening. The West Virginia primary election campaign has already been characterized by the unique and the unusual, and that tradition is being followed in spectacular and unusual fashion tonight with a face-to-face debate between Senator Hubert H. Humphrey of Minnesota and Senator John F. Kennedy of Massachusetts. */2*

For weeks the attention of the nation has been focused on the voters of West Virginia and on the efforts of these two men to enlist their support in the presidential preference balloting next Tuesday. In that voting, only registered Democrats can cast their ballots for these presidential candidates, and the outcome of the voting is not binding on the Democratic delegates to the July convention in Los Angeles. Still, it is generally

From **The Charleston Gazette**, May 5, 1960. Text emended for this book after comparison with a tape of the broadcast.

agreed that the results of next week's election in West Virginia will be important to the presidential ambitions of the winner and of the loser. /3

With a desire to crystallize for the voter the issues in the West Virginia presidential race, *The Charleston Gazette*, WCHS-TV, and participating stations in and out of the state have brought Senators Humphrey and Kennedy together for this encounter. /4

Formal debate will begin the program. A question-and-answer period will follow the debate. The questions which will be asked have been sent in to *The Charleston Gazette* by its readers. The questions will be put to the senators by the two men on either side of me, Ned Chilton, Assistant to the Publisher of *The Charleston Gazette*, and by Dale Schussler of the News Department of WTRF-TV in Wheeling. Gentlemen, in the debate, you will each have an opportunity for an opening five-minute statement. Then, you will have five minutes for rebuttal. In a toss of the coin before broadcast time tonight, you won, Senator Kennedy, and then chose to go second in debate. The order to be followed in opening statements and rebuttal, therefore, is: the opening, Senator Humphrey, then an opening by Senator Kennedy, rebuttal by Senator Humphrey, and rebuttal by Senator Kennedy. Now, the sound of this buzzer will indicate that your time is at an end, and I ask your cooperation in observing the limitations placed upon you. And so, Senator Humphrey, may we begin with your opening five-minute statement. /5

Humphrey: Thank you, Mr. Ames, and fellow Americans. Now, every political campaign should make a truly constructive contribution to American democracy. We should learn, and become informed, and I have learned that here in West Virginia that you want a government which never rests in this all-important and vital effort to build a secure and an enduring peace. I have learned that you want a government that cares and acts for the people, and understands the needs of the people, and you want a government that isn't blinded by budget-balancing slogans, but rather is deeply dedicated to a balanced nation in which the pockets of depression and unemployment and poverty are erased. /6

Now, the problems of this wonderful and beautiful West Virginia are much the same as those of other states, and, indeed, of the world itself. And, mind you, these problems are growing and spreading like a cancer throughout our very land. There is one thing to me that's crystal clear: America needs a Democratic victory, and I pledge my wholehearted and active support to any forward-looking Democrat who may win the nomination, and I mean that to my friend, John Kennedy, as well. /7

Richard Nixon must not be the next President of the United States. We've had too many years of caretaker government that ignores problems and avoids opportunities, too many years of shameful neglect of America's needs at home, and waste and loss of America's prestige abroad. We have, in fact, friends, been the victims of a "no go—go slow—not now—veto" administration. /8

Popularity has been substituted for leadership, and mediocrity for principle. Slogans have been offered in place of programs, and public relations instead of genuine public service. America, yes, West Virginia deserves a much better deal. Now, we have one basic problem: a conservative Republican government in Washington that is content with standing still in a changing America and a very rapidly changing world, and talk—talk has been substituted for deeds. Little or nothing has been done about distressed industry, such as coal, or depressed areas, or the problems of technological unemployment and automation, or, indeed, little or nothing about the growing demands and needs of education or the care of our elderly. */9*

The Republican administration has put on the brakes on the American economy when we should be moving ahead with giant strides. It has complained about growing surpluses of food and fiber while in many parts of America, yes, in West Virginia, children suffer from inadequate diet. It shouts of inflation as it adds to the cost of living by hiking up the interest rates, and tightening up the credit, and we pay a terrible price for this indifference. Now, these problems in West Virginia and the other states of our Union are, in fact, however, not the worst that America faces. */10*

Time has caught up with America. For the past seven years the Soviet Union has been eating up the lead that America inherited, indeed, from past administrations, and it's going to be a pitiful inheritance that our next President will receive from this administration when he sits across the table from the Soviet dictator, Mr. Khrushchev. */11*

Now, the next ten years may well decide whether the United States is to be a first-class power or become a second-class nation. More than a year ago, I sat across the table from Mr. Khrushchev for better than eight hours. I saw him as he is, tough and able, a Communist, a Bolshevik, determined to surpass the United States, and he is determined that Communism will rule the world, and I am determined that it will not. */12*

Now, the next President must arouse this nation to heroic deeds. He must courageously search for a lasting peace with justice and freedom, and he must understand the complexities of disarmament negotiations, the workings of diplomacy, the United Nations. He must develop a force for peace, using our food and our fiber surplus to feed the hungry, our medical knowledge to heal the sick, and our education to teach the illiterate. */13*

I have tried to prepare myself for this. Now, the West Virginia primary is more than a popularity contest. There are differences between the candidates, but the basic difference has been very accurately assessed by the journalists as one of temperament, and one of attitude, and one of approach. */14*

Now, how you should vote, I think, depends on your sober assessment of the needs of West Virginia, America, and the world. If you're satisfied with things as they are, then you'll vote for Mr. Nixon. If you think that only a little change, an obvious change, is needed, for my friend; if you believe that a vigorous, hard-hitting, constructive action is required, you know my record, and I hope you'll find me your man. Thank you. */15*

Ames: And now, Senator Kennedy, it's your turn for five minutes of an opening statement. */16*

Kennedy: Ladies and gentlemen, I run for the presidency after eighteen years in the service of the United States—four years in the Navy and fourteen years in the Congress, because I believe the presidency is the key office—it is the center of action; and because I believe strongly in my country and in its destiny; and because I believe the power and influence of the next President and his vitality and force are going to be the great factor in meeting the responsibilities that we're going to face. So I run for the presidency. And because the presidency is the people's office as no other office is, it is my judgment that any candidate for the presidency should be willing to submit their name, their fortunes, their record, and their views to people in primaries all over the United States. */17*

West Virginia has such a primary, and that is the reason that I am here. I did not have to come; I came of my own free will; there are no delegates involved; a setback here, a defeat, would be a major one; but nevertheless I came; and I must say I am extremely glad I came. I think this is the best experience and the best education that an American political leader can have, whether he serves in the presidency or serves in the Senate. */18*

Many of you who may be watching television in other parts of the country have been seeing a good deal of West Virginia through your TV, and I wonder whether you realize what a varied state it is, and how unusual is its past, and how bright is its promise. */19*

If there is one quality which I think this state can be justly proud of, it is the quality of courage. More men from West Virginia lost their lives in the Korean War than from any state in the Union of its size. More West Virginians served in World War II than for any state of its size. I was in Hinton this morning, which is the home of the navigator who flew with my brother before he was killed. */20*

This is a state which has sent men to die in every section of the world. And also here in the state of West Virginia you have to have courage to work in the basic industry of this state—coal mining. Eight West Virginians die in the coal mines of this state every month. These people are tough and hard; they've lived in the mountains; there are probably more descendants of American revolutionary soldiers here in West Virginia than in any state of the country. */21*

George Washington said many years ago, "Let me plant a banner in those mountains and I will set men free." This is a state that deserves an opportunity. It deserves recognition from our federal government. Last night I was in McDowell County. That county produces more coal than any county in the world. There are more people on relief in that county than in any county in the country. Now, why should there be 250,000 people living on a subsistence and below-subsistence distribution from the federal government who only want to work—a hundred thousand able-bodied men who want a job and can't find it, who have spent their lives in the coal mines, who have spent their lives underground working in thirty-five or forty inches and who want to get a job again, who want to work? That is the problem of West Virginia. This state can really do a good deal. I don't think I've seen a more vigorous industrial complex than I've seen along the Ohio Valley and the Kanawha River, or better farms. */22*

The people of this state only need a chance, and I think that they're going to get it. I think this election is probably as important to West Virginia as any state in the country, and I hope the people of this country regard carefully what's happened here, because the problem that West Virginia is facing is the problem that all America is going to face. That is the problem of what happens to men when machines take their place. We produce more coal than we did twenty years ago in West Virginia, but there are thousands of men who mined in 1940 who can't find a job. */23*

What is happening in the coal industry in the last ten years in West Virginia is going to spread all over the country. When a machine takes the job of ten men, where do those ten men go? What happens to their families? They live on unemployment compensation and that runs out; they live on a subsistence diet distributed by the federal government which is beyond the living standard for any American; and then they wait for a chance and a job. I must say I am delighted I came here to West Virginia. I think everyone who seeks the office of the presidency should be willing to come. The lesson is hard but it's important for all Americans. */24*

Ames: Thank you very much, Senator Kennedy. You have been shy ten seconds of your five minutes. We move on now to the rebuttal portion of the formal debate. Senator Humphrey . . . in accordance with the order established by the flipping of the coin, it is your turn now to rebut. You will have five minutes for this as well, and you may begin, sir. */25*

Humphrey: Thank you, Mr. Ames. It would be, of course, very undesirable and foolish to attempt to rebut the fine and splendid and pleasant statement as to the—the wonderful assets and the great qualities of the state of West Virginia and its people, this state that has this marvelous history of freedom, and this great contribution to our American system. But I do think there are points that well ought to be emphasized, once having made the generalized statements. While it is true that automation and technological improvements have taken jobs, it is equally true that a government that is worthy of the respect of the American people will move into action with private industry, and with labor, and with the local communities, to find new jobs to retrain workers, to provide for new industries, and to diversify the economy. */26*

It is equally true that a government has a responsibility, not the total responsibility, but a responsibility, to the total economy of the nation, and when you break that down you make it into the respective jurisdictions such as our states. /27

Now, West Virginia's problems, as I indicated in my opening statement, are characteristic of this country. In fact, I might say that I wish that the television camera that is—that has become so much a part of the American scene would not only focus upon certain areas of West Virginia where there is unemployment and distress, but that it would find its way into parts of New York City and Philadelphia and Baltimore and Boston and, yes, Minneapolis and Chicago, to look into those slums where people live in munic-, in metropolitan areas in conditions that are incredible. And yet we have a government that says we have prosperity. /28

I must say without arguing with my associate from Massachusetts that we have been taught in recent days by our current government not to care, and I consider this to be immoral. It is absolutely necessary for us to care for one another. The strength of the American economy is best judged by the weakness of any section or any person or any part, and wherever there is an area of unemployment or distress or suffering, wherever there is a slum, wherever there are conditions that degrade humankind, it weakens America, and it surely weakens our moral posture in the world, and it takes a terrible toll in terms of the economics of our country. /29

You see, I was trying to emphasize in my opening statement that America needs to be strong. We're facing the toughest competition of our lives, tougher than anyone ever dreamed. And the Soviet Union, and Mr. Khrushchev as he symbolizes it, is determined to surpass us; and he's fighting us, competing with us on every area, not merely military. He's competing with us economics—in economics, in education, science and technology, and culture, and we have to be prepared to meet that competition and to surpass it, to expand the areas of freedom. /30

Now, you can't do that if you ignore problems at home. For example, if we're going to have a foreign policy which is willing to loan economic assistance to every nation of the world under the International Development Loan Fund, which I have supported, it seems to me we must have a domestic policy which will make possible loans to local communities, to local industries, to Americans for the improvement of economic conditions in our own country. In other words, our ability to maintain our strength abroad will be dependent in no small part upon our capacity to have full production and employment at home, with social justice. /31

Now, I have some programs that I have mentioned. I don't think that generalities are any—are accurate or adequate. I think I know what it means to be in trouble, to be poor, to be without a job. I learned something about that in the depression of South Dakota. I've seen it in the iron mines of Minnesota. I didn't have to go to the coal mines of West Virginia for first-hand knowledge. I've seen it; I've tasted it; I don't like it. And therefore I propose that we have area redevelopment; that we find new uses for coal and find new outlets for this great source of power; that we build generating plants at the mouth of the mine, for example; that we distribute electricity throughout this whole eastern seaboard, which is a great power center of America, the great industrial center; that we develop the great recreational facilities of West Virginia; that we make it the people's playground; that we give our young people a chance to work in the forests and out in the public lands, in the parks, in a youth conservation corps program; that we spend time and money upon conservation. All of this is an asset; all of this is an investment in the future. Those are my views for the future of this state. */32*

Ames: And now, Senator Kennedy, it is your turn to rebut the statements made by Senator Humphrey. Our thanks to you, Senator Humphrey. Senator Kennedy, your time begins right now. */33*

Kennedy: During my speech, I think that—in considering the problems of West Virginia, I think the people of West Virginia are concerned about what can be done, and I think the people of the United States are concerned. */34*

This is a problem which goes beyond West Virginia. In Massachusetts we lost our textile industry and we had through four, five, or six years in the great mill towns an extremely difficult time. Pennsylvania, southern Illinois, Kentucky, parts of Indiana, parts of Ohio have all been hard hit by technological change. The question is, what shall we do about them, what shall we do about West Virginia? */35*

I said that there were 250,000 people getting surplus food from the government. I received a letter the other day, April 23rd, from A. F. Johnston, Box 17, Montcalm, West Virginia. Here's what he gets every month from the government: "I'm a man with TB and I happen to get surplus food. I have seven children. This is what I receive: five bags of flour, four cans of eggs, three 5-pound bags of meal, eight pounds of shortening, four pounds of rice, which we can't use if we don't get it clean, and four powdered milk. We do not get any butter, cheese, or beans, as Mr. Benson stated. I would challenge anybody on the surplus food situation, on what we get, what we don't get." */36*

These are the powdered eggs. For a family of four, you get three of these per month. It says "for distribution to needy persons." There's 250,000 people in West Virginia getting this kind of assistance every month. It's an inadequate diet. There are a good many children who get their only good meal when they go to school and who bring some of it home to share with their brothers and sisters. This is a national problem, not a problem just for West Virginia, and it certainly is a problem which needs the devoted effort of the federal government, the President, the administration, and the Congress. */37*

There are, I think, some things we ought to do immediately. First place, we ought to send a better diet to those who are dependent upon the government. This is not a satisfactory diet for Americans. We should certainly add decent food. We send many of them overseas; we sell them for local currency overseas; we should send them here. Secondly, we should add to the unemployment compensation benefits. After twenty-four weeks, a man goes out. He waits on relief. He waits for surplus food. I think we should give him the thirty-nine weeks that the administration has recommended, make it a part of federal minimum standards, because no state has adopted the thirty-nine weeks. Thirdly, I think we ought to do as Senator Humphrey said, pass the Area Redevelopment Bill, which makes it possible for small businesses to come in, which makes it possible for communities to clean the water, to attract industry, which makes it possible to retrain workers in a new work, vocational retraining. All these things can be done if the force of the federal government is put behind them. */38*

Then, I think we can do a good deal more about West Virginia and other states in sending defense contracts to them. Do you know that West Virginia, which had the most serious unemployment in the United States last year, was the lowest in number of defense contracts it received? West Virginia received twenty million dollars in defense contracts from the Pentagon, which was spending over forty billion dollars. My own state of Massachusetts received a billion, four hundred million. Virginia, which borders right next to you, received one billion, twenty-eight million. */39*

I think that the Defense Department should set aside of every contract a percentage which would go into those areas where there was a high level of unemployment. Then, I think we ought to begin to consider long-range recovery, of how we can attract new industries into this area, how we can provide new uses for coal. */40*

The administration vetoed the Coal Research Bill. I think the administration should approve it. I think that the federal government must recognize that as machines come in and men are thrown out of work, it presents a problem, not just to the community, but also to the country. I think in every industry in the United States in the next ten years, there should be councils between labor and management, with government representatives, so that as machinery comes in which throws people out of work, we can find new jobs for them, new training, that the machines come in in a way that will help people rather than just provide unemployment. This is the lesson of West Virginia. This is why West Virginia should be a matter of greatest concern to us all. Because what has happened to these people can happen in every state of the country. West Virginia needs help and I think it ought to be on the desk of the next President of the United States. */41*

Ames: Thank you, Senator Kennedy, Now, gentlemen, we have concluded the formal portion of the program, the formal debate with opening statements and their rebuttals. And we come to the portion which will be devoted to questions and answers. */42*

Now, I'll remind you again that the questions have all been sent to *The Charleston Gazette* by its readers, and that they've been screened by the editorial board of *The Gazette* to avoid repetition and to make a representative selection of the hundreds that were received. */43*

Now, the ground rules regarding the answering of questions are as follows: The questions will be asked of you alternately and you have two minutes in which to give your answer. Now, at the end of the two minutes, the familiar buzzer—the buzzer with which you've now become familiar—will sound as it has before, and you will stop. And I must ask your cooperation in observing that. */44*

The candidate to whom the question was not directed—some have been directed to you both—but the candidate to whom the question was not directed will have the optional comment if he so desires, and the time limit on comment will also be two minutes. Now, may we have the first question, first from Ned Chilton of *The Charleston Gazette.* */45*

Chilton: The first question is addressed to both of you gentlemen, and I'll ask Mr. Humphrey first. "Should Red China be permitted to join the United Nations?" It is sent in by Charles W. Simpson of Syracuse, New York. */46*

Humphrey: Mr. Simpson and Mr. Chilton, I would not, as a delegate of the United Nations representing this country, nor would I, if responsible for the nation's foreign policy, recommend, at least at this time, the admission of Red China to the United Nations. She has demonstrated a kind of arrogance and a kind of intransigence which I believe is anything but worthy of the respect and of the consideration of our country. */47*

May I further add that the Charter of the United Nations requires that the nations that are members thereof should be peace-loving nations. Now, I know there are some members of the UN that surely don't qualify too well for that particular description, but I would add they came in at the time of the United Nations' inception, and now we have an opportunity to weigh the admission of new members very carefully. Now, I qualify my statement by saying that you don't take a position in terms of the indefinite future. You take it in terms of the present circumstances. */48*

Ames: Thank you, Senator Humphrey. Senator Kennedy, do you . . . this question was directed, was it not? */49*

Voices: To both. Yes. To both. */50*

Kennedy: Yes, I would agree with Senator Humphrey. Unless the Chinese Communists demonstrated a change in their foreign policy—and we've seen a very belligerent phase of their foreign policy in their relations with India during the past year—unless they're willing to demonstrate that they desire to live with peace with the neighbors to the south of them, work out a solution to the problems facing us, including the problems of disarmament, then I would not recognize them. But if they indicated that they would, then I would begin negotiations to see if it's possible to establish more intimate relations. After all, we desire peace and harmony. They are one quarter of the world, but I do think that they have to meet certain standards before recognition should be coming. */51*

Ames: Thank you, sir. The next question comes to us with Dale Schussler of WTRF-TV as the questioner. */52*

Schussler: It's addressed to you, Senator Kennedy. It comes from a reader in White Sulphur Springs, Charlotte Cabot. She asks: "In your opinion, are the Soviets acting in good faith when they press the case for disarmament?" */53*

Kennedy: Well, not for disarmament. When they say that they want complete disarmament, then quite obviously that's impossible, unless they would agree to the kind of inspection which they have been unwilling to disagree—to agree to. In addition, I don't think that they have shown particular vigor in good faith, because they've failed to agree to the efforts we've made to provide for the disarmament of outer space, which would be possible, as no country today dominates outer space. */54*

I am hopeful, however, that it would be possible to reach out—to reach some agreement with the Soviet Union on nuclear testing. I think this is an area where it may be to our mutual advantage, where it may be to the self-interest of the Soviet Union and the United States, to agree to the cessation of tests, to agree to a realistic and workable inspection system; and if that should be, then I'm hopeful we can proceed on that basis. But on the general thesis which Mr. Khrushchev advanced many months ago—of immediate disarmament—I don't think they're working in good faith. */55*

Humphrey: May I comment, please? */56*

Ames: Mr. Humphrey. */57*

Humphrey: Well, I would agree that there is considerable evidence of the lack of what one might call "good faith, " but I do have some hopes about the Summit conference, particularly if the Summit conference, the first Summit conference, is limited to the phase of disarmament discussions. Now, at that conference I think the most that we could expect is to be able to lay down or to get an agreement upon the ground rules for the present ten-nation disarmament conference that's under way in Geneva. If we could get the ground rules clearly understood—in other words, how—what they were to do in the ten-nation conference—this would be a forward step, particularly if there was a firm agreement. Secondly, there is one basic problem in the field of the nuclear test suspension—with adequate inspection and control—and that problem is the number of on-site inspections where the mobile teams, the international inspection teams, can move into an area where there seems to be a suspicious event. Now, if we could come to an agreement upon the number of on-site inspections, then I think we would be making some forward progress in the field of disarmament, and this is a prospect that lends some hope. I think the Soviet Union needs peace for at least the next seven to eight years if it's to fulfill its Seven-Year Plan. */58*

Chilton: Senator Humphrey, the next question is addressed to you from J.A. Asbury of Glasgow, West Virginia: "What stand do you take on the proposal to raise federal income-tax exemptions from six hundred to eight hundred dollars?" */59*

Humphrey: I took a stand early on that, and this is one of the differences between my colleague from Massachusetts and myself—a difference of degree, I might add. I voted for the amendment offered by the senator from Texas, Mr. Yarborough, to increase the exemption from six- to eight hundred dollars. I also voted for the George amendment—of the late Senator Walter George—to increase the exemption from six- to seven hundred dollars as a—it was a—a similar measure but of less degree. Now, I felt this was important at the time that it was up, because there was considerable recession in the country, growing unemployment, and genuine economic distress. */60*

I feel that the use of the tax laws to be able to stimulate purchasing power and to broaden the base of the . . . consumers, or the consumption ability of the people, is very important. Now, I would have made up that loss of revenue—and it was a loss of revenue—I would have made it up by having withholding taxes upon dividends and interest, upon closing tax loopholes, such as reducing the amount of depletion allowance on gas and oil—I voted to decrease it from 27½ per cent to 15 per cent—and those two items alone—the reduction in the depletion allowance, which I submit is fair—the present law is special privilege—closing the tax loophole on interest and dividends would more than have compensated for the loss of revenue; and the individual family—head of family—would have had more money with which to make his purchases, to educate his family, to take care of the medical needs of his family, and to be a better customer. I think it was a sensible vote. */61*

Ames: Thank you, sir. The next question, Dale. Oh, excuse me, Senator Kennedy, do you have any— */62*

Kennedy: As I understood, the question was, am I in favor of it today? Is that the question? */63*

Ames: What stand do you take on the proposal to raise federal income-tax exemptions from six hundred to eight hundred dollars? */64*

Kennedy: Well, I'm not—I think it would be a mistake and misleading for me to suggest that I'm going to favor a good many of the programs that I've talked about earlier—also a stronger national defense, federal aid to education, assistance to this state and other states—and at the same time say that I'm going to reduce income taxes this year. I don't think that's possible. I think it's—I think that we—in the final analysis, the President of the United States has to make a determination of what is in the long-range interest of this country. And I don't think, therefore, that at the present time, until the economy has moved up, I think it's going to be possible to reduce income taxes. Now, secondly, I am heartily in favor of closing the loopholes; I hope that can be done. We've been defeated on many occasions since I've been in the Senate. In the eight years I've been in the Senate, the vote has come up on many times, and it's been defeated on every occasion. I hope we can do something about the oil depletion allowance. I think 27 percent is too much, so I do agree that we ought to try to close the loopholes. There are many things that can be done, but until we do it, until we're able to bring in enough revenue to make up for the loss, I cannot advocate at this time that reduction in taxes. */65*

Schussler: The next question is addressed to both of you gentlemen. The name has been withheld; the reader lives in Bluefield, West Virginia. Senator Humphrey, former President Harry Truman has said that if he were a merchant faced with a lunch-counter sit-down demonstration by Negroes, he would chase them out of his store. "What would you do?" is the question asked. */66*

Humphrey: Well, I surely wouldn't. As a matter of fact, I feel that the young men and women who have engaged in these respective demonstrations have been orderly, they've been standing up for their rights as they see them as American citizens, and they've been applying what I would call a higher moral law. Now, there may be instances in localities where the local ordinances give protection to existing inequities, injustices. If that's the case, those ordinances should be changed; and in the meantime, I would suggest to those who are the operators of private business establishments, that they have some consideration for not only the constitutional rights of people under the Fourteenth Amendment—because no state is supposed to pass any law which falls unequally upon its citizens. And I would suggest also they might practice some good business sense by treating customers with equity and with equality. I'd like to add, however, if I may go back to another question on this—is that within the rules?—on the tax question? */67*

Ames: I believe, sir, that you have one minute left. */68*

Humphrey: Yes; I'd just like to point this out, that the tax act of 1954, passed by the eighty-third Republican Congress, is not Divine script; it's not sancrosact—sacrosanct. It is man-made law; it is filled with inequities and injustices; I refuse to accept it without protesting against it; I did not vote for it; I thought that it was injustice consummate; and I feel that the tax loopholes will not be closed until there is a firm determination on the part of more of us in the Congress, like myself, to demand some equity in the tax laws. And that's why I would have supported, and do support, an increase in the deduction for the average family, because I think it will lend itself to the health of the economy and compel this government to do justice in the tax laws rather than to continue to spread the benefits to a handful of people who do not need them. */69*

Ames: Senators, before we proceed—you have an answer to the question that was raised, Senator Kennedy, but let me point out this fact. Senator Humphrey raised the point, and it was a legitimate one: If you finish your answer to a specific question and you have some comments you would like to throw in on some subject raised before, you will have the option to use up the two-minute time in that kind of reply should you so desire. This will be true of both. The question that was asked of you, sir, Senator Kennedy, was, "If you were faced with a lunch-counter sit-in demonstration by Negroes, would you chase such demonstrators from your store?" */70*

Kennedy: No, I wouldn't, providing the demonstrations were peaceful and respect the rights of others. It is in the great American tradition of peaceful protest, which goes back to the beginning of this country. I certainly wouldn't chase them out. */71*

Chilton: Senator Kennedy, the next question is asked of you, sent in from Bill Buchanan of Beckley: "In view of the recent troubles in Cuba, do you feel we should continue to purchase Cuban sugar at prices above the world trade prices?" */72*

Kennedy: Well, I think the best thing to do about Cuba at the present time is to put the quota and its maintenance in the hands of the President. The administration has recommended that, and as a member of the Senate Foreign Relations Committee, which both Senator Humphrey and I are, I would suggest that that is the most appropriate course. Then we can carry it on on a month-by-month basis, and we can make a determination as events change; they're constantly changing, and we don't know what's going to be the situation six months from now. For the present, therefore, I would continue it as it is. To merely cut it on the basis that you suggest would be an annoying act, would have no serious effect on Mr. Castro; in fact, it would make him be able to say to the world that we were carrying on economic discrimination against him. There is no doubt he would take reprisals against Americans who were there. Therefore, for the present, I must say in the case of Cuba I agree with the administration policy. */73*

Humphrey: This is one of the few times, may I say, where I have agreed that the administration's reluctance to act has had a positive and affirmative position or policy. I thoroughly agree with the comments of my colleague from Massachusetts that this kind of patience which we've exercised is creditable and desirable and I, too, have the feeling that the President, whoever the President may be, must have within his power the opportunity to take timely action as the national security requires. I believe that that flexibility would be a highly desirable development and I surely support it. */74*

Schussler: Senator Humphrey, would you agree with this statement from a reader in Lake, West Virginia, T. V. Saunders by name: "How do you feel in regard to foreign aid? Doesn't it make more enemies than it does friends?" */75*

Humphrey: Well, it can, but I don't think it does. In the main, the foreign aid program has been a constructive force in American life, in American foreign policy. There has been a tendency, however, of late to emphasize primarily the monetary aspects of foreign aid rather than the manner in which it is—it is utilized and the manner in which it is effectuated. */76*

Take, for example, some time ago I wrote to the State Department about our foreign aid program in Korea. I had information which led me to believe that it was being poorly administered; in fact, there were some elements of corruption. The administration didn't seem to feel that that was the case. I made a speech in the Senate. In fact, I made five speeches over two years in the Senate on Korea, pointing out what was happening over there—which finally developed, as you know, into riots, with the government having to be changed; and we now discover that the foreign aid program has been poorly managed and has cost the American taxpayers substantial amount through mismanagement and corruption. But, in the main, I must say that foreign aid is required. I don't think that we ought to take it—that we ought to do away with it. What we need are administrators of foreign aid, continuity of administration, who follow through to see that this foreign aid does some direct good for the people for which it is intended. */77*

Ames: Senator Kennedy. */78*

Kennedy: I think that it would be to the advantage of both the United States and the countries involved if more and more foreign aid could be put in the form of loans, if we could strengthen the Development Loan Fund, make it possible for them to pay back, not put so much emphasis on the disposition of surplus military equipment which they're not able to sustain. We gave Laos, I think, something like three hundred million dollars and yet they weren't able to defend themselves against a five thousand-guerilla invasion. */79*

So I would say, I would strengthen the Development Loan Fund, put it on the basis of loan. Then when people ask for it, they will have projects which are worth while, and it would be done on a more businesslike basis. It does serve a useful function, because so much of the world is in a—going through a period of transition—Latin America, and Africa, and Asia—we want them to maintain their freedom; you've seen what's happened to the balance of power in the world when China went Communist. We want to make sure that these other countries have a chance to develop under a free system. Our security is protected when they do so. Therefore, I think the best way, in a measured, careful way: Strengthen the loan provisions—put the major emphasis into those—and also help get the countries of Western Europe, whom we assisted ten years ago, to play their proportionate role in assisting these countries. */80*

Chilton: This question is asked of both. I'll query Mr. Humphrey first—Senator Humphrey first: "Vice-President Nixon by inference has said this country has nothing to fear until such time as an individual with no religion, an atheist or an agnostic, is a candidate for President. Would you care to comment on this?" */81*

Humphrey: Well, I believe it is quite well understood, or at least it should be, that the Constitution of the United States makes no religious requirement for any candidate for office; and my comment is that a good deal of this discussion on a subject that is as sensitive and as volatile and as personal and intimate as one's religious convictions could be well relieved if there was a little less talk about it and a little more understanding about the personal matter of one's religious faith and convictions. */82*

I have said, and I shall repeat it, that the most important thing for a voter to understand about religion and politics is the moral laws, the ethical standards, or the moral standards of the individual candidates, and the party that he may represent. In other words, we ought to have some religion, some faith in our heart, and by that I mean some love of fellow man, a recognition of our humility before Divine Providence, and the need of prayerful guidance and advice. */83*

Ames: Senator Kennedy. */84*

Kennedy: Well, of course, as Senator Humphrey said, the Constitution is quite explicit and says there shall be no religious test for office in Article 6; and, of course, in the First Amendment, says Congress shall make no laws. So, therefore, of course, this country was founded on the basis of religious freedom, and that means that we all believe as we want to believe, and I don't think that the Vice-President, and I'm sure he doesn't intend to, or anyone else—how could we decide whether somebody is irreligious or not religious? It's far better that we let them carry on their own life, believe as they choose to do so, providing they have given adequate demonstration that they believe in the constitutional system, that they believe in the First Amendment, that they believe in the rights of others to worship as they want, that their decisions are made based on their own experience and their own best judgment. These are the great factors which I think motivate men as different as Jefferson and Lincoln, men who had entirely opposite in some ways, or in some ways the same, religious beliefs. This country—this is perhaps the most important ingredient in the development of American character from the beginning of this country, which was founded on the principle of religious freedom. Therefore, I'm devoted, and I know Senator Humphrey is, to the maintenance of this tradition, and I'm confident that they are, too, in West Virginia. */85*

I—that's my experience, and I continue to believe that, because I think it's such an important quality in the American character and the American experience. If this were lost—if we've started to apply religious tests of one kind to another, then really something important in American life would go out. So, I must say that I believe that people should be free. That's the important thing: to believe as they wish, providing they are loyal Americans and devoted to constitutional principles. */86*

Ames: Senator Humphrey, Jerry Carney of Dunbar directs this question to you: "Are you in favor of a national fair trade law?" */87*

Humphrey: I have been. I feel that fair trade laws have a place in the American economy. The biggest problem has been in the area of enforcement. I believe that there ought to be rules of conduct in the economic market place just as there are rules of conduct in banking, in railroading, in utilities. I happen to believe that loss leaders lend themselves to the warfare—to jungle warfare in the economic market place, threaten the very existence of private enterprise, particularly individually owned enterprise or partnerships. I have seen through experience, not through theory, the impact of the powerful, large interests upon the independent retailer—and he is in need, particularly in those areas where there are nationally advertised brands, of some kind of price protection lest these nationally advertised items be used as come-ons to draw people into a business establishment and ultimately to destroy the independent merchant, who is, in fact, as important to the American social and economic structure as the family farmer, or, indeed, as the schoolteacher or the independent school district. These are the—these are the ways that we develop an America that has a degree of independence and a degree, I would say, of social justice and fair play, which is so important a part of our national make-up. /88

Ames: Senator Kennedy, do you wish to reply to that question? /89

Kennedy: Well, I think we want to be careful in protecting small businessmen—and I must say I think they need protection, because I think in this administration particularly the credit policies and all the rest have worked to their disadvantage—to make sure that it doesn't provide that the consumers are going to have to pay a unnecessarily high cost. I remember Senator Neely from this state making a speech on the Senate floor in which he said a fair trade bill would cost his people millions and millions of dollars, so that I think we want to be extremely careful before we push a national fair trade law, that we are providing protection where it is needed and not merely permitting a higher cost for a good many people. /90

Chilton: Gentlemen, Mrs. Elsie Osborne of Clendenin asks: "Why do Senator Kennedy"—this is a question directed at both of you—"Why do Senator Kennedy and Senator Humphrey blame all the ills of West Virginia on the Eisenhower Administration when we have a Democratic Congress of which both are members and which has done nothing yet toward helping us?" /91

Kennedy: Who are you going to let answer that one first? /92

[Laughter]

Ames: —choose up sides. /93

Humphrey: Since I've been getting all the hot ones first, I'll take this one. [Laughs] Go ahead, John, if you wish. /94

Kennedy: Oh, no; well, I was just going to say—and I'll let Senator Humphrey answer half of this question—I remember that—taking the lead in Defense Manpower Policy No. 4 in 1953 to steer defense contracts into distressed areas, of which my state of Massachusetts had a good many. This administration committed themselves to maintaining it by executive order, and it was never done. Senator Knowland led the fight against our effort. I was the floor manager in the first Area Redevelopment Bill which was intended—and both of us have mentioned this—to assist areas like West Virginia which had high unemployment. The President vetoed that bill. Now I'm going to let Senator Humphrey give a couple of other examples. /95

Humphrey: Well, one other good example is the Coal Research Bill, which was passed with the support, of course, of the members of the West Virginia delegation; and by the way, the Coal Research Bill had a very modest appropriation to it that would have been of help to the coal industry of this state and, indeed, the entire economy. The President vetoed that; I might add, however, that we have nineteen such research programs going in foreign countries which the taxpayers of America pay for, but not one dime is to go into West Virginia. */96*

Furthermore, the administration has taken a very dim view upon such programs as the Food Stamp Plan, which we passed, that would have been of help right here in the state of West Virginia. Now, I am the author of the Food Stamp Plan. We attached it to the so-called Surplus Food Disposal Program last year. It would have provided for a balanced diet for the needy people in this state. There is over four hundred millions of dollars of monies not paid in by taxpayers, but collected by tariffs on food imports into this country, that are available—those dollars are available—to purchase poultry, meat, milk, butter, cheese, oleomargarine, soybean oil—whatever would be necessary for a balanced diet, including fruits and vegetables. */97*

The administration has vetoed 147 times acts of Congress, and we have not had the two thirds to override the vetoes. I am fully familiar with the Area Redevelopment Bill, having been, with Senator Kennedy, a co-sponsor of it; and, by the way, we passed it again in the Senate and I am hoping that tonight the House of Representatives will have passed it for the second time so that the President will have it on his desk once more. */98*

Kennedy: I think—if I may say—that this indicates the importance of the presidency. Regardless of what action is taken by the members of Congress from this state or any other state, the presidency is the key office. The President can veto programs, as this administration has done—housing, water pollution, unemployment compensation—can oppose minimum wage—and you can't get action. All the President needs is one third plus one in either the House or the Senate to stop any bill from passing, and in addition the power of the President to suggest action to the Congress. This is the key office. Make no mistake about it. The Congress is an equal and coordinate branch, but the power, and influence, and the prestige is of the presidency. That makes it the key office. And that's why I think it's important for West Virginia and the United States to have a change in administration. */99*

Humphrey: You know, I might add, gentlemen, that I remember the days of 1936 when Franklin Delano Roosevelt visited my home state of South Dakota, at that time in the drouth period. He came to see the conditions. I wish the President of the United States would come to see some of the conditions that we've seen in this state and other states. I can't help but feel that any man who occupied that high office with the tremendous power of the presidency would advocate programs of action and insist upon prompt action. But instead of that, I read the other day where the President thought that there was a liberal allowance for foodstuffs in this state. */100*

Ames: Senators Kennedy and Humphrey, you've put a mathematical burden on me there that I hope I've fulfilled, but jointly you've each had two minutes. [Laughter] Mr. Chilton, I think you have the next question. */101*

Chilton: Senator Kennedy, this one is submitted to you by J. Hugh Cummings of Parkersburg: "Are you willing to take a definite stand on Senator McCarthy?" */102*

Kennedy: Yes, I have. I said that I support the censure. On many occasions I've stated that. */103*

Humphrey: I supported the censure in the Senate at the time of the vote and spoke in favor of it. */104*

Schussler: Senator Humphrey, Betty Twaddle, I believe is the name, from St. Albans, West Virginia, asks this question of you: "Do you honestly feel that if you should win the West Virginia primary you would have a chance of getting the Democratic nomination?" */105*

Humphrey: I surely do, and I suppose it's at this point where I disagree most sharply with my friend from Massachusetts. No Democrat has this nomination tied up. There are a number of Democrats that are potential Democratic nominees, and the West Virginia primary is a significant primary. It isn't the alpha and the omega, the beginning and the end, but it is a very significant primary. If I should win this primary, I will surely have additional impetus in my efforts to obtain the nomination. */106*

I believe that, at the best, any candidate going to the Democratic convention will not have over 500 votes, and 500 votes is about 165 less than he needs; and if you have 200 votes, you're just as much alive politically as the man with 500 votes; and when it gets right down to it out at Los Angeles at the Democratic convention, the Democratic party is going to want a candidate who will take this battle to the Republicans, who will speak up unequivocally, who will stand on the platform, who will be able to wage a battle against Mr. Nixon, the Republican nominee, and who will not back off. */107*

I waged that battle in my opening statement tonight because I believe that the Republican administration has been costly to this country, and it has been an unhappy administration for the future of America, and I want no more of it. */108*

Ames: Senator Kennedy, do you care to comment? */109*

Kennedy: Well, I think that Senator Humphrey has stated, and he stated it the other day in the District of Columbia, that he hoped to have at the convention 200 votes, and I agree with you that there probably won't be any candidate who goes in at the beginning with 500. I think this primary may well be key, however, in the state of West Virginia. I ran in the New Hampshire primary. I have run in the Wisconsin primary, where I was successful against Senator Humphrey and Mr. Nixon. I ran in the

Indiana primary yesterday. In the Pennsylvania primary we received 175- or -80,000 write-in votes, which was a good many more, I think—which was 75 per cent of all the write-ins—and I am running in Maryland, and we run again in Oregon. This is a key primary. I think that what happens here could very well determine what will happen at Los Angeles. No one knows who's going to win, but I would say it may well be decided in West Virginia. */110*

Ames: Senator Kennedy— */111*

Kennedy: I will say, if I may, further, that there are other candidates. Their supporters, who are supporting Senator Humphrey in this state, they're not supporting me. Now, they must make a judgment that if Senator Humphrey wins it eliminates me, but Senator Humphrey does not serve as a major threat to them. Otherwise, I don't see why every candidate who is opposing me for the nomination with their supporters in the state are supporting Senator Humphrey. */112*

Ames: Next question. */113*

Chilton: Mr. Kennedy, Senator Kennedy, sir, this question has been sent in, name withheld, from Charleston: "The Roman Catholic Church's position on truth versus error assumes a right to discriminate against Protestants in some countries where Catholics are in the majority. Do you agree with the Church's reported attitude that where Protestants are a minority they shouldn't be permitted equal status?" */114*

Kennedy: No, I wholly disagree. I couldn't disagree more. I think that using the power of the state against any group, forcing, using the state to force a group to be of one faith or another, or of a faith, I think, is wholly repugnant to our experience; I wholly disagree with that. */115*

Now, there are some states where there is no separation between church and state. The Queen of England is the head of the Church of England as well as the state. There're other states in Europe where the relationship is intimate. In Spain, the relationship between church and state has been intimate. I disagree with that. This country was founded on the principle of separation of church and state. This is a view that I hold against any other view, and it's the view that I subscribe to in the Constitution. Now, other countries have less fortunate experiences. I wish they all provided for the separation of church and state, but we do in this United States and we're going to continue to do it, because I don't know of anyone who holds any position of responsibility that isn't devoted to that and wishes that that system could spread throughout the world. */116*

Ames: Senator Humphrey. */117*

Humphrey: That was stated very well; this obviously is my position. I have always believed in and will continue to believe in the separation of church and state because it is fundamental, to my mind, to the basic political democracy that this country enjoys and that it wants to enjoy in the years ahead. */118*

Now, in the brief time that I have left I should like to comment on a matter which was raised by my friend from Massachusetts, about the support that we have here in the state of West Virginia. Now, Senator, Jack, I haven't had any endorsement from Lyndon, or from Stu. As a matter of fact, their neutrality has been so conspicuous that it's almost been icy. */119*

I must say, however, that I've seen in other areas of the country where there was considerable support for you. I know that in Wisconsin, for example, that a number of Republicans were very strong for you. It's quite well recognized that they were. I also know that there were those—for example, a congressman came out very strongly for you. Sort of ganged up on me. Congressman Zablocki, nice fellow, don't misunderstand me, but he could have been neutral. And I must say that I haven't— */120*

Kennedy: Isn't he a Democrat? */121*

Humphrey: Good Democrat, yes, but isn't Johnson a Democrat? He's the majority leader and even if—I would think he— */122*

Kennedy: I don't think Congressman Zablocki is a candidate for the President, however. */123*

[Laughter]

Humphrey: Never can tell, it's wide open. */124*

Ames: Gentlemen, Senator Humphrey has the floor— */125*

Kennedy: Excuse me, I'm sorry— */126*

Ames: —for thirty more seconds. */127*

Kennedy: I'm sorry— */128*

Humphrey: I'm through. */129*

Ames: The next question. */130*

Kennedy: Let's talk about—I don't know where the primary in Wisconsin—you could vote in either primary—I don't know how the votes divide. . . . There were congressmen, Democrats, supporting Senator Humphrey and some supporting me. The only point I make is that there have been the statement, including the statement by, I think, Senator Humphrey's campaign manager, that Senator Humphrey was his third choice. */131*

Ames: Senator Kennedy, we have two minutes left to the end of the program. I will give you each one minute apiece to debate on this subject. You have the floor, sir, for one minute. */132*

Kennedy: To debate on the subject— */133*

Ames: On the subject that you have just opened. That you are replying on now. You have one minute. */134*

Kennedy: Oh, well, I merely say that Senator Humphrey runs and—and he's a very able, vigorous senator. All I stated was that those who are supporting other candidates have uniformly supported the candidacy of Senator Humphrey in West Virginia. Now, that is their privilege, but that is because, in my opinion, the other candidates believe, and their supporters, that if we can be stopped here in West Virginia, that it will be difficult to be nominated. That is why I say this is the key primary, and therefore I'm running as hard as I can, and I'm running against what I consider to be a coalition of those who choose a good many other candidates. That is their privilege. All I have is the privilege of pointing it out. /135

Ames: Senator Humphrey, one minute, sir. /136

Humphrey: Well, Senator, let me just say this, that I welcome the support of the good people of West Virginia and I haven't given them any blood test. I happen to believe that if they wish to support Senator Humphrey, that they have every right to do so. I can recall here not long ago that a poll showed you ahead 70 to 30 per cent and there was no complaint at all about who the support was for. And when the race tightened up a bit, well, at once we had some complaints about who was supporting whom. I merely want to say that in this primary election I have had generous support from the rank and file of our people. In the District of Columbia yesterday, I saw Kennedy's support for Senator Morse, one of his prime workers. Now, despite that, I didn't call it a gang-up; I went ahead and proceeded with the election and won it. I hope to be able to do exactly the same thing here in West Virginia, but to do it honorably, without recrimination. Thank you. /137

Ames: Thank you, gentlemen, both for appearing on this open, face-to-face debate this evening from West Virginia. /138

We know that Kennedy defeated Humphrey in that primary. In fact, in the spring and early summer, Kennedy achieved impressive victories in every primary he entered. At Los Angeles he was selected on the first ballot as the Democratic presidential candidate of 1960.

Perhaps the most distinctive feature of the 1960 presidential campaign which followed were the "Great Debates" between Kennedy and Richard M. Nixon. Nixon had been a champion debater since high-school days. Kennedy's debate training was less apparent, having been gained largely in deliberations within his family. Yet in the crucial television encounters of September and October 1960, John F. Kennedy emerged the victor.

QUESTIONS

1. On what specific issues, if any, do the speakers clash in this debate? Is there a word or phrase other than *debate* which more accurately describes this encounter?

2. Who appears to be Humphrey's principal opponent in this debate? Why should this be so?

3. Why do you suppose Kennedy chose to speak second? Is there not usually an advantage in speaking first in a debate? Who speaks last in this debate, and why?

4. What does Humphrey feel the federal government should do about unemployment caused by automation?

5. What specific proposals to improve economic conditions in West Virginia are made by each candidate?

6. What bills did a Democratic Congress pass to overcome the ills of West Virginia, according to Kennedy and Humphrey? Did they receive the President's signature?

7. The West Virginia primary was viewed by many as a test of Kennedy's acceptability on the basis of his religious views as well as his political popularity. Why were some Americans skeptical about a Roman Catholic's chances of attaining the presidency?

8. What efforts did Kennedy make in West Virginia to overcome the political liability of great wealth? Is he wise to refer to his visits about the state in his speech?

PROJECTS

1. Read James M. Burns' *John Kennedy: A Political Profile* (New York: Harcourt, Brace and Company, 1960). Note the specific events in Kennedy's background which contributed to his development as a speaker.

2. Compose in 300-500 words a biographical sketch of Hubert H. Humphrey. Cite events that contributed to the development of his speaking ability.

3. What liabilities did Humphrey and Kennedy have as presidential candidates, according to Eric Sevareid in *Candidates 1960* (New York: Basic Books, Inc., 1959)? Did later events confirm Sevareid's judgment?

4. Humphrey maintains (par. 67) that sit-in demonstrators are applying a "higher moral law." Read Henry David Thoreau's essay "On Civil Disobedience" in *The Portable Thoreau,* ed. Carl Bode (New York: The Viking Press, Inc., 1947), pp. 109-137. Would you agree with Humphrey and Thoreau? Why or why not?

5. In this text of the debate you may have noticed some slight grammatical errors. How are such errors handled in texts of speeches in the *Congressional Record?* What limits, if any, must senators and representatives observe in altering their speeches before they appear in print? Why do our national representatives have the privilege of congressional immunity for their remarks in the House or Senate?

6. Read Edmund Burke's speeches to the Bristol Corporation in 1780 in *Select British Eloquence,* ed. Chauncey A. Goodrich (Indianapolis: The Bobbs-Merrill Company, Inc., 1963), pp. 292–311. What two concepts of public service does Burke discuss? Explain why you agree or disagree with his view.

7. Read Theodore White's *The Making of the President 1960* (New York: Atheneum Publishers, 1961). How important a factor, in the view of this writer, were Kennedy's speeches in his election to the presidency?

8. What advantages and disadvantages accrue to a presidential candidate who chooses "the primary route" to the White House? Investigate and discuss the view former President Harry S Truman takes of this procedure.

9. Describe the number and nature of the Lincoln-Douglas debates. For what office

were the debaters campaigning? Why did these debates achieve nation-wide interest? What immediate and long-range effects did the debates have on Lincoln's political career?

10. Prepare a five-minute oral report on the speaking of Stephen A. Douglas. Use Forest Whan's essay in *The History and Criticism of American Public Address,* Vol. II (cited in Project 1, p. 141) as a reference.

11. Read Sidney Kraus' account of *The Great Debates* (Bloomington, Ind.: Indiana University Press, 1962). Describe the special broadcast arrangements, and explain their purpose. Contrast the format with the Lincoln-Douglas format. Why do you suppose the latter was avoided for these debates?

PART FIVE

THE PROBLEM OF ESTABLISHING CREDIBILITY

Adjectives which denote "good" and "bad" in a moral or ethical sense are as old as any language; they appear in every tongue known to man. So it is not surprising that we use such terms—apply ethical standards—when we listen to speakers, read speeches, or discuss the art of speaking.

Some theorists maintain that the skills of effective speech are merely tools to be used. Both good men and bad men, statesmen and demagogs, may speak effectively, in the sense that either may sway an audience to their way of thinking.

Yet the fact remains that we do distinguish between statesmen and demagogs—we do follow some ethical guidelines in reacting to speakers, although these guidelines may sometimes be vague in our thinking.

The speeches which follow serve to (1) clarify these ethical guidelines, (2) show a speaker establishing himself as trustworthy in the eyes of his listeners, and (3) show a speaker defending himself when his integrity has been questioned.

RIGHT AND WRONG IN ORAL DISCOURSE

Karl R. Wallace, Head of the Department of Speech and Theatre, University of Illinois at Urbana, made the search for an ethical basis of communication the theme of a series of addresses in 1954. As President of the Speech Association of America, Wallace wanted a subject that would prove of both contemporary and lasting interest to the speech teachers he would address across the country. The speech which follows is part philosophical essay, part public address; happily, Wallace's remarks preserve the spontaneity of a speech designed for an immediate audience.

AN ETHICAL BASIS OF COMMUNICATION

KARL R. WALLACE

On a recent plane trip a friend of mine sat beside a citizen of Wisconsin. Inevitably the conversation came around to the junior senator from that state. Part of the dialog went like this:

Friend: What do you think of Mr. McCarthy?

Citizen: Well, I happen to know him personally, and I just don't like him at all. And I don't like his investigation methods, either—his badgering people and twisting their words around and acting like he owned the whole committee.

Friend: It's too bad you Wisconsin people don't have a chance of turning him out of office.

Citizen: What'd we want to do that for? He's doing a darn good job of blasting out those Communists. There ought to be more of it.

Friend: If there were an election tomorrow, would you vote for McCarthy?

Citizen: Yes, I would. */1*

The conversation points up the age-old problem of judging the right and wrong of human conduct. There is a similar difficulty when we come to judge the right and wrong of communication. The problem is essentially this: Does the end warrant our using any means which seem likely to achieve it? Is the public speaker or debater who believes his purpose worthy justified in using any methods and techniques which he thinks would be successful? Is the play director, convinced that his educational objectives are right, free to select any play and employ any methods of interpretation and production which seem likely to be "effective"? Is the speech correctionist, profoundly motivated to help the child with deviant speech behavior, free to adopt any techniques which seem workable? */2*

From **The Speech Teacher** (January 1955), 1–9. Reprinted with permission.

This is an ethical problem. It is time that teachers of communication confronted it squarely. The signs of warning are about us. One of the more prominent signs is implicit in the widespread growth of research in communication, as may be seen in the serious study of polling techniques designed to measure the effectiveness of persuasive methods, the new interest of political scientists and bureaucrats in methods of propaganda, the progress made by linguists and psychologists in applying scientific methods to the analysis of language behavior. The facts and data thus compiled are, of course, valuable; nevertheless, it is somewhat disquieting to observe that such research is centered overwhelmingly on processes, operations, mechanisms, and techniques. There seems to be little, if any, prevailing interest in the *character* of the communicator or in the quality of the communicative product. Some parent groups, of course, have shown concern over the character of radio and television programs and over the comic books, but their activities have been largely sporadic and spotty. We are fascinated—often hypnotized—by what happens, how it happens, and why it happens, but we seem to be utterly unexcited by the question: *Ought* it to happen thus? What would be *better?* /3

There is room to mention here but one other sign of our apathy toward the ethics of communication. We can read it from our own behavior as teachers of speech. As we start out a new class in speech, or as we confront the thoughtful student who wonders if his praiseworthy purpose allows him to give his audience what it wants, we have been known to speak like this: "Remember, in this class we are studying and applying methods and techniques of speaking. Communication is a skill, a tool, and because it is a tool we are not directly concerned with who uses it and what he says. These are matters which the individual speaker must decide for himself. The main business of this course is to help you to become an effective speaker, a successful speaker. After all, the art of speaking is like the art of reasoning, or like mathematics and science, in that morality lies outside them; it is not *of* them; it is not *in* them." This kind of professional position, this disinterested attitude, this kind of easy reasoning, is leading many persons to look anew at the ethics of both the teacher and his student. Communication is in danger of being regarded as merely an art of personal success and prestige, and of being forgotten as the indispensable art of social persuasion. /4

Any professional field which has reached maturity is ever alive to its ethics. Law, medicine, engineering, and journalism have their codes of ethics. The profession of teaching, too, has its code of behavior. The field of speech shows some evidence of recapturing the maturity and stability it once enjoyed, under the name of *rhetoric*, in the educational systems of centuries past. Is it not time for the teacher of the arts of speech to face up to his special commitments? We must confront questions like these: Is there an ethic of communication? Specifically, is there an ethic of oral communication, a morality of rhetoric? I believe that there are ethical standards which should control any situation in which speaker and writer endeavor to inform and to influence others. I shall try to indicate where we find these standards and what they are like. /5

In the first place, ethical standards of communication should place emphasis upon the means used to secure the end, rather than upon achieving the end itself. A political speaker may win the vote, or a competitor in a speech contest may win the prize, but it is far more important that his means and methods, the character of his skill, and, indeed, the quality of his entire product, should conform to standards formulated by competent judges and critics of speech-making. Let us discover why. /6

If we give much weight to the immediate success of a speech, we encourage temptation. To glorify the end is to invite the use of any means which will work. The end can be used, for example, to sanction distortion and suppression of materials and arguments. We need here only to mention that there are still popular books on speech-making which sometimes offer shocking advice. A recent manual advises the speaker that he may, if necessary, remodel a pet quotation to fill the bill, for, after all, no one will know the difference! Such advice is on a par with the shoddy ethics of the debate coach who exclaims, "If my boys misquote, it's up to their opponents to spot it." The end, moreover, can be readily called upon to justify the misleading maneuvers, the innuendoes, and the short-cut tricks of the propagandists. The advertiser, in his zeal to sell, is constantly tempted to promise more than he can deliver. In brief, to exalt the end is often to be indifferent about means. As a result, we gradually undermine confidence in communication and, indeed, in all human relations; and with confidence gone, nothing is left but distrust and suspicion. /7

If we give first prize to the speaker who wins his goal, we not only unnecessarily tempt the honest and sincere man; we undermine the character of the communicator. We associate with "success" such values as popular prestige and personal ambition. We thus give a premium to the man with a compulsive drive, to him who must win at any cost; and we handicap the man who places the welfare of others above his personal gain. We give the advantage to Senator McCarthy; we hand a disadvantage to Secretary Stevens. John Morley, one of the best English critics of public address in the nineteenth century, has clearly described the risk which the popular persuader incurs when he measures his utterance by its immediate effect. To do so may undermine

> a man's moral self-possession. . . . Effect becomes the decisive consideration instead of truth; a good meeting grows into a final object in life; the end of existence is a paradise of loud and prolonged cheering; and character is gradually destroyed by the [parasite of] vanity.

Finally, the worst evil which follows from an indifference to means is that we make easy the intent of the dishonest, insincere speaker. It is easy to assert high-sounding purposes; it is difficult for the listener to assess the sincerity of these assertions. In short, as Mahatma Gandhi often told us, "Evil means, even for the good end, produce evil results." /8

There is a better ethic than that which justifies the means by the end. It is an ethic which respects the means more than the end. It governs both the selection and the presentation of materials. Above all, the ethic measures the quality of the communicative product in terms of the communicator, rather than according to its immediate effect upon the audience. Some 2300 years ago Aristotle suggested the standard:

> [The function of speech-making] is not simply to succeed in persuading, but rather to discover the means of coming as near such success as the circumstances of each particular case allow. In this it resembles all other arts. For example, it is not the function of medicine simply to make a man quite healthy, but to put him as far as may be on the road to health; it is possible to give excellent treatment even to those who can never enjoy sound health.

What does such a standard suggest? It implies, first, that a speaker does the best job he can under the circumstances; and doing his best job means that he has education, training, and competence in the art of communication. In the second place, the comparison of the speaker with the physician and with other arts implies that the standards of communication are determined by those who best know the art, that is, by the teachers and critics of communication. Finally, the passage suggests that since immediate success is not always possible, anyway, the end or purpose of a speech operates principally as a guide or direction. Purpose serves to give organization and shape to the speech, the discussion, or the play; it aids in the choice of means, but it should not dominate the moral values of either the product or the speaker. /9

It seems clear that the ethical standards of communication should be set by persons who know communication best, and that the standards or code they formulate will express their judgment as to what means are good, what means are bad. If the standards were clearly stated and widely understood, they could be freely used by expert and layman alike to measure the character of any case of communication. /10

Where does one look for such standards? They are derived from the function of an art. The function of any art takes its ultimate meaning from what it tries to accomplish in its social setting. What, for example, does a speaker do not only for himself, but also for society, the community? /11

Although there are many sides to society, its indispensable side is political. Indeed, when society behaves politically it has the technical name, *state*. And *the state* is simply another name for an association of men. Because it is the largest, most inclusive association we know of, its values and ends are reflected in nearly everything that its citizens do. They are reflected particularly in education and in the arts and sciences.

The influence of the political society is stated in this passage from the *Ethics* of Aristotle:

> If . . . there is some end of the things we do which we desire for its own sake . . . clearly this must be the good and the chief good. . . . If so, we must try, in outline at least, to determine what it is, and of which of the sciences or capacities it is the object. It would seem to belong to the most authoritative art and that which is most truly the master art. And politics appears to be of this nature; for it is this which ordains which of the sciences should be studied in a state, and which each class of citizens should learn and up to what point they should learn them; and we see even the most highly esteemed of capacities to fall under this, e.g., strategy, economics, rhetoric; now, since politics uses the rest of the sciences, and since, again, it legislates as to what we are to do and what we are to abstain from, the end of this science must include those of the others, so that this end must be the good for man. */12*

The passage demands that we recognize two basic facts. First, the political society aims to help its citizens to secure whatever they consider to be the good life. Indeed, the dominant tone of a political group is set by its ethical values. Thus Communism, for example, has one set of values, democracy a quite different set. Second, the arts and sciences serve the ideals of the political society. Indeed, they share the same ethical values and goals. The art of rhetoric—and all the arts of communication—thus embraces the ethical part of politics. This point Aristotle states flatly in his book on rhetoric, and for this reason in his system of communication he incorporates materials which he borrows directly from the fields of political science and ethical science. For example, in discussing the materials of political oratory, he talks of the good, of happiness, of virtue, and of the general welfare. He even advises the political speaker to study ways of political life in different kinds of society. In discussing the speaking of the law courts, he treats of justice and equity. Thus, the instrumental art, rhetoric, shares the controlling ideas of the master art, politics. Hence, communication inevitably must stand for and must reflect the same ethical values as the political society of which it is a part. It is clear, furthermore, that this principle is as true today as it was in Aristotle's time. Although government and politics are much more complex than they were in the days of ancient Greece, the modern political scientist acknowledges that the foundations of the state are laid in ethics. */13*

Is it not becoming clear, therefore, that we look for the ethical basis of communication in the ideals of our own political society? That society, for all its manifest defects, is still a free and democratic society. If we can clearly state the essential values of democracy, we can then suggest an ethic of communication and the ethics of the teacher of speech. */14*

A free and democratic society, first of all, is built on the notion that the individual has dignity and worth. Our society holds that government exists to uphold and preserve the worth and dignity of each and every person. A totalitarian society, on the other hand, holds that the individual lives for the state. In a democracy people are supreme and wield the ultimate power. In totalitarianism the state is almighty and is the final source of all power. The difference is crucial; it is as sharply different as black and white, as tyranny and freedom. The phrase, "dignity and worth of the individual," leads to a state of mind best described by the old-fashioned word, *respect.* Each man respects his fellow man. This fact has led some students of political science to describe a democratic society as a "commonwealth of mutual deference." */15*

Respect for the individual leads us to a second basic belief: a profound faith in equality of opportunity. We believe that a man can best reach his greatest maturity if he has the chance. If we can say with Wordsworth that the child is father of the man, we believe that the child must have the opportunity to become the best possible father of the best possible man. We believe, furthermore, that so far as we are able, every child must be given the *same* chance. Out of such beliefs we have developed the all-important notion of *fairness.* Like the rules of any game, the laws of the political game must be as fair as we can possibly make them. */16*

We hold a third belief that has become one of the great hallmarks of a democratic society. It is the belief in freedom. Difficult as it may be to define *freedom,* we know well enough that each individual must be given as wide a field to roam in as he wishes. The word also means that if a person in his roaming prevents another man from ranging widely, he must so modify his behavior as to give his fellow a similar opportunity. He can do what he wants to do, so long as he does not hinder another from exercising a like range of choice and of action. So freedom always implies restraint. A person can behave as he wishes in his own home so long as he does not become a nuisance to his neighbors; he can drive his car where and how he wishes so long as he does not endanger others; he can compete as he may desire in business, in sports, in speech contests, so long as he respects the rules. */17*

In a free and democratic society, individuals acting in concert and with deliberation make their own restraints. The restraints are called *legislation* or *laws.* They are policies or guides of conduct. Indeed, they are no different in their origin and effect from the rules of family life or the regulations of a school. Furthermore, individuals through their government set up agencies to which they delegate power for administering the laws, and they create courts charged with the responsibility of enforcing the restraints. Lincoln showed deep wisdom in saying that our political society was of us, by us, and for us. In our democratic society, moreover, we insist that the laws bear equally upon everyone. In effect, we say to our legislators and judges: "You must do your best to make laws which will be fair to everybody, and you must enforce the laws in the spirit of fairness and justice." */18*

A free and democratic society rests upon a fourth deep and abiding belief. It is a conviction closely linked to the idea that each individual must have the opportunity of growing and developing to the limits of his ability. The conviction is that every person is capable of understanding the nature of democracy: its goals, its values, its procedures and processes. This belief assumes that persons can acquire the knowledge necessary to form opinions and decisions and to test them by means of discussion and action. As a result of this conviction, a democracy demands that knowledge be made available to all, rather than to the few; it requires that the sources and channels of communication be wide and diverse, rather than limited and one-sided. It cannot tolerate restriction and distortion. Consequently, it must cherish and protect certain special freedoms: freedom of speech, freedom of press, and freedom of assembly. Without these freedoms democracy is meaningless; the life of a free society depends upon them. */19*

Is it not evident that each person participates in a political society? that he reflects its values and uses its procedures? In his role as communicator, whether he be playwright or play producer, public reader or public speaker, he must also reveal his political character. What he says and his method of saying it reveal his choices, and the choices a man makes are always an index to his character. Theoretically, of course, a man need not speak at all; or he can choose to speak only to himself, or to refuse to discuss matters of public interest. But if he chooses to speak, he reveals his political soul. */20*

What, then, are the ethics of the teacher of speech? They are grounded in the public character of public utterance in a free society. */21*

First, a communicator in a free society must recognize that during the moments of his utterance he is the sole source of argument and information. His hearers know this fact, and they defer to him. He in turn must defer to them. Accordingly, his speech must reveal that he knows his subject, that he understands the implications and issues relevant to the particular time and occasion, that he is aware of essential and trustworthy opinions and facts, that he is dealing with a many-sided, rather than a one-sided, state of affairs. Although the speaker might find it difficult to know when he has met such standards, he can always direct a test question to himself: Can I answer squarely, without evasion, any relevant question that a hearer might ask? If he can answer *yes* in all honesty, he has met the standard of knowledge. In the learning situation, the teacher of speech has an obligation to teach the art of inquiry and investigation, to inculcate respect for scope and depth of fact and opinion—in a word, to help build the habit of *search*. The teacher has this duty because a free society demands that communication be informative and that knowledge be shared. */22*

How can the teacher help his students develop the habit of searching widely for both fact and opinion? There is no simple answer, of course. Many teachers, both in high school and in college, are well aware of this duty and have developed their own methods of teaching the art of inquiry. But we shall not hurt ourselves if we periodically confront these questions: Am I keeping up with information and opinion on problems that are currently discussed, so that my chances are better, rather than worse, of being a good guide and critic of what my students know or do not know? Am I making sufficient use of discussion methods, in both the classroom and private conference, to stimulate interest and inquiry? Am I habitually encouraging the classroom audience, upon hearing a student speak, to discuss the adequacy of the speaker's knowledge and the trustworthiness of his materials? */23*

Second, the communicator who respects the democratic way of life must select and present fact and opinon *fairly*. One of his great tasks is to help preserve a kind of equality of opportunity among ideas. He must therefore be accurate in reporting fact and opinion; he must *respect* accuracy. Moreover, he must not intentionally warp and distort ideas. Nor must he suppress and conceal material which his audience would need in justly evaluating his argument. He must, furthermore, avoid the short-cut methods of the propagandist. He cannot make one word guilty by loosely associating it with another guilty word. He cannot indulge in the tricks of emotion, cannot juggle with reason, at the expense of sound argument. In helping himself meet the standard of justice, a communicator can always quiz himself: In the selection and presentation of my materials, am I giving my audience the *opportunity* of making fair judgments? The speaker who can answer *yes* understands what is involved in the sharing of information and opinion. He knows that he has had a special opportunity to observe, to learn, to evaluate, which most of his hearers may not have had. He knows, accordingly, that one of his jobs as a communicator is to help his hearers compensate for the lack of special opportunity. He realizes that he cannot possibly give them the same chance he has had, but he can give them the best chance that time and occasion will allow. Speaker and hearer, writer and reader, cannot have had the same experience, but they can feel that they have had. In the classroom, accordingly, the teacher of speech must inculcate what I shall call the *habit of justice*. The habit is based on respect for truth and accuracy, and respect for fair dealing. Neither can be disassociated from communication in a free society. The teacher of speech must stand for truth and justice in communication because the health and welfare of a free society depend upon the integrity of the communicator. */24*

Third, the communicator who believes in the ultimate values of democracy will invariably reveal the sources of his information and opinion. As Al Smith said, a public figure must keep the record straight. A speaker before any audience is by that fact a public person, and he is no exception to the rule. A communicator, moreover, will help his hearers to weigh any special bias, prejudice, and private motivations which are inherent in source materials. He knows that argument and fact are unacceptable if their springs are contaminated. As an investigator preparing for his speech, he has had the opportunity of discovering whether private motives, such as those of self-interest, personal prestige, and personal profit, have merely imparted a special flavor to the source or have made it dangerous to drink. Such information he should share with his hearers. And if he is not already a public character well known to his audience, he should be willing to reveal frankly his own motivations. The critical question which he poses to himself is this: Have I concealed information about either my source materials or my own motives which, if revealed, would damage my case? The communicator who can answer *no* is in the tradition of public integrity. */25*

In the high school and the college, the teacher of speech must devise methods and techniques which will form the *habit of preferring public to private motivations.* Public communication is responsible communication; it remembers who said what under what circumstances and for what reasons. In this respect it is utterly unlike gossip and rumor which, if not malicious, we may tolerate as idle talk for idle pleasure. */26*

How can the teacher of speech help his young communicators toward habits of fairness, justice, and public accountability? I do not wish to preach here. Let him who is without blemish cast the first stone. Nevertheless, we shall do well occasionally to examine ourselves as objectively as we can and to conduct the inquisition mercilessly. We may ask: In all my relationships with my students, am I as fair as I can be? Do I keep clear the differences between opinion and fact, and do I distinguish between my opinion and somebody else's? When I express an opinion, do I explain its basis, or do I take a short cut and let the opinion rest on my own authority and prestige? Do I respond to questions frankly, without evasion? Am I withholding information, as "not being good for young persons," especially under the circumstances? What kind of censor am I? */27*

Sometimes teachers effectively employ examples of what not to do. For a ready source of illustrations of unfair tactics in public address, the speeches and press releases of Senator McCarthy offer a rich hunting ground. One could start his collection of negative examples by reading Professor Barnet Baskerville's article, "Joe McCarthy, Brief-Case Demagogue," in the September number of *Today's Speech.* Baskerville cites one careful study whose author checked McCarthy's initial charges of Communism in the State Department with the ascertainable facts. The investigator, Professor Hart of Duke University, examining only the charges as presented up to the fall of 1951, found that McCarthy's "assertions had been radically at variance with the facts in fifty specific instances." Another examination of two 1952 campaign speeches reveals them as "*a most amazing demonstration of studied inaccuracy.*" McCarthy's nationally televised address which attacked Adlai Stevenson (the speech making use of documents from a Massachusetts barn) yields "no less than eighteen 'false statements or distortions' in the text which McCarthy described as having 'complete, unchallengeable documentation.'" Baskerville comments on the senator's documents, often raised aloft for all to see, "The deceit lies in the significant omissions, and in unwarranted inferences drawn from impressive but often completely irrelevant documents." The article could well be the beginning of a case study in personal and public integrity. */28*

Fourth, a communicator in a democratic society will acknowledge and will respect diversity of argument and opinion. His selection of issues, his analysis of the situation, the style of his address will reflect the attitudes which signify admission, concession, and compromise. Nevertheless, his communication will not sacrifice principle to compromise, and he will prefer facing conflict to accepting appeasement. For such a communicator, the test question will ever be this: Can I freely admit the force of opposing evidence and argument and still advocate a position which represents my convictions? The great duty of the teacher of speech is to devise ways and means and to maintain a climate which will favor the *habit of respect for dissent.* Can he teach what it means to hold convictions without loss of integrity and at the same time respect the convictions of others? The teacher who can do so is not merely skillful; he is a true representative of the free society. */29*

It is these four "moralities": the duty of search and inquiry; allegiance to accuracy, fairness, and justice in the selection and treatment of ideas and arguments; the willingness to submit private motivations to public scrutiny; and the toleration of dissent, which provide the ethic of communication in a free society. */30*

In view of these moralities, as teachers of speech we can no longer tell even the most elementary student of our discipline that speech skills and techniques, like tools, are divorced from ethical values. We can no longer say that how he uses his art is his own private affair. But we need not be content with an ethic which is external to communication. We need not rely solely upon the familiar, classic positions: "You'd better be good, or your audience may find you out"; or "A good man skilled in speaking will in the long run be more effective than a bad man skilled in speaking." As I have tried to indicate, communication carries its ethics within itself. Public address of any kind is inseparable from the values which permeate a free and democratic community. A speaker is in a deep and true sense a representative of his constitution which defines his way of life, and therefore defines in part the social goals and methods of rhetoric. His frame of political reference is not that of an aristocracy, an oligarchy, a monarchy, or a tyranny. In a word, there are ethical guides in the very act of communicating; and it seems to me that the guides are the same for all communicators, no matter whether they speak as politicians, statesmen, businessmen, or professional men. */31*

Wallace's address is regarded as an important milestone in the teaching of speech in America. Often it is quoted at speech association conventions and is assigned reading for students of speech.

QUESTIONS

1. Wallace indicates early in his presentation that instructors of speech face ethical decisions much as people in other professions do. What are some of the ethical problems faced by a doctor? lawyer? political speaker? speech correctionist? play director?

2. Wallace suggests (pars. 6–8) that victory in a speech contest is less important than the communicative behavior of the participant. What difference does it really make if a contestant cheats a little?

3. Have you ever been duped by a salesman's promises? What was your reaction when you discovered that you had been misled? Did you ever purchase anything from that salesman again?

4. Can you recall a speech in which immediate success in communication proved impossible to attain? How did the speaker behave? Would you act differently if you were the speaker and could relive the experience?

5. How does Wallace contrast the roles of the individual in a free society and a totalitarian society?

6. What does Wallace mean when he says (par. 17) that "freedom always implies restraint"? Illustrate your answer.

7. What specific freedoms does Wallace deem essential to a democratic society? Why does he maintain this view?

8. What difference is there between the public and the private motivations of a speaker, according to Wallace in paragraphs 25–26? Cite an example of each form of motivation.

9. Why is diversity of opinion inevitable in a free society? Should even Communists be allowed freedom to speak in this country?

PROJECTS

1. Read Barnet Baskerville's "Joe McCarthy, Brief-Case Demagogue" in *Today's Speech* (September 1954), 8–15. To what extent does the evidence support Baskerville's conclusions?

2. The ideal orator "is a good man skilled in speaking"—so wrote Quintilian, a schoolmaster of ancient Rome. Describe Quintilian's conception of *goodness* as it is revealed in his *Institutes of Oratory.*

3. Describe the principal ethical problems which face the college debater, according to authors who discuss debating in *The Quarterly Journal of Speech* and other speech journals. Which of these problems would you personally find most difficult to resolve?

4. Examine the study of opinion determinants in the 1940 election by Paul Lazarsfeld and others, entitled *The People's Choice: How the Voter Makes Up His Mind in a Presidential Campaign* (New York: Duell, Sloan & Pearce, Inc., 1944). What community was chosen as the representative sample? Why? What do the results of this investigation suggest about the relative impact of the various communication media?

5. Read Vance Packard's *The Hidden Persuaders* (New York: David McKay Co., Inc., 1957). What persuasive techniques of American advertisers does Packard describe?

6. Wallace mentions the importance of search and inquiry (par. 22). Read Josephine Tey's *The Daughter of Time* (New York: The Macmillan Company, 1952). What details led Grant and Carradine to question the accepted verdict of history regarding the character of Richard III? To what extent can their ultimate conclusions be supported?

7. Read Dale Carnegie's *How To Win Friends and Influence People* (New York: Simon and Schuster, Inc., 1937). What position does Carnegie take on the question of whether a speaker should tell an audience what it wants to hear? Would Wallace defend or oppose this view?

8. Read Chapter 5, "Speaking and Listening Responsibly," in S. Judson Crandell, Gerald M. Phillips, and Joseph A. Wigley, *Speech: A Course in Fundamentals* (Chicago: Scott, Foresman and Company, 1963). What distinguishes a fact from an opinion? How do these authors define *prejudice*? What advice do they offer for drawing valid inferences?

9. Explain the meaning of *guilt by association*. Describe three implications of guilt by association that appeared in political speeches you have heard or read. Explain what Senator Joseph McCarthy meant by *Fifth-Amendment Communist*.

10. Prepare a 500-word essay defending or attacking the following proposition: *Speech censorship in any form is incompatible with a democratic society.*

11. Read one of A. Conan Doyle's Sherlock Holmes mysteries. What can we learn from Holmes about the art of observation?

THE SPEAKER AS A MAN TO BE TRUSTED

The Second World War produced a host of American heroes, possibly the greatest of whom was a former Kansas farm boy, Dwight D. Eisenhower. As Supreme Allied Commander in Europe, Eisenhower was faced with the task of defeating Nazi Germany. It was "Ike's" responsibility to coordinate the armed might of a dozen nations in the invasion of the Continent. His success in this effort and his personal popularity in the years that followed caused both the Democratic and Republican parties to seek him as a presidential candidate. It looked as if any gift the American people could make to Eisenhower was his for the asking . . . including the presidency.

In the 1952 campaign, Eisenhower was the Republican nominee for President. Americans thronged to see and hear the General, not only because of what he might say about political issues, but also because of his appeal as a national hero. Eisenhower's personality won him friends everywhere, even among the opposition.

Presidential candidates are expected to give a great many speeches during a campaign. Many come to rely heavily, therefore, on speech writers. In June 1952, Dwight Eisenhower was new to the ways of American politics, so it is not altogether surprising to find him departing from custom and addressing his supporters directly, in impromptu fashion.

The following short speech was presented at a campaign breakfast in Detroit. As you read it, notice the speaker's informality and especially his efforts to win the trust of his listeners.

SPEECH TO DETROIT SUPPORTERS

DWIGHT D. EISENHOWER

Ladies and gentlemen, I think sometimes my military training may not have been as thorough as it could have been, because one of the principles of military life is never to be surprised. I am touched, astonished, and surprised this morning, and I expect it is due to deliberate intent on the part of my associates, now normally labeled as political advisers. */1*

They get some inkling of the way I get tired of my own voice, and so I think they conceal from me at times that I am expected to battle again with one of these microphones. */2*

In any event, as you know, I am scheduled for two talks here today. For a simple fellow like myself, that is quite a chore. */3*

From **The New York Times**, June 15, 1952. Reprinted with permission of General Dwight D. Eisenhower.

I am delighted that such a group as this should invite me to their breakfast hour to give me a chance to say to them, "Thank you for coming," and to express my almost amazement that they are interested in the views I may hold about today's life and problems, and to give me a chance to meet just some more Americans, always something that is valuable and instructive to any of us. */4*

I am going to tell you one thing about my talks today, in which you may have some interest. */5*

When I told Mr. Summerfield[1] that I would come out here, I began to think, as would anyone else, what message could I bring that was worth while to the people of Detroit. And I worked pretty hard on numbers of drafts of ideas and putting them together. And during the past week I have been going through an experience that, for me, if not for you, is certainly strange, and it has been again very instructive, and I have listened to many questions that people have asked me. And so, finally, coming down on the train last night and this morning, I made a decision to this effect: All my prepared talks are thrown out of the window. Today, whatever I do, I am going to try to take the questions that have been coming to me over the past week and do my best to show to you and to the people of this city how I feel about them as a matter of conviction. */6*

On many of them I have no details of solution. I am not a medicine man and I have no panaceas for anything. All I can do, therefore, is to show how I would approach these problems. I can show by them my basic concern for, and my love of, America. */7*

If what I have got to offer in the way of honest, decent approach, as I see it, for Americans to this problem is not enough, there is nothing more I can do. Such as I have is yours and all the rest of America's to use freely, and that is exactly what I intend to try to say today, without benefit of paper. And I am telling you—and I see among you some of my intimate friends—if I make blunders, I know my friends will excuse it. I hope the others will realize at least that I am sincere. */8*

I have used the vertical pronoun very much in this little talk and I don't like it, but at least let me say again, thank you very much indeed for coming here and letting me meet with you for this brief moment. Thank you. */9*

There were other speeches the General gave, many of which were formal addresses designed for formal occasions. But on no future occasion did the Eisenhower personality reveal itself more openly than on that crowded morning in Detroit. As Isocrates of Athens summed up the matter centuries ago, "The argument which is made by a man's life is of more weight than that which is furnished by words."

[1]Arthur E. Summerfield, then Republican National Committeeman from Michigan, and later Postmaster General during the Eisenhower Administration.

QUESTIONS

1. Why is the first paragraph of this speech likely to appeal to an audience? What other direct references does Eisenhower make to the audience?

2. What statements are likely to elicit sympathy for Eisenhower as a presidential candidate? Is it desirable or undesirable for a candidate for high political office to appear human?

3. In the course of his talk, Eisenhower mentions (pars. 2, 3, and 7, respectively) getting "tired of my own voice," two talks being "quite a chore," and having "no panaceas for anything." Are such remarks typical of political candidates? Do they make a speaker appear more, or less, trustworthy? Why do some Americans suspect the fluent, knowledgeable speaker?

4. The General mentions (par. 8) that he speaks "without benefit of paper." "All my prepared talks are thrown out of the window," he says (par. 6). Is this approach one every office-seeker should follow? Why is a manuscript speech sometimes less effective than an extemporaneous or impromptu one?

PROJECTS

1. Procure a copy of Eisenhower's *Peace with Justice: Selected Addresses* (New York: Columbia University Press, 1961) and Adlai E. Stevenson's *Major Campaign Speeches, 1952* (New York: Random House, 1953). Compare the style of these two speakers in terms of clarity, directness, and impressiveness. Why do you suppose Stevenson's speeches became best sellers almost as soon as they appeared in print?

2. What other military men have been elected to the presidency? Did any of them campaign extensively? Read Fletcher Knebel and Charles Bailey, *Seven Days in May* (New York: Harper & Row, 1962). Is the danger of a military dictatorship in America real? If so, to what degree?

3. Discuss the principal issues of the 1952 presidential campaign, and the position the two major candidates took on each. Discuss also Stevenson's use of humor in the campaign, and public reaction to it. Check relevant issues of *The New York Times* as a reference in investigating these topics.

4. Read this study by Marie Hochmuth [Nichols]: "Ghost Writing: Implications for Public Address," in *Rhetoric and Criticism* (Baton Rouge, La.: Louisiana State University Press, 1963). What special problems does the ghost writer present to the student of public address?

5. Examine the pages of *The New York Times* for the three-month period after the 1952 election. What reaction did political commentators have to Stevenson's insistence upon principal authorship of his campaign speeches? Using later issues of this same source, investigate the extent to which John F. Kennedy wrote his own speeches.

6. Read Norman Thomas' *Mr. Chairman, Ladies and Gentlemen . . . Reflections of Public Speaking* (New York: Hermitage House, Inc., 1955). Describe Thomas' background as a public speaker. What advice about speaking does he present in Chapters 5–8?

THE SPEAKER IN DEFENSE OF HIMSELF

A speech in self-defense may be required of any public figure on short notice. Such an address occurred in September 1952 at Los Angeles, California. The speaker was Richard M. Nixon, vice-presidential candidate on the Republican ticket. A New York newspaper accused Nixon of unethical conduct in accepting $18,000 from California businessmen. The suspicion of corruption troubled Eisenhower-Nixon supporters, for one of their campaign slogans was "Let's clean up the mess in Washington." Americans wondered whether Eisenhower would keep Nixon as his running mate. The radio and television speech Nixon presented to a national audience on this occasion and the response of his audience to the speech would determine his political future. Recall Karl R. Wallace's four standards of ethical communication (pp. 187–190) as you read the following address.

THE EXPENSE FUND SPEECH

RICHARD M. NIXON

My fellow Americans: I come before you tonight as a candidate for the vice-presidency and as a man whose honesty and integrity has been questioned. Now, the usual political thing to do when charges are made against you is to either ignore them or to deny them without giving details. I believe we have had enough of that in the United States, particularly with the present administration in Washington, D.C. To me the office of the vice-presidency of the United States is a great office, and I feel that the people have got to have confidence in the integrity of the men who run for that office and who might attain them. I have a theory, too, that the best and only answer to a smear or to an honest misunderstanding of the facts is to tell the truth. And that is why I am here tonight. I want to tell you my side of the case. */1*

I am sure that you have read the charge, and you have heard it, that I, Senator Nixon, took $18,000 from a group of my supporters. Now, was that wrong? And let me say that it was wrong . . . I am saying it, incidentally, that it was wrong, not just illegal, because it isn't a question of whether it was legal or illegal; that isn't enough. The question is, was it morally wrong? . . . I say that it was morally wrong—if any of that $18,000 went to Senator Nixon, for my personal use. I say that it was morally wrong if it was secretly given and secretly handled. And I say that it was morally wrong if any of the contributors got special favors for the contributions that they made. */2*

Text from **U.S. News and World Report** (October 3, 1952), 66–70.

And now, to answer those questions, let me say this: Not one cent of the $18,000 or any other money of that type ever went to me for my personal use. Every penny of it was used to pay for political expenses that I did not think should be charged to the taxpayers of the United States. /3

It was not a secret fund. As a matter of fact, when I was on "Meet the Press"—some of you may have seen it, last Sunday—Peter Edson came up to me, after the program, and he said, "Dick, what about this fund we hear about?" And I said, "Well, there is no secret about it. Go out and see Dana Smith, who was the administrator of the fund," and I gave him his address. And I said, "You will find that the purpose of the fund simply was to defray political expenses that I did not feel should be charged to the government." /4

And, third, let me point out, and I want to make this particularly clear, that no contributor to this fund, no contributor to any of my campaigns, has ever received any consideration that he would not have received as an ordinary constituent. I just don't believe in that, and I can say that never, while I have been in the Senate of the United States, as far as the people that contributed to this fund are concerned, have I made a telephone call for them to an agency, nor have I gone down to an agency in their behalf. And the records will show that, the records which are in the hands of the administration. /5

Well, then, some of you will say, and rightly, "Well, what did you use the fund for, Senator? Why did you have to have it?" Let me tell you in just a word how a Senate office operates. First of all, the senator gets $15,000 a year in salary. He gets enough money to pay for one trip a year—a round trip, that is—for himself and his family, between his home and Washington, D.C.; and then he gets an allowance to handle the people that work in his office to handle his mail. And the allowance for my state of California is enough to hire thirteen people. And let me say, incidentally, that this allowance is not paid to the senator. It is paid directly to the individuals that the senator puts on his payroll, but all of these people and all of these allowances are for strictly official business—business, for example, when a constituent writes in and wants you to go down to the Veterans' Administration and get some information about his GI policy—items of that type, for example. But there are other expenses which are not covered by the government. And I think I can best discuss those expenses by asking you some questions. /6

Do you think that when I or any other senator makes a political speech, has it printed, should charge the printing of that speech and the mailing of that speech to the taxpayers? Do you think, for example, when I or any other senator makes a trip to his home state to make a purely political speech, that the cost of that trip should be charged to the taxpayers? Do you think when a senator makes political broadcasts or political television broadcasts, radio or television, that the expense of those broadcasts should be charged to the taxpayers? /7

I know what your answer is; it is the same answer that audiences give me whenever I discuss this particular problem. The answer is *no*. The taxpayers should not be required to finance items which are not official business but which are primarily political business. */8*

Well, then the question arises: You say, "Well, how do you pay for these, and how can you do it legally?" And there are several ways that it can be done, incidentally, and it is done legally in the United States Senate and in the Congress. */9*

The first way is to be a rich man. I don't happen to be a rich man. So I couldn't use that. */10*

Another way that is used is to put your wife on the payroll. Let me say, incidentally, that my opponent, my opposite number for the vice-presidency of the Democratic ticket, does have his wife on his payroll and has had her on his payroll for the past ten years. Now, just let me say this: That is his business, and I am not critical of him for doing that. You will have to pass judgment on that particular point, but I have never done that for this reason: I have found that there are so many deserving stenographers and secretaries in Washington that needed the work that I just didn't feel it was right to put my wife on the payroll—my wife sitting over here. */11*

She is a wonderful stenographer. She used to teach stenography and she used to teach shorthand in high school. That was when I met her. And I can tell you folks that she has worked many hours nights and many hours on Saturdays and Sundays in my office, and she had [sic] done a fine job, and I am proud to say tonight that in the six years I have been in the House and in the Senate of the United States, Pat Nixon has never been on the government payroll. */12*

What are other ways that these finances can be taken care of? Some who are lawyers, and I happen to be a lawyer, continue to practice law, but I haven't been able to do that. I am so far away from California and I have been so busy with my senatorial work that I have not engaged in any legal practice; and also, as far as law practice is concerned, it seemed to me that the relationship between an attorney and the client was so personal that you couldn't possibly represent a man as an attorney and then have an unbiased view when he presented his case to you in the event that he had one before the government. */13*

And so I felt that the best way to handle these necessary political expenses of getting my message to the American people and the speeches I made—the speeches that I had printed, for the most part, concerned this one message, of exposing this administration, the Communism in it, the corruption in it—the only way that I could do that was to accept the aid which people in my home state of California, who contributed to my campaign and who continued to make these contributions after I was elected, were glad to make. */14*

And let me say I am proud of the fact that not one of them has ever asked me for a special favor. I am proud of the fact that not one of them has ever asked me to vote on a bill other than my own conscience would dictate. And I am proud of the fact that the taxpayers by subterfuge or otherwise have never paid one dime for expenses which I thought were political and should not be charged to the taxpayers. */15*

Let me say, incidentally, that some of you may say, "Well, that is all right, Senator; that is your explanation, but have you got any proof?" And I would like to tell you this evening that just an hour ago we received an independent audit of this entire fund. I suggested to Governor Sherman Adams, who is the chief of staff of the Eisenhower campaign, that an independent audit and legal report be obtained, and I have that audit in my hand. It is an audit made by Price Waterhouse & Co. firm, and the legal opinion by Gibson, Dunn and Crutcher, lawyers in Los Angeles, the biggest law firm and, incidentally, one of the best ones in Los Angeles. */16*

I am proud to report to you tonight that this audit and this legal opinion is being forwarded to General Eisenhower, and I would like to read to you the opinion that was prepared by Gibson, Dunn and Crutcher, based on all the pertinent laws and statutes, together with the audit report prepared by the certified public accountants:

> It is our conclusion that Senator Nixon did not obtain any financial gain from the collection and disbursement of the funds by Dana Smith; that Senator Nixon did not violate any federal or state law by reason of the operation of the fund; and that neither the portion of the fund paid by Dana Smith directly to third persons, nor the portion paid to Senator Nixon, to reimburse him for office expenses, constituted income in a sense which was either reportable or taxable as income under income tax laws.
>
> (signed)
> Gibson, Dunn and Crutcher,
> by Elmo H. Conley

That is not Nixon speaking, but that is an independent audit which was requested because I want the American people to know all the facts, and I am not afraid of having independent people go in and check the facts, and that is exactly what they did. */17*

But then I realized that there are still some who may say, and rightly so—and let me say that I recognize that some will continue to smear, regardless of what the truth may be—but that there has been, understandably, some honest misunderstanding on this matter, and there are some that will say, "Well, maybe you were able, Senator, to fake this thing. How can we believe what you say—after all, is there a possibility that maybe you got some sums in cash? Is there a possibility that you might have feathered your own nest?" And so now what I am going to do—and, incidentally, this is unprecedented in the history of the American politics—I am going at this time to give to this television and radio audience a complete financial history, everything I have earned, everything I have spent, everything I own, and I want you to know the facts. */18*

I will have to start early. I was born in 1913. Our family was one of modest circumstances, and most of my early life was spent in a store, out in East Whittier. It was a grocery store, one of those family enterprises. The only reason we were able to make it go was because my Mother and Dad had five boys, and we all worked in the store. I worked my way through college and, to a great extent, through law school. And then, in 1940, probably the best thing that ever happened to me happened. I married Pat, who is sitting over here. */19*

We had a rather difficult time, after we were married, like so many of the young couples who might be listening to us. I practiced law. She continued to teach school. */20*

Then, in 1942, I went into the service. Let me say that my service record was not a particularly unusual one. I went to the South Pacific. I guess I'm entitled to a couple of battle stars. I got a couple of letters of commendation. But I was just there when the bombs were falling. And then I returned. I returned to the United States, and 1946, I ran for Congress. When we came out of the war, Pat and I—Pat during the war had worked as a stenographer, and in a bank, and as an economist for a government agency—and when we came out, the total of our savings, from both my law practice, her teaching, and all the time that I was in the war, the total for that entire period was just a little less than $10,000. Every cent of that, incidentally, was in government bonds. Well, that's where we start, when I go into politics. */21*

Now, whatever I earned since I went into politics—well, here it is. I jotted it down. Let me read the notes. First of all, I have had my salary as a congressman and as a senator. Second, I have received a total in this past six years of $1600 from estates which were in my law firm at the time that I severed my connection with it. And, incidentally, as I said before, I have not engaged in any legal practice, and have not accepted any fees from business that came into the firm after I went into politics. I have made an average of approximately $1500 a year, from nonpolitical speaking engagements and lectures. And then, fortunately, we have inherited a little money. Pat sold her interest in her father's estate for $3000, and I inherited $1500 from my grandfather. We lived rather modestly. */22*

For four years we lived in an apartment in Parkfairfax, Alexandria, Virginia. The rent was $80 a month. And we saved for the time that we could buy a house. Now, that was what we took in. */23*

What did we do with this money? What do we have today to show for it? This will surprise you, because it is so little, I suppose, as standards generally go of people in public life. First of all, we've got a house in Washington, which cost $41,000 and on which we owe $20,000. We have a house in Whittier, California, which cost $13,000, and on which we owe $3000 [see par. 25]. My folks are living there at the present time. I have just $4000 in life insurance, plus my GI policy, which I have never been able to convert, and which will run out in two years. I have no life insurance whatever on Pat. I have no life insurance on our two youngsters, Patricia and Julie. I own a 1950 Oldsmobile car. We have our furniture. We have no stocks and bonds of any type. We have no interest of any kind, direct or indirect, in any business. Now, that is what we have. What do we owe? */24*

Well, in addition to the mortgage, the $20,000 mortgage on the house in Washington, a $10,000 one[1] on the house in Whittier, I owe $4500 to the Riggs Bank, in Washington, D.C., with interest at 4 per cent. I owe $3500 to my parents, and the interest on that loan, which I pay regularly because it is a part of the savings they made through the years they were working so hard—I pay regularly 4 per cent interest. And then I have a $500 loan, which I have on my life insurance. */25*

Well, that's about it. That's what we have. And that's what we owe. It isn't very much. But Pat and I have the satisfaction that every dime that we have got is honestly ours. */26*

I should say this, that Pat doesn't have a mink coat. But she does have a respectable Republican cloth coat, and I always tell her that she would look good in anything. */27*

One other thing I probably should tell you, because if I don't they will probably be saying this about me, too. We did get something, a gift, after the election. A man down in Texas heard Pat on the radio mention the fact that our two youngsters would like to have a dog, and, believe it or not, the day before we left on this campaign trip we got a message from Union Station in Baltimore, saying they had a package for us. We went down to get it. You know what it was? */28*

It was a little cocker spaniel dog, in a crate that he had sent all the way from Texas, black and white, spotted, and our little girl, Tricia, the six-year-old, named it Checkers. And, you know, the kids, like all kids, loved the dog, and I just want to say this, right now, that regardless of what they say about it, we are going to keep it. */29*

It isn't easy to come before a nation-wide audience and bare your life, as I have done. But I want to say some things before I conclude, that I think most of you will agree on. */30*

Mr. Mitchell, the Chairman of the Democratic National Committee, made the statement that if a man couldn't afford to be in the United States Senate, he shouldn't run for the Senate. And I just want to make my position clear. I don't agree with Mr. Mitchell when he says that only a rich man should serve his government, in the United States Senate or in the Congress. I don't believe that represents the thinking of the Democratic party, and I know it doesn't represent the thinking of the Republican party. */31*

[1]Nixon indicates (par. 24) that the mortgage on the $13,000 home in Whittier is $3000, and here that it is $10,000. The latter figure is correct, Nixon's secretary, James Bassett, told reporters later, explaining the discrepancy as "a verbal error."

I believe that it's fine that a man like Governor Stevenson, who inherited a fortune from his father, can run for President. But I also feel that it is essential in this country of ours that a man of modest means can also run for President, because, you know—remember Abraham Lincoln—you remember what he said—"God must have loved the common people, he made so many of them." /32

And now I'm going to suggest some courses of conduct. /33

First of all, you have read in the papers about other funds, now. Mr. Stevenson apparently had a couple. One of them in which a group of business people paid and helped to supplement the salaries of state employes. Here is where the money went directly into their pockets, and I think that what Mr. Stevenson should do should be to come before the American people, as I have, give the names of the people that contributed to that fund, give the names of the people who put this money into their pockets, at the same time that they were receiving money from their state government and see what favors, if any, they gave out for that. /34

I don't condemn Mr. Stevenson for what he did, but until the facts are in there is a doubt that would be raised. And as far as Mr. Sparkman is concerned, I would suggest the same thing. He's had his wife on the payroll. I don't condemn him for that, but I think that he should come before the American people and indicate what outside sources of income he has had. I would suggest that under the circumstances both Mr. Sparkman and Mr. Stevenson should come before the American people, as I have, and make a complete financial statement as to their financial history, and if they don't it will be an admission that they have something to hide. /35

And I think you will agree with me—because, folks, remember, a man that's to be President of the United States, a man that is to be Vice-President of the United States, must have the confidence of all the people. And that's why I'm doing what I'm doing, and that is why I suggest that Mr. Stevenson and Mr. Sparkman, if they are under attack, that should be what they are doing. /36

Now, let me say this: I know that this is not the last of the smears. In spite of my explanation tonight, other smears will be made. Others have been made in the past. And the purpose of the smears, I know, is this, to silence me, to make me let up. Well, they just don't know who they are dealing with. I'm going to tell you this: I remember, in the dark days of the Hiss trial, some of the same columnists, some of the same radio commentators who are attacking me now and misrepresenting my position, were violently opposing me at the time I was after Alger Hiss. But I continued to fight, because I knew I was right, and I can say to this great television and radio audience that I have no apologies to the American people for my part in putting Alger Hiss where he is today. And as far as this is concerned, I intend to continue to fight. /37

Why do I feel so deeply? Why do I feel that in spite of the smears, the misunderstanding, the necessity for a man to come up here and bare his soul, as I have—why is it necessary for me to continue this fight? And I want to tell you why. Because, you see, I love my country. And I think my country is in danger. And I think the only man that can save America at this time is the man that's running for President, on my ticket, Dwight Eisenhower. */38*

You say, why do I think it is in danger? And I say, look at the record. Seven years of the Truman-Acheson Administration, and what's happened? Six hundred million people lost to the Communists. And a war in Korea in which we have lost 117,000 American casualties, and I say to all of you that a policy that results in a loss of 600,000,000 people to the Communists and a war which costs us 117,000 American casualties isn't good enough for America, and I say that those in the State Department that made the mistakes which caused that war and which resulted in those losses should be kicked out of the State Department just as fast as we can get them out of there. */39*

And let me say that I know Mr. Stevenson won't do that, because he defends the Truman policy, and I know that Dwight Eisenhower will do that, and that he will give America the leadership that it needs. */40*

Take the problem of corruption. You have read about the mess in Washington. Mr. Stevenson can't clean it up because he was picked by the man, Truman, under whose administration the mess was made. You wouldn't trust the man who made the mess to clean it up. That is Truman. And, by the same token you can't trust the man who was picked by the man who made the mess to clean it up, and that is Stevenson. And so I say, Eisenhower, who owes nothing to Truman, nothing to the big-city bosses—he is the man who can clean up the mess in Washington. */41*

Take Communism. I say that as far as that subject is concerned the danger is great to America. In the Hiss case they got the secrets which enabled them to break the American secret State Department code. They got secrets in the atomic-bomb case which enabled them to get the secret of the atomic bomb five years before they would have gotten it by their own devices. And I say that any man who called the Alger Hiss case a red herring isn't fit to be President of the United States. */42*

I say that a man who, like Mr. Stevenson, has pooh-poohed and ridiculed the Communist threat in the United States—he said that they are phantoms among ourselves—he has accused us, that have attempted to expose the Communists, of looking for Communists in the Bureau of Fisheries and Wildlife. I say that a man who says that isn't qualified to be President of the United States. And I say that the only man who can lead us into this fight to rid the government of both those who are Communists and those who have corrupted this government is Eisenhower, because General Eisenhower, you can be sure, recognizes the problem, and knows how to handle it. */43*

Let me say this, finally. This evening I want to read to you just briefly excerpts from a letter that I received, a letter which after all this is over no one can take away from us. It reads as follows:

Dear Senator Nixon: Since I am only nineteen years of age, I can't vote in this presidential election, but believe me, if I could, you and General Eisenhower would certainly get my vote. My husband is in the Fleet Marines in Korea. He is in the front lines. And we have a two-months-old son he has never seen. And I feel confident that with great Americans like you and General Eisenhower in the White House, lonely Americans like myself will be united with their loved ones now in Korea. I only pray to God that you won't be too late. Enclosed is a small check to help you in your campaign. Living on $85 a month, it is all I can afford at present, but let me know what else I can do. */44*

Folks, it is a check for $10, and it is one that I shall never cash. And just let me say this: We hear a lot about prosperity these days, but I say why can't we have prosperity built on peace, rather than prosperity built on war? Why can't we have prosperity and an honest government in Washington, D.C., at the same time? Believe me, we can. And Eisenhower is the man that can lead the crusade to bring us that kind of prosperity. */45*

And, now, finally, I know that you wonder whether or not I am going to stay on the Republican ticket or resign. Let me say this: I don't believe that I ought to quit, because I am not a quitter. And, incidentally, Pat is not a quitter. After all, her name was Patricia Ryan and she was born on St. Patrick's Day, and you know the Irish never quit. */46*

But the decision, my friends, is not mine. I would do nothing that would harm the possibilities of Dwight Eisenhower to become President of the United States. And for that reason I am submitting to the Republican National Committee tonight through this television broadcast the decision which it is theirs to make. Let them decide whether my position on the ticket will help or hurt. And I am going to ask you to help them decide. Wire and write the Republican National Committee whether you think I should stay on or whether I should get off. And whatever their decision is, I will abide by it. */47*

But just let me say this last word. Regardless of what happens, I am going to continue this fight. I am going to campaign up and down America until we drive the crooks and the Communists and those that defend them out of Washington, and remember, folks, Eisenhower is a great man, and a vote for Eisenhower is a vote for what is good for America. */48*

The response to Nixon's remarks was immediate and generally favorable. Affirmative telegrams and letters from all over America flooded the Republican National Committee, state committees, the Eisenhower and Nixon staffs, and the broadcasting stations. In a conversation with this author, Robert T. Oliver labeled the Nixon address one of the ten most effective speeches ever delivered in America.

QUESTIONS

1. Nixon says that his "honesty and integrity" have been questioned. What is the difference in the meaning of these two terms? How do they differ from *probity* and *veracity?*

2. In his first paragraph, the speaker says that "the best and only answer to a smear . . . is to tell the truth." Are you convinced that Nixon accepted $18,000 from his supporters for political purposes only? Can a clear-cut distinction be made between political expenditures and personal expenditures?

3. Senator Paul Douglas of Illinois once said that he never accepts a personal gift worth more than $2.50. Does this policy strike you as commendable or foolhardy for a political figure who is not independently wealthy?

4. Is Nixon rationalizing when he says (par. 3) that "every penny" of the $18,000 "was used to pay for political expenses that I did not think should be charged to the taxpayers"? Explain your answer.

5. Is it possible for a political party to pay some of the admittedly large, routine political expenses of a member of Congress? Why or why not?

6. Since the acceptance of funds from political supporters for political purposes is not illegal, why was Nixon's television address necessary?

7. Although this speech is predominantly defensive, Nixon does attack his opponents from time to time. What examples of political attack do you find?

8. Nixon twice indicates that the Democrat vice-presidential nominee, Senator Sparkman, employs his wife as an office staff member. The speaker further indicates that he is not criticizing Sparkman for this; why then do you think he includes these references?

9. What was the special significance of such terms as *Communism, corruption,* and *mink coats* in 1952?

10. Did Stephen Mitchell say that only a rich man should serve in Congress (par. 31), or is this an interpretation by Nixon?

11. How does Nixon try to identify himself with significant blocs of voters?

12. Some opponents described Nixon's speech as "political corn." What does this slang expression mean? Why do you think the label is, or is not, justified?

PROJECTS

1. Investigate and report on the number of Americans who saw or heard Nixon deliver this speech. How many followed his suggestion to contact the Republican National Committee, according to *The New York Times?*

2. Get a copy of Nixon's book *Six Crises* (Garden City, N.Y.: Doubleday & Company, Inc., 1962) and read his account of "The Fund." What new information is presented here which does not appear in the speech?

3. Would Karl R. Wallace (pp. 181–190) consider this address ethical? Prepare a 500-word essay in defense of your answer.

4. To what events preceding his speech does Nixon refer in paragraph 1? Check Section 4 of *The New York Times* for that period.

5. Discuss provisions of the Hatch Act that relate to political expenditures. Why has it been so difficult to enact legislation limiting the amount a candidate may spend? How do senators and representatives who are not wealthy finance their campaigns?

6. Examine back issues of *The New York Times* relating to the trial of Alger Hiss. Who is Hiss, and what crime was he charged with? What part did Nixon play in the trial? What was the verdict? Where is Hiss now?

7. Describe events which led up to Communist seizure of Poland, East Germany, and the Balkans. What agreements were made respecting this part of the Continent at Yalta? Why were these agreements later ignored?

8. Describe the State Department's *policy of containment.* Have Presidents from both political parties supported this policy? What troop concentrations of the United States stand ready to enforce this policy?

9. Compare the "Red Scare" of the early 1920's with the Communist scare of the 1950's. What caused these periods of fear? Why did these fears subside? Consult Robert K. Murray's *Red Scare: A Study in National Hysteria, 1919–1920* (Minneapolis, Minn.: University of Minnesota Press, 1955) as a reference for the earlier period.

APPENDIX

SPEECH AS A LIBERAL STUDY

GORDON F. HOSTETTLER

It is paradoxical that speech, one of the oldest studies known to man, is called upon so often to defend its claim to a place amid the liberal arts. For rhetoric, which to Greeks and Romans alike meant persuasion through speech, was not only a major area for study in classical civilization; it was, even more, the essential core of higher learning.[1] From the days of Plato, however, the effective speaker and his art, rhetoric itself, have been frequently regarded with suspicion and at times subjected to downright condemnation. As Charles Sears Baldwin has said: "Again and again educational practice has found that it cannot do without rhetoric; again and again educational theory has grudgingly inquired what to do with it."[2] It is the purpose of this paper to define the role of speech in liberal education; to consider major objections which have been laid to speech as an academic subject; and to set forth principles upon which the modern department of speech should, and does, function.

Language, symbolic communication, differentiates man from other life forms. In the words of anthropologist Leslie White: "All culture (civilization) depends upon the symbol. . . . Without the symbol there would be no culture, and man would be merely an animal, not a human being."[3] Unlike other forms of life, man is a "time-binder"—Korzybski's term—because language enables him to profit from the experiences of previous generations, to accumulate knowledge, and to establish complex systems and institutions.[4] Modern society, with its intricate divisions of labor and its interdependent human activities, would be impossible if man did not possess the ability to symbolize—to communicate through speech and writing. These truths have long been recognized. In ancient Greece, Isocrates observed: "Because there has been planted in us the power to persuade each other and to make clear to each other whatever we desire, we not only have escaped the life of wild beasts, but we have come together and founded cities and made laws and invented arts; and . . . there is no institution devised by man which the power of speech has not helped us to establish."[5]

In 1651 Thomas Hobbes declared: "The most notable and profitable invention of all others was that of speech . . . without which there had been amongst men neither Commonwealth, nor Society, nor Contract, nor Peace, no more than amongst Lyons, Bears, and Wolves."[6] And a modern student, Henry Lee Smith, concurs: "Language is . . . the very mask of humanity, for man is human only by virtue of *human* communication systems, of which language is the hub and center. To understand language and the communication processes

From **The Pennsylvania Speech Annual** (September 1962), 12–28. This paper was written at the request of an administrator at Temple University, where Dr. Hostettler was Chairman of the Department of Speech and Dramatic Arts, to explain the aims and practices of speech courses as they relate to liberal education.

[1]Charles Sears Baldwin, **Ancient Rhetoric and Poetic** (New York: The Macmillan Company, 1924), pp. 85–86. For a detailed account of the centrality of rhetoric in ancient education, see Donald Lemon Clark, **Rhetoric in Greco-Roman Education** (New York: Columbia University Press, 1957). Quintilian's **Institutio Oratoria** is the best contemporary account of the role of rhetoric and of the ways other subjects were related to it.

[2]**Medieval Rhetoric and Poetic** (New York: The Macmillan Company, 1928), p. 2.

[3]"The Symbol: The Origin and Basis of Human Behavior," **Philosophy of Science** (October 1940), 460.

[4]The concept of "time-binding" was first expounded by Alfred Korzybski in **The Manhood of Humanity** (New York: E. P. Dutton & Co., Inc., 1921). His basic idea was later developed into his system, General Semantics. See his **Science and Sanity** (Lancaster, Pa.: Science Press Printing Company, 1933).

[5]**Antidosis**, trans. George Norlin, Vol. I (London: William Heinemann, Ltd., Loeb Classical Library, 1928), XVI.

[6]**Leviathan** (London: J. M. Dent & Sons, Ltd., Everyman's Library, 1934), p. 12.

clustered about it is, then, in a very real sense to understand the essence of our humanity."[7] It seems not immoderate to claim that a study which would lead students "to understand the essence of our humanity" should have a place, even a central place, in a liberal curriculum.

But should that study be speech? There are many who hold that courses in written composition and in literature provide an ample understanding of language processes and that speech, therefore, is not needed as an academic subject. The view is erroneous. Speech precedes writing and is fundamental to it. Although written and spoken language have some characteristics in common, there are sharp differences between them. An effective speech is not "an essay on its hind legs." Written language must be ultimately intelligible to the reader; spoken language must be instantly intelligible to the hearer. What may be an aid in one form may hinder communication in the other. Vocabulary and even structure differ. Effective spoken language is more idiomatic, more direct, more specific.[8] Auditors react to more than words. They respond, as well, to bodily motions, facial expressions, tones of voice (paralanguage), and these are vital culture clues in communication. Speech is closer than writing to culture because speech is essential to it. As Smith, himself a professor of English, declares: "But language is not words. It is far more than that. It is a system, a pattern, a structure of communication. Writing is for the most part no more than an incomplete and inconsistent *symbolization* of the communicative processes associated with language. But for the group that speaks it, language symbolizes the common experience, the culture, of the group. Writing, then, actually is *a symbolization of a symbolization.*"[9]

The foregoing is established not to deprecate the art of writing, but to make clear the case for speech. The writer agrees that "writing is certainly one of the two or three greatest of all man's inventions,"[10] and that it deserves a prominent place in a liberal curriculum. The indispensable points are that the ability to symbolize makes us human and that speech is the more basic mode of language. To acquire an understanding of the processes essential to speech and to develop skills in speaking are simply more fundamental than to gain an understanding of and skills in writing. Failure to recognize these inherent facts accounts, in large measure, for the reluctance of many scholars to support speech as a necessary academic subject. Again Smith well makes the point: "But language precedes writing. We must constantly remind ourselves that language is as old as man. Writing, on the other hand, has a history of only a few thousand years. The distinction is a critical one. Speech is prior to writing in every sense, but the unhappy confusion between language and writing continues to be universal among all literate people. This universal confusion between speech and writing is today the principal obstacle to a clear understanding of the nature and function of language."[11]

If "this universal confusion between speech and writing" can be recognized and eliminated, the case for speech will have been far advanced; for if "speech is prior to writing in every sense," it would seem to have a compelling claim upon the liberal curriculum. Few, to this writer's knowledge, call for the elimination of written composition. Indeed, there seems to be almost unanimous agreement that skill in writing is so important that it should be required of all students.

But the case is not complete. Are there objections to the study of speech, to the ways in which it is conceived and taught, which may tend to mitigate arguments to this point? There are, and they must be considered to establish the case for speech. In general, there are two major positions which

[7]"Linguistics: A Modern View of Language" in **An Outline of Man's Knowledge of the Modern World**, ed. Lyman Bryson (New York: McGraw-Hill Book Co., Inc., 1960), p. 344.

[8]Raymond F. Howes, "The Talked and the Written," **The Quarterly Journal of Speech** (April 1940), 231–234.

[9]Smith, p. 344. The italics are Smith's.

[10]Smith, p. 345.

[11]Smith, p. 345. Howes, p. 231, makes the same point.

opponents of speech have taken. One is an argument of substance; the other is not. The latter will be examined first.

The argument is often advanced that speech is a mere skill and, hence, is entitled to no legitimate place in liberal education. The position is spurious. That the ability to communicate effectively is something of a skill no one would deny. So the first part of the argument is conceded. But what of the second? Can we safely and consistently take the position that all courses which involve skill are to be eliminated from liberal studies? If we do, we shall find precious little left. First, let it be observed that the argument is rarely, if ever, advanced against written composition. Is not the ability to write with effect also a skill? And what of other areas? Is not skill involved in speaking, writing, and reading a foreign language? In solving problems in algebra and calculus? In manipulating equipment and measuring devices in science laboratories? In judging syllogisms? In the memorization essential in any course? No, it is not "skill" *per se* which bothers critics of speech. Instruction in skills often constitutes a significant part of their own disciplines. It is something more, and that "more" we shall examine shortly.

But there is yet another facet to the argument which rests upon the issue of skills. When confronted with the preceding argument, academicians opposed to speech sometimes respond with the declarations that, although skill may play a part in their own disciplines, it is not the central core and that a significant body of worthwhile knowledge provides the main focus. The implication in such a reply is that a similar claim cannot be made for the study of speech. Here the argument seems to resolve to a charge that speech is *only* a skill. Such a contention can only be contradicted, for it simply is not true. Space contravenes against a detailed account of speech as an academic discipline. Suffice it to say that the process of oral communication is most complex. Every speaking situation involves a speaker, a subject, a speech, an occasion for speech, an audience, and the interaction of these factors. From another point of view, every act of speech includes motivation for talk, thought and feeling, symbolization, vocalization and delivery, sound transmission, physical reception, reaction of auditors, and the response of the speaker to these reactions. An adequate understanding of oral communication and its role in society—objectives by no means yet attained—necessitates a knowledge of anatomy, acoustics, phonetics, language, semantics, psychology, logic, ethics, history, and the social sciences. Pertinent materials from these areas are incorporated, synthesized, and taught in speech; for modern speech courses are directed toward attaining an understanding of the processes and effects of speech as well as toward developing skills in formal and informal communication. As a president of the Speech Association of America has said: "The field of speech is an area whose twin aims are to understand the functions, processes, and effects of oral communication and to teach the principles and methods that make the spoken word effective."[12] Moreover, speech commands a significant province of its own. From Aristotle's day and before, teachers of rhetoric, the art of effective speech, have been concerned with principles essential for efficient oral communication. These embrace logical analysis of controversy, collecting and evaluating evidence, proper reasoning, clear organization of thought, the ethics needed in any communicative situation, audience analysis, clear and artistic use of language, methods of presentation, and criteria for critical listening and evaluation. This writer maintains that these principles constitute a significant body of content and that they are essential for a liberally educated man. If there are those who deprecate them, he is content to rest his argument and rely upon the judgment of those who understand and cherish humane studies.

And even if for the sake of argument (but *only* for the sake of argument) it were granted that courses in oral communication are primarily concerned with skills, the case for speech as a humane study is still compelling. One

[12]Karl R. Wallace, "The Field of Speech, 1953—An Overview," **The Quarterly Journal of Speech** (April 1954), 117.

definition of liberal education, comparable to most, declares that its "central purpose . . . is to develop men of tempered mind, civilized taste, and independent convictions, men fit to take their place as citizens of a free society."[13] Now, a free society is posited on the assumptions that we shall be governed by persuasion and reason; that its leaders, both in and out of power, shall communicate their programs and policies to the electorate; and that the people, responding through elections and other free institutions, can be trusted to exercise final authority in the state. Freedom of speech, of the press, of assembly are recognized universally as fundamental prerequisites to our democratic way of life. So we may well ask, how can a man be fit to take his place in a free society if he does not possess the abilities, yes, the skills, essential to the operation of that society? How can our students exercise effectively the right of free speech if they receive no instruction in the practice and principles of speech? Truth and knowledge, unaided, will not necessarily prevail. If free society is to survive, good men must know how—yes, possess the skills—to win their fellow men to truth. "More than once," Norman Thomas testifies, "I have heard good men come out second best to demagogs because they have depended upon their righteous indignation. . . . "[14] And George Saintsbury, the noted historian of literary criticism, adds: "Book-education by itself is education of the most wretchedly inadequate character."[15] The difficulties of many scholars, standing almost inarticulate when called upon to communicate their knowledge and ideas, are all too familiar. It is here contended that liberal education is obligated to provide its graduates with the ability to communicate effectively—by oral as well as written means. To do less is to deprive them of requisites for meaningful participation in free society. Even if speech is regarded as "merely a skill," it provides a skill essential for free men.

But there is a more substantial objection to speech, and from this view springs the basic, and most meaningful, argument against it as a needed liberal study. Reference is to the charges that effective speakers are often dangerous, that persuasion is an essential tool of demagogs, and that "tricks of oratory" are frequently employed to delude or inflame. In short, this view holds that instruction in speech encourages sophistical chicanery. It was from these conceptions that Plato, especially in the *Gorgias*, inveighed against rhetoric, calling it a form of flattery and likening it to cookery. The argument has continued since his day. "The first persuader was the devil," declares Everett Lee Hunt, "and . . . there always has been and always will be something devilish about persuasion."[16] Norman Thomas observes that "not without reason, oratory has been called the harlot of the arts, so subject it is to abuse and degradation."[17] As Baldwin states: "Plato's distrust of rhetoric is a permanent reminder. It is so significantly typical that it recurs throughout the history of education, and must recur."[18] It must recur because there has been, and there is, ample basis for it. The sophistical practice and teaching which Plato condemned is not restricted to antiquity. There are direct lines running from Gorgias, to Seneca, to Philostratus, to Dio Chrysostom, to Geoffrey of Vinsauf, to Richard Sherry and Henry Peacham, to Thomas Sheridan and John Walker, to Delsarte and MacKaye, to Dale Carnegie and the hucksters of Madison Avenue. All these men represent an aspect of the sophistic tradition. All treat rhetoric

[13]Carl Billman, Secretary of Phi Beta Kappa, in a letter to members, November 11, 1960.

[14]"Random Reflections on Public Speaking," **The Quarterly Journal of Speech** (April 1954), 146.

[15]**A History of Criticism**, 2nd ed., Vol. I (Edinburgh: William Blackwood & Sons, Ltd., 1934), 139.

[16]"Rhetoric as a Humane Study," **The Quarterly Journal of Speech** (April 1955), 114.

[17]Thomas, p. 146. Similar views are voiced by Aldous Huxley, **The Devils of Loudun** (New York: Harper & Brothers, 1953), pp. 18–19; Hugh Nibley, "*Victoriosa Locquacitas*: The Rise of Rhetoric and the Decline of Everything Else," **Western Speech** (Spring 1956), 57–82; and V. E. Simrell, "Mere Rhetoric," **The Quarterly Journal of Speech** (June 1928), 359–374.

[18]**Medieval Rhetoric and Poetic**, p. 2.

as an art of personal display or as an instrument of personal power. They differ in emphasizing various aspects of rhetoric; but, whatever their centuries, they are governed by a common motivation. In Baldwin's words: "The conception animating the practice and teaching of sophistic, far from being limited to antiquity, is medieval as well, and modern. Apparently it is permanent."[19]

If the preceding told the whole story, if the primary functions of rhetoric are, and have been, "to make the worse reason appear the better" and to serve as a mere vehicle for personal power and aggrandizement, this writer would abandon his argument and join with the opponents of speech. Happily, rhetoric is not, and has not been, so limited. There is another tradition —a tradition as old, more constant, more nobly conceived. Indeed, its existence enables us, by contrast, to apply the label "sophistic" to its rival. It, too, dates from antiquity. It, too, has lines—lines which run from Aristotle, to Cicero and Quintilian, to Saint Augustine, to Leonard Cox and Thomas Wilson, to Thomas Hobbes and Francis Bacon, to George Campbell and Richard Whately, to John Quincy Adams, to Chauncey Goodrich and Edward Channing, to Winans, O'Neill, Phillips, Hudson, Hunt, Wichelns, Baird, and other founders and leaders of modern speech departments. Plato himself helped found the better tradition when in the *Phaedrus* he had Socrates say: "But perhaps rhetoric has been getting too roughly handled by us, and she might answer: What amazing nonsense you are talking! As if I forced any man to learn to speak in ignorance of the truth! Whatever my advice may be worth, I should have told him to arrive at the truth first, and then come to me. At the same time I boldly assert that mere knowledge of the truth will not give you the art of persuasion."[20]

Moreover, after outlining the kinds of knowledge essential for an orator,[21] Plato specifically approves the study of rhetoric: "And this skill [rhetoric] he will not attain without a great deal of trouble, *which a good man ought to undergo*, not for the sake of speaking and acting before men, but in order that he may be able to say what is acceptable to God . . . as far as in him lies."[22]

Taking such cues from his mentor, Aristotle composed his *Rhetoric*. Called "one of the world's best and wisest books,"[23] it is "the most important single work in the literature of speechcraft."[24] Aristotle viewed rhetoric as "the counterpart of dialectic"[25] and defined it as "the faculty of discovering in the particular case what are the available means of persuasion."[26] Its basic function, he asserted, is to make "truth and justice" prevail.[27] Here, then, is the answer of traditional rhetoric to sophistic. As Baldwin declares: "The ultimate, the only final answer to Plato's challenge is the *Rhetoric* of Aristotle. . . . The true theory of rhetoric as the energizing of knowledge, the bringing of truth to bear upon men, is there established for all time. Aristotle amply vindicated rhetoric by defining its place among studies, its necessary correlation with inquiry and with policy, its permanent function. He settled the question of rhetoric philosophically."[28]

The classical rhetorical tradition, the basis of modern speech instruction, stems from Aristotle. Rhetoric, as taught by Cicero, Quintilian, and other Aristotelians, was conceived as containing five major canons: *inventio, dispositio, elocutio, pronuntiatio*, and *memoria*—investigation and analysis of subject matter, arrangement, style, delivery, and memory. Of these the touchstone is *inventio*. When speech is taught and practiced as an agency for making truth prevail, primary emphasis must be given to methods of

[19]**Medieval Rhetoric and Poetic**, p. 3.
[20]**The Dialogues of Plato**, trans. Benjamin Jowett, 3rd ed., Vol. I (New York: Random House, Inc., 1937), 264.
[21]Jowett, pp. 274–275.
[22]Jowett, p. 277. The italics are Hostettler's.
[23]Lane Cooper, **The Rhetoric of Aristotle** (New York: D. Appleton & Company, 1932), p. vii.
[24]Lester Thonssen and A. Craig Baird, **Speech Criticism** (New York: The Ronald Press Company, 1948), p. 57.
[25]**Rhetoric**, 1354a, in Cooper, p. 1.
[26]**Rhetoric**, 1355b, in Cooper, p. 7.
[27]**Rhetoric**, 1355a, in Cooper, p. 5.
[28]**Medieval Rhetoric and Poetic**, p. 3.

discovery and analysis which lead to sound ideas. Under these conditions the other rhetorical divisions, concerned primarily with techniques, are subordinated to *inventio* and are studied only as means necessary to make ideas effective.

Whenever another of the divisions, for whatever reasons, occupies the center of teaching and practice, a form of sophistic is the inevitable result. Ornate style and clever verbalisms characterized the Second Sophistic during the latter centuries of the Roman Empire.[29] The elocutionary movement of the eighteenth and nineteenth centuries went to absurd extremes in its emphasis upon pronunciation, vocal inflection, and delivery.[30] Sophistic stress on style or delivery arises when rhetoric is conceived as an art of providing a speaker with techniques which will enable him to gain personal power or triumphs. Baldwin phrases it well: "What has intervened to deviate rhetoric and frustrate its best use again and again has been the preoccupation with giving effectiveness not to the message, but to the speaker."[31] Given the ambitions of men and given the fact that communication is requisite for all human enterprise, debasement of traditional rhetorical concepts is an omnipresent danger. We must agree with Hunt that: "The history of rhetoric shows how often and how readily it slips from its high estate and well deserves all the harsh things said about it by Plato. In its protean forms it is at home in institutes of salesmanship, in seminaries of charm and personality, in the psychology of advertising, in propaganda machines that wage hot and cold wars, in defense of intolerance, racial hatred, and special privilege. . . ."[32]

"There may be a better rhetoric," some may conclude, "but if it is so subject to debasement, we had better agree that it is too dangerous for a liberal curriculum and devote our attention to less hazardous arts and sciences. Let us remain safe by patiently seeking knowledge for its own sake." This doctrine, the idea that liberal education is complete when a student has learned "the best that has been thought and said," is all too common. It lies at the base of the "ivory tower" theory. To accept it is to abdicate, to hold that liberal study sustains no meaningful hope for men who must contend with the problems and crises of our time. For as Sir Philip Sidney cried: "To what purpose should our thoughts be directed to various kinds of knowledge unless room be afforded for putting it into practice?"[33] Implicit in the argument that to know is sufficient unto itself is the notion that truth will prevail on its own account. The view is naive. As Bryant notes, "In the Kingdom of Heaven truth may be its own sole advocate, but it needs mighty help if it is to survive in health among the nations on earth."[34] And rhetoric, its study and practice, is the major agency to make truth effective among men. Moreover, the view is inconsistent. If truth will prevail on its own accord, if persuasion is inherent in it, why should opponents of speech be so concerned about misuses of rhetoric? Their concern reveals that

[29]See Harry Caplan, "The Decay of Eloquence at Rome in the First Century," **Studies in Speech and Drama in Honor of Alexander M. Drummond** (Ithaca, N. Y.: Cornell University Press, 1944), pp. 293–325; Nibley, pp. 57–82; Thonssen and Baird, pp. 96–105; Baldwin, **Ancient Rhetoric and Poetic**, pp. 87–101; and Baldwin, **Medieval Rhetoric and Poetic**, pp. 8–50.

[30]See William P. Sandford, **English Theories of Public Address, 1530–1828**, 2nd ed. (Columbus, Ohio: Harold L. Hedrick, 1938), pp. 127–137. See also Frederick W. Haberman, "English Sources of American Elocution," pp. 105–128; Marie Hochmuth and Richard Murphy, "Rhetorical and Elocutionary Training in Nineteenth Century Colleges," pp. 153–177; Mary M. Robb, "The Elocutionary Movement and Its Chief Figures," pp. 178–201; and Claude L. Shaver, "Steele MacKaye and the Delsartian Tradition," pp. 202–218, all in **A History of Speech Education in America**, ed. Karl R. Wallace (New York: Appleton-Century-Crofts, Inc., 1954).

[31]**Medieval Rhetoric and Poetic**, p. 4.

[32]Everett Lee Hunt, "Rhetoric and General Education," **The Quarterly Journal of Speech** (October 1949), 277.

[33]As cited by Donald Lemon Clark, "The Place of Rhetoric in a Liberal Education," **The Quarterly Journal of Speech** (October 1950), 292.

[34]Donald C. Bryant, "Rhetoric: Its Functions and Its Scope," **The Quarterly Journal of Speech** (December 1953), 409.

all too often, as they really know, charlatans and fools defeat truth and are successful in winning assent to falsehood or nonsense. Only a classically oriented rhetoric, understood and capably practiced by men of goodwill, supplies the needed corrective.

"Whether we will or no," Bryant declares, "we cannot escape rhetoric, either the doing or the being done to. We require it. . . ."[35] We require it because man lives by communication. Even the opponents of speech, including Plato in his *Gorgias*, must resort to rhetorical argument to assail rhetoric itself.[36] If truth is to prevail it must be communicated. A resolution by the American Association for the Advancement of Science underlines this obvious fact: "The work of the scientist is not truly completed until his significant results are communicated, not merely to other scientists, but to the public at large."[37] The essential question posed for the liberal curriculum is: Shall it provide its students, we hope the bearers of truth, with means for making it effective? Echoing the tradition of Aristotle, Cicero, and Quintilian, Saint Augustine provides us with the response of classical rhetoric. Faced with the contention that Christian preachers should forego the study of rhetoric, the art of pagan *declamatores* of the Second Sophistic, he replied: "Who dare say that the defenders of truth should be unarmed against falsehood? While the proponents of error know the art of winning an audience to goodwill, attention, and open mind, shall the proponents of truth remain ignorant? While the [sophist] states facts concisely, clearly, plausibly, shall the preacher state them so that they are tedious to hear, hard to understand, hard to believe? While the one attacks truth and insinuates falsehood by fallacious argument, shall the other have too little skill either to defend the truth or refute the false? Shall the one, stirring his hearers to error, urging them by force of oratory, move them by terror, by pity, by joy, by encouragement, and the other slowly and coldly drowse for truth?"[38]

The modern department of speech takes its stand with Augustine and the classical tradition. It holds, with Aristotle, that the function of instruction in speech is to help men of goodwill make the truth prevail. It holds that ignorance of rhetoric is no defense, no haven of safety. All men, evil and good, must of necessity resort to communication if they would attain their purposes. Armed with knowledge of rhetoric, a man of goodwill is better able to combat demagoguery and chicanery; ignorant of it, he may stand powerless before them. The position is well stated by Bryant: "Knowledge of the devices of sophistry will always be acquired by those whose purposes are bad; ignorance of them will provide no defense for the rest. No great force can be used without hazard, or ignored without hazard. The force understood, rather than the force not understood, is likely to be the force controlled."[39] Moreover, reprehensible though sophistry is, to be unable to defeat it may be even more deplorable. "We may agree," writes Simrell, "that the man who makes the worse appear the better reason is a sinner, and still agree that the man who makes the better reason appear the worse is a greater sinner, for . . . he is also equally deceptive."[40] For liberal graduates to possess truth and to be unable to make it prevail, to be unequipped to communicate it effectively to their fellow citizens, holds dire consequences for a free society.

Finally, note well that the position of speech in regard to the age-old conflict of sophistic and the classical tradition is not unique among humane studies. Sophistic is not limited to rhetoric. Its typical deviation of aim may infest any art or science. Sophis-

[35]Bryant, 1953, p. 410.

[36]Everett Lee Hunt, "From Rhetoric Deliver Us," editorial, **The Quarterly Journal of Speech** (April 1928), 262. Hunt states: "The profession of ignorance or distrust of tricks of rhetoric is often itself a rhetorical trick." **Ibid.**

[37]As cited by J. Jeffery Auer, "Speech as a Social Force," **NEA Journal** (November 1960), 22. See also Bower Aly, "The Scientists' Debt to Rhetoric," **The Quarterly Journal of Speech** (December 1936), 584–590.

[38]As trans. by Baldwin in **Medieval Rhetoric and Poetic**, pp. 57–58.

[39]Bryant, 1953, p. 411. See also Hunt, 1949, p. 277.

[40]Simrell, p. 363.

tic goes to motivation for study and practice and, as such, may deflect the aim of any field of learning; for "all education helps in giving a man power to overreach and overpersuade his fellows, if disposed to do so."[41] Who shall guarantee that a student of logic will not use his knowledge to obfuscate truth, that he will not become adept merely at "logic-chopping"? We all know that the lawyer, the physician, the artist, the scientist, even the teacher may come to be motivated by greed, reputation, or personal power and, as a result, to misuse knowledge and skills at his command. Indeed, science today possesses the knowledge to destroy all society—all mankind. Its mastery of atomic weapons and biological warfare poses threats incomparably greater than those inherent in rhetoric. Who is to vouch for proper use of such knowledge? Shall we eliminate such areas of study because of their potential dangers? Or shall we admit them all, confident that with proper guidance, under a competent faculty, their students will learn to love truth, to develop an abiding respect for humanity, and to act in the interests of truth, justice, and their fellow beings? This writer accepts the second alternative, and he claims the same arguments for the study of speech; for "it is never the purpose of rhetoric to promote cheap, gaudy talk any more than the purpose of poetic is to promote cheap, shallow, dishonest popular art."[42] We have learned to live with the debasement of other arts. We analyze their problems, attempt corrective action, and continue their teaching and practice. But when rhetoric is debased, we are more shocked, more prone to advocate drastic remedies, even the abolition of the art itself. We are more shocked because we know, or sense, that any debasement of communication goes to the heart of our humanity. But we cannot escape. We must employ rhetoric if we would have truth prevail. Let us, then, recognize that speech must have a central role in any meaningful liberal education; and let us, ever aware of the dangers of sophistic, give encouragement to those who would teach youth the high precepts of the classical tradition.

One major question remains. Do modern speech departments, in fact, operate in accordance with the classical tradition of rhetoric? If they do not, this writer will agree that their claim upon the liberal curriculum is suspect. But if they do, he will claim for speech an important role in any system of humane study. Obviously the question affords no blanket response. Each department—even each course—must be appraised on its own merits. Any able speech faculty would welcome such scrutiny. Too many critics do not really understand the field of speech, and often they seem unwilling to learn. An examination to ascertain whether current practice in speech measures up to its best tradition and purpose—a procedure which might be usefully applied to any department in the liberal college—would undoubtedly prove fruitful to critics of speech as well as to its proponents.

If we can assert no universal conclusion applicable to every department or course, we can at least do two things. First, we can point out that the main tendency, the prime motivation, of the modern speech movement is to restore the field, with precepts modified by research, to its ancient values and purpose.[43] Second, we can enunciate the basic principles which must govern instruction in speech if

[41]Hunt, 1928, p. 264.

[42]Donald C. Bryant, "Aspects of the Rhetorical Tradition—I, The Intellectual Heritage," **The Quarterly Journal of Speech** (April 1950), 176.

[43]Sentiments of the sources cited throughout this paper should serve to document this statement. Space, of course, is insufficient for a detailed discussion of the aims and motives of modern speech education which arose about fifty years ago to counteract and displace the elocutionary movement. The volume **A History of Speech Education in America**, cited above, gives an excellent account of the rise of the modern speech field. See also Robert T. Oliver and Marvin G. Bauer, eds., **Re-Establishing the Speech Profession: The First Fifty Years** (Speech Association of the Eastern States: 1959). For an account of changing concepts of rhetorical theory see Wilbur E. Howell, "Renaissance Rhetoric and Modern Rhetoric: A Study in Change," in **The Rhetorical Idiom**, ed. Donald C. Bryant (Ithaca, N. Y.: Cornell University Press, 1958), pp. 53–70.

sophistic is to be avoided and if the promise of the classical tradition is to be fulfilled. To help make truth prevail, the fundamental purpose of rhetoric, the following principles must obtain in speech instructions:

First, only subject matter of substance can be admissible in the speech classroom. Frivolous, shallow topics—"My Weekend at the Shore," "How to Park a Car," "My Hobby," and the like—can serve only to sap and impoverish the minds of students and to debase the study of speech. Such practice undermines the heritage of rhetoric and makes speech suspect, and properly so, in the academic world. The point is stressed again and again by our best writers. "Rhetoric is so inextricably moral," Baldwin maintains, "that it should never be divorced from subject matter of real significance."[44] Thonssen and Baird agree: "Great public speaking should, first of all, be a demonstration of significant ideas. This is a principle of the art."[45] The objective can be attained in several ways. In the public speaking course at Temple University, for example, each student is assigned a broad topic relating to an important social, political, educational, or economic problem. He works with this subject for most of the semester, gathering and evaluating facts, formulating arguments, preparing outlines, and delivering speeches of information, analysis, and persuasion. In another approach, topics for the various assignments are drawn from other courses, especially the social sciences and humanities. There has always been a close affinity between rhetoric and politics[46]—rhetoric has often been defined as dealing with *quaestiones civiles*—so it is a natural arrangement when subject matter for speeches is derived from political science, sociology, economics, and comparable areas. Whatever procedure is employed, sound instruction demands significant ideas in speeches. When it does not, it becomes sophistical; but when it does, it becomes a valuable part of humane study.

Second, as a corollary to the foregoing, speech instruction must be equally insistent upon rigorous intellectual application in analysis, preparation, and presentation of subject matter. A significant topic is essential for speeches, but it will avail but little if it is dealt with in a superficial way. Emphasis upon adequate research and knowledge, logical analysis, and sound reasoning is a *sine qua non* of speech instruction. And so it has always been in the best tradition. The combination of knowledge and thought is inherent in *inventio*, the core of healthy rhetoric. In Bryant's words: "Knowledge and thought, ideas and understanding, information and contemplation—the steady and superior application of the superior intellect—this is the cry of rhetoric throughout the tradition. Whatever else is taught . . . there is nothing except a good character which more persistently underlies and justifies rhetorical teaching than the insistence upon intellectual processes in the speaker and intellectual content in the speech and in the preparation of the speech."[47] Thus, stimulation to greater mental achievement is, and must be, a goal of speech, no less than for any other academic field.

The third essential principle has been implicit throughout this paper. If speech through the process of time-binding makes human society possible and if the primary function of rhetoric is to make truth prevail, the proper study of speech is inextricably bound to ethics and morality. Unanimous agreement on this point is found in the ancient writers and in modern

[44]**Medieval Rhetoric and Poetic**, p. 5.

[45]Thonssen and Baird, p. 382. The point is also made in the following articles in **The Quarterly Journal of Speech**: Herbert A. Wichelns, "Our Hidden Aims" (November 1923), 322–323; William P. Sandford, "Content and Form" (November 1923), 329; H. M. Karr, "The Central Task Restated" (June 1933), 339; Angelo M. Pellegrini, "Public Speaking and Social Obligations" (June 1934), 350; and Edward Z. Rowell, "The Conviction-Persuasion Duality" (November 1934), 474–475. See also Clark, 1950, p. 295.

[46]See, for example, Karl R. Wallace, "Rhetoric, Politics, and the Education of the Ready Man," in **The Rhetorical Idiom**, pp. 71–96.

[47]Bryant, 1950, pp. 172–173. See also Wilbur E. Gilman, "Logic and Public Speaking," **The Quarterly Journal of Speech** (December 1940), 668.

students of language and culture.[48] In 1718 [in a work published posthumously], Fénelon bluntly and succinctly stated the classical view: "The speaker, to be worthy of persuading the people, ought to be an incorruptible man. Without that, his talent and art become a deadly poison in the republic itself. Hence . . . the first and most essential attribute of the speaker is virtue."[49] These words reflect the admonitions of Plato, Isocrates, Aristotle, Cicero, Quintilian and the other founders of traditional rhetoric. "The good man speaking well" has been the persistent goal of the tradition. Thonssen and Baird iterate the modern view when they insist that teachers of speech have an "obligation of inculcating moral principles in speakers, and of advising future citizens of the necessary duty of holding themselves strictly accountable for what they say."[50] Ethical theory and study, of course, is a province of philosophy, but it finds essential application in the speech classroom.

Fourth, instruction in speech must be cognizant of the consequences of communication. From one point of view this principle embodies the three already discussed, for the demands for significant content, rigorous thinking, and high ethical standards are all concerned with the effects of speeches. But there is still another aspect. Just as in the past rhetoric has been subjected to sophistics of style and delivery, it seems today to be threatened by the cult of success. Reference is made to "the disposition to regard rhetoric as an instrument of power, by which a speaker may improve himself, make more money, control people. . . ."[51] Too often this view governs the view of Madison Avenue and of commercialized speech instruction. Success or effectiveness is, of course, a legitimate goal of persuasion; but it must be success in terms of truth, of the audience, of society. As Robert D. Clark puts it: "When we say that one of the general purposes of speech training . . . is to teach students how to persuade, we do not really mean it. Such a statement of aim is *partial;* it is removed from the social context, and so removed has a doubtful place in the . . . curriculum. . . . The purpose of speech training is not simply to develop skill in persuasion but to develop those skills which may be used under certain conditions; namely, within a social context."[52] The best rhetoric, as expounded by ancients and moderns alike, is alive to the danger of success *per se* in persuasion. Wallace only echoes Aristotle[53] when he declares: "A theory of persuasion which calls for a man's always hitting his mark and losing success and prestige if he doesn't, is indefensible in any free society."[54] When success alone is the end of persuasive discourse, justification of almost any means becomes easy. Sound speech teaching avoids such emphasis and perversion.

Fifth, techniques of speech—articulation, voice, delivery, linguistic style, organizational skills, audience adaptation—must always be treated as means, never as ends. They must be held subservient to subject matter. When any or all assume an importance equal to the message, speech instruction and practice, as we have seen, becomes sophistical.

Sixth, precepts for speaking must be derived from a knowledge and

[48]See, for example, S. I. Hayakawa, "The Ethics of Time-Binding," in **Papers from the Second American Congress on General Semantics,** ed. Marjorie Mercer Kendig (Lakeville, Conn.: Institute of General Semantics, 1943), pp. 17–27; and Harry L. Weinberg, **Levels of Knowing and Existence** (New York: Harper & Brothers, 1959), pp. 144–176.

[49]**Dialogues on Eloquence,** ed. and trans. Wilbur S. Howell (Princeton, N. J.: Princeton University Press, 1951), p. 76.

[50]Thonssen and Baird, p. 471. See also Pellegrini, pp. 349–350; and Richard Murphy, "Preface to an Ethic of Rhetoric," in **The Rhetorical Idiom,** pp. 125–144.

[51]Thonssen and Baird, p. 471.

[52]"These Truths We Hold Self-Evident," **The Quarterly Journal of Speech** (December 1948), 446. See also Pellegrini, p. 348; A. Craig Baird, "The Educational Philosophy of the Teacher of Speech," **The Quarterly Journal of Speech** (December 1938), 549; and Arleigh B. Williamson, "Social Standards in Public Speaking Instruction," **The Quarterly Journal of Speech** (October 1939), 376.

[53]**Rhetoric,** 1355b, in Cooper, p. 6.

[54]Wallace, 1954, p. 128. See also Bryant, 1950, p. 176.

understanding of *oral* communication. Artificial cultivation of technique or reliance upon rules for writing can lead only to awkward, stilted speaking. When either occurs, attention is deflected from matter and directed to technique. Henry Lee Smith agrees with modern speech texts when he writes: "The student of language and culture is aware of the difference between the spoken and written language. He realizes that one form cannot be translated directly into the other, that what may be effective in one may actually bring about disruption of communication in the other. He knows that 'correctness' as laid down in a set of prescriptive rules for effective writing may well lead to awkwardness and incongruities of speech that draw attention from *what* is being said to *how* it is said. He is aware that most effective speech and writing is that which draws the least attention to itself, which strikes the receiver as the most appropriate for the situation as defined by the culture."[55]

These six principles should obtain in the various areas of study embraced by a department of speech in the liberal college. They have direct application to public address, to courses in speech fundamentals, public speaking, persuasion, argumentation and debate, discussion, and rhetorical theory and history. So conceived and taught, such courses fulfill the promise of the classical tradition of rhetoric and thus hold a wide potential for liberal education. Indeed, they may serve as excellent vehicles to integrate knowledge from other fields while simultaneously providing students with instruction and practice in effective and responsible communication.

When examined in relation to liberal education, courses in dramatic arts pose problems with new dimensions, for we encounter here further basic questions relative to the role of the fine arts in humane study. But the theater is a means of communication as well as an art form. So considered, courses in dramatics are affected by the principles enunciated. They, as well, must insist upon significant ideas in dramatic productions and rigorous application of intellect in analysis of plot, character, and execution. They, too, must subordinate technique to content. When the program in dramatics is directed toward attaining professional competence or when it is devoted primarily to the presentation of entertainment, its claim upon the liberal curriculum is weakened. When it is so organized and taught as to meet the requirements of wholesome communication, however modified by the requisites of an art form, it can provide much that is desirable and necessary in humane education.

The study of literature, foreign and English, has long been regarded as essential in liberal study, and the drama is universally accorded a prominent place in literature courses. The values of literary study, the drama included, are well known and need not be defended here. But plays, ancient and modern, were written to be seen and heard by audiences—not merely to be studied as literary forms or as agencies to heighten historical or cultural insights. Indeed, it may be argued successfully that a drama does not really exist, in a significant way, until it has been lifted from the pages of the text and made to live on a stage as the playwright intended. A dramatics program which presents plays which otherwise could only be studied in the classroom makes a valuable contribution to students who attend, as well as to those who profit from direct participation. Thus, a sound program in drama, one which stages plays of literary, historical, and cultural significance, can make a double contribution to liberal education.

Courses in speech science and pathology center upon speech as a physical *act*. Here the act of speech is approached as an entity capable of detailed study in much the same ways a geologist is concerned with rock structures, a biologist with plants or animals, an economist with the production and distribution of goods and services. These and comparable areas of study focus upon important aspects of man's environment or activities. They seek to understand the complexities of a given area, to describe accurately, to establish relationships. In so far as such objectives are attained, these fields enable man to predict

[55]Smith, p. 348.

what may occur under certain circumstances and, hence, to control such occurrences for the betterment of mankind. And so it is in speech science, for the object of study here is to understand the exceedingly complex act of speech so that it may be known and controlled. Such knowledge is essential in a department of speech, for the *art* of oral communication depends upon understanding and control of the *act* of speech.

The study of speech as an act leads inevitably to consideration of abnormalities of production and reception, just as mental disorders become important in psychology, or disease is analyzed in biology, or depressions are examined in economics, or delinquency and crime are investigated in sociology. The purpose of such study is always to better understand the normal and to better control the abnormal. Viewed in this light, speech pathology is as appropriate for inclusion in a liberal department as are comparable courses in other departments. Too often, however, courses in speech science, pathology, and audiology are conceived and taught with the view of imparting professional competence to therapists. When this is the case, such courses should not be eligible for inclusion in liberal, undergraduate education. But such conditions need not obtain—no more than for courses in comparable areas. The scientific study of the production and reception of speech, with its attendant complications, is a rigorous, extensive, and complex field. Courses in this area must draw upon aspects of anatomy, neurology, linguistics, acoustics, psychology, and statistics. When taught with the view of inculcating an understanding of the act of speech and its abnormalities, these courses provide an exciting, difficult, and rewarding area of study. Under these circumstances, even "clinical practice," the course most often deemed necessarily "professional," becomes a vehicle for demonstration, observation, and direct experience with problems of speech production and reception. It serves a purpose similar to that of the laboratory periods which are integral parts of courses in natural and biological sciences. Perhaps those responsible for courses in speech science and pathology would have been better advised to make laboratory a part of each course, as the other sciences have done; but whatever the form of course structure, "clinical practice" cannot be condemned out of hand on the basis of its title alone. Whether it has a proper place in a liberal department of speech must be ascertained on the basis of its aims, methods, and content. Studied as an integral part of oral communication, speech science and pathology may not constitute an area to be recommended for all liberal arts students, but it certainly represents a legitimate field of study for those whose interests lead them to it.

Although the area of radio and television is not always a part of a department of speech, as is the case at Temple University, it, too, is concerned with oral communication. In fact, a major portion of work in courses in this area is concerned with adapting basic principles of speech and dramatic arts to the requirements of mass media. It may be proper, therefore, to note that the principles essential to sound, liberal training in communication apply to this area as well as to the others. When courses in the mass media are professionally centered, they can have no claim upon the liberal curriculum. So conceived and taught, courses in radio and television are prone to regard programming as entertainment and the media themselves are mere agencies for salesmanship. "Success," as measured by ratings or by the value of goods sold, easily becomes the only meaningful end of programming. But, again, such a situation need not obtain. Radio and television have revolutionized the role and the potential role of oral communication in our century. Their capacity for evil or good is almost boundless. They can remain a "vast wasteland," as Newton Minow has termed them, or they can become vital agencies in a free society, bringing needed information and cultural enrichment to our citizens. When they are studied so as to provide students with a grasp of their potential, when they are approached as operating in a social context, when "success" and techniques are held subservient to content and ethics, then courses in radio and television provide a valuable aspect of liberal education.

What, then, is the case for speech as a liberal study? First, it is the ability to symbolize, to speak and to write, which makes us human and makes human society possible; so that to understand speech is "to understand the essence of our humanity." Second, speech is prior to writing as a mode of language, and principles for efficient writing will not ensure effective speech. Third, the study of speech includes broad areas of knowledge and involves a great deal more than mere "skill"; but even if it did not, ability in speech is essential for meaningful participation of a liberally educated man in democratic society. Fourth, although rhetoric has been and is subject to sophistic, the main tradition has been and is otherwise. The primary function of rhetoric and of modern speech instruction is to help make truth prevail. Knowledge, unaided, will not obtain among men; and ignorance of the arts of persuasion is no safeguard against sophistical demagoguery. Truth must be made effective in a free society, and to this goal speech can and does make a major contribution. Fifth, modern speech instruction, loyal to the classical tradition, insists upon significant subject matter, rigorous intellectual application, high ethical standards, responsible communication, and the subordination of techniques to ideas in speeches. Speech, thus conceived and taught, in all its areas, is liberal in aim and spirit. It may serve as an excellent medium for integration of other fields of study. On these bases, speech surely can claim a place—yes, a high place—among liberal studies. As Everett Lee Hunt, former Dean at Swarthmore College, has said: "The problems of persuasion become more significant as society becomes more complicated, and . . . only make the ancient rhetoric, based on experience, more significant. . . . If competitive academic organization rules otherwise, so much the worse for it. Neglect of rhetoric always brings its own penalties and limitations, and the academic pendulum is always swinging."[56]

[56]"Herbert A. Wichelns and the Cornell Tradition of Rhetoric as a Humane Study," in **The Rhetorical Idiom**, p. 3.